# ME

## TH⎯ ⎯⎯ GUIDE

There are more than one hundred Rough Guide travel,
phrasebook and music titles, covering destinations
from Amsterdam to Zimbabwe, languages from Czech
to Thai, and musics from World to Opera and Jazz

## Forthcoming titles include

Cuba • Dominican Republic
Las Vegas • Sardinia
Scottish Highlands & Islands

## Rough Guides on the Internet

www.roughguides.com

## Rough Guide Credits

Text editor: Gavin Thomas. Series editor: Mark Ellingham
Typesetting: Judy Pang and Katie Pringle
Cartography: Nichola Goodliffe

## Publishing Information

This first edition published October 1999 by
Rough Guides Ltd, 62–70 Shorts Gardens, London WC2H 9AB

### Distributed by the Penguin Group:

Penguin Books Ltd, 27 Wrights Lane, London W8 5TZ
Penguin Books USA Inc., 375 Hudson Street, New York 10014, USA
Penguin Books Australia Ltd, 487 Maroondah Highway,
PO Box 257, Ringwood, Victoria 3134, Australia
Penguin Books Canada Ltd, 10 Alcorn Avenue,
Toronto, Ontario, Canada M4V 1E4
Penguin Books (NZ) Ltd, 182–190 Wairau Road,
Auckland 10, New Zealand

Typeset in Bembo and Helvetica to an original design by Henry Iles.
Printed in Spain by Graphy Cems.

# MELBOURNE

## THE MINI ROUGH GUIDE

### by Stephen Townshend

**W**e set out to do something different when the first Rough Guide was published in 1982. Mark Ellingham, just out of university, was travelling in Greece. He brought along the popular guides of the day, but found they were all lacking in some way. They were either strong on ruins and museums but went on for pages without mentioning a beach or taverna. Or they were so conscious of the need to save money that they lost sight of Greece's cultural and historical significance. Also, none of the books told him anything about Greece's contemporary life – its politics, its culture, its people, and how they lived.

So with no job in prospect, Mark decided to write his own guidebook, one which aimed to provide practical information that was second to none, detailing the best beaches and the hottest clubs and restaurants, while also giving hard-hitting accounts of every sight, both famous and obscure, and providing up-to-the-minute information on contemporary culture. It was a guide that encouraged independent travellers to find the best of Greece, and was a great success, getting shortlisted for the Thomas Cook travel guide award, and encouraging Mark, along with three friends, to expand the series.

The Rough Guide list grew rapidly and the letters flooded in, indicating a much broader readership than had been anticipated, but one which uniformly appreciated the Rough Guide mix of practical detail and humour, irreverence and enthusiasm. Things haven't changed. The same four friends who began the series are still the caretakers of the Rough Guide mission today: to provide the most reliable, up-to-date and entertaining information to independent-minded travellers of all ages, on all budgets.

We now publish more than 150 titles and have offices in London and New York. The travel guides are written and researched by a dedicated team of more than 100 authors, based in Britain, Europe, the USA and Australia. We have also created a unique series of phrasebooks to accompany the travel series, along with an acclaimed series of music guides, and a best-selling pocket guide to the Internet and World Wide Web. We also publish comprehensive travel information on our Web site: **www.roughguides.com**

# Help Us Update

We've gone to a lot of effort to ensure that this first edition of *The Rough Guide to Melbourne* is as up to date and accurate as possible. However, if you feel there are places we've underrated or over-praised, or find we've missed something good or covered something which has now gone, then please write: suggestions, comments or corrections are much appreciated.

We'll credit all contributions, and send a copy of the next edition (or any other Rough Guide if you prefer) for the best letters. Please mark letters "Rough Guide Melbourne Update" and send to:

Rough Guides, 62–70 Shorts Gardens, London WC2H 9AB, or
Rough Guides, 375 Hudson St, New York NY 10014.

Or send email to: mail@roughguides.co.uk
Online updates about this book can be found on
Rough Guides' Web site (see opposite)

# The Author

Stephen Townshend was born in New Zealand in 1962. Before settling in Melbourne in 1994, he worked as a music journalist in Perth and as an editor in Sydney, where he also published a series of magazines showcasing local writing. Since then he has travelled extensively in Southeast Asia, the USA, and in Cuba, which was the subject of his first guidebook; he has also written another guide to Melbourne. While in Melbourne he met and married his wife Kate; they now have three children.

# Acknowledgements

Thanks go to Swanston Trams for letting me reproduce their transport maps. Special thanks go to Giselle Cattapan, Daniel Batt, David Tarranto, Ian Russell, Chris Wommersley and Trish Maunder, who provided invaluable insights into Melbourne. Very special thanks are reserved for my editor Gavin Thomas, and to Steve Wommersley, Crusader Hillis and David McLymont, whose efforts helped me enormously in preparing, researching and writing this guide.

At Rough Guides, thanks also to Charles Hebbert and Olivia Mandel for UK and US research, Nikky Twyman for proofreading, Judy Pang and Katie Pringle for typesetting, and Nichola Goodliffe for her usual monumental contribution to all things cartographic.

# CONTENTS

CONTENTS

# INTRODUCTION

**A**ustralia's second-largest city and capital of the State of Victoria, **Melbourne** prides itself on being a place that knows how to live well. Although it lags behind Sydney in terms of population and prestige, its less brazen charms offer a quality of life which other Australian cities find difficult to match. Magnificent landscaped gardens and parklands have made the city one of the greenest in the world, while beneath the skyscrapers of the arresting Central Business District an understorey of elegant Victorian-era facades presents Melbourne on an agreeably human scale. This is a cosmopolitan and sophisticated city – one that is undeniably a good place to live in, and enjoyable to visit too. Residents and visitors alike can take pleasure in its interesting and affordable cuisine; in the revitalized city-centre laneways and arcades which now house some of Australia's coolest cafés and bars; in its successful mix of ethnically diverse people; and in its leading role in Australian cultural and sporting life.

There's a staid and even boorish side to Melbourne too, as you might expect from a city that had – in comparison to Sydney's incontrovertibly brutal origins – relatively genteel beginnings, when the discovery of gold brought sudden wealth to the infant settlement. Reminders of the old conservatism linger on in the city's uniform layout and relentless suburbanization, and in the way that locals like bragging about inconsequential things like the possibility of having the world's tallest building (the on-again, off-again Grollo Tower) or fussing over nothing, such as when visiting American comedian Jerry Seinfeld remarked that Melbourne was "the anus of the world". That the city has been able to shake off the cultural cringe which haunted it for years is largely the result of the **postwar immigration** which, since 1945, has brought the world to Melbourne, shaking up the city's Anglo-Celtic mindset for good. Whole villages have arrived from Lebanon, Turkey and Greece (and, more recently, from Vietnam and China), and it is these new immigrants who have enriched and energized Melbourne's formerly inward-looking and parochial character.

Over the last decade, Melbourne has also undergone an amazing **economic transformation** in a huge variety of fields – multimedia, architectural design, fashion, food, drinking and gambling among them – partly thanks to a forward-thinking state government which has spent billions of dollars on infrastructure and major sporting and cultural events. Development has come at a cost – older city and suburban buildings have been demolished, eroding Melbourne's past, and wealth is now more unevenly distributed, with increasing numbers of homeless people and drug addicts on the streets – but despite these growing pains, Melbourne today is a city humming with vigour, and looking forward to a confident and prosperous new millennium.

Outside Melbourne and easily accessible by public transport or car are a host of rewarding day-trips. Nearby on the coast is **Phillip Island**, with its famous Little Penguins, and the beach resorts of the **Bellarine** and **Mornington peninsulas**. Inland on the city's doorstep, the scenic

**Dandenong Ranges** and the prestigious wineries of the **Yarra Valley** present convenient escapes from the pace of city life, while slightly further afield the salubrious spa towns of **Daylesford** and **Hepburn Springs** and the grandiose architecture of the former goldmining town of **Ballarat** offer reminders of the area's nineteenth-century heritage. Heading westwards along the coast, the magnificent **Great Ocean Road** winds 300km through some of Australia's most spectacular coastal scenery.

## When to visit

Melbourne's **climate** is variable, being warm to hot in summer (Dec–Feb), mild in autumn (March–May), cold and damp in winter (June–Aug), and cool in spring (Sept–Nov). The warmest months are generally January and February, which are often dry and prone to barbaric hot spells when temperatures can climb into the forties. The coldest months are June and July, when frosts sometimes occur during the night, while October is the wettest. A feature of Melbourne's climate is its changeability, particularly during spring and summer – dramatic falls in temperature sometimes occur within a few minutes, both intriguing and infuriating locals, who describe the atmospheric transformations as "four seasons in one day".

# Melbourne's Climate

| | °F | | °C | | Rainfall | |
| | Average daily | | Average daily | | Average monthly | |
| | max | min | max | min | in | mm |
|---|---|---|---|---|---|---|
| Jan | 79 | 59 | 26 | 15 | 1.8 | 48 |
| Feb | 79 | 60 | 26 | 16 | 1.9 | 50 |
| March | 75 | 57 | 24 | 14 | 2.1 | 54 |
| April | 70 | 53 | 21 | 12 | 2.3 | 59 |
| May | 63 | 50 | 17 | 10 | 2.2 | 57 |
| June | 57 | 44 | 14 | 7 | 1.9 | 50 |
| July | 57 | 44 | 14 | 7 | 1.8 | 48 |
| Aug | 59 | 44 | 15 | 7 | 1.9 | 49 |
| Sept | 63 | 48 | 17 | 9 | 2.2 | 58 |
| Oct | 68 | 50 | 20 | 10 | 2.6 | 67 |
| Nov | 71 | 53 | 22 | 12 | 2.3 | 59 |
| Dec | 75 | 57 | 24 | 14 | 2.2 | 58 |

# BASICS

---

# Getting there from Britain and Ireland

The quickest way to get to Melbourne from the UK is to **fly direct** with British Airways or Qantas from London Heathrow, with a journey time of around 21 hours. Plenty of other airlines have **indirect flights** (involving at least one change of plane) to Melbourne, taking longer but costing significantly less. There are no direct flights from **regional airports** in the UK or from Ireland, but plenty of connections to London or flights via other European capitals.

## Fares

Fares are most expensive from mid-June to mid-August and in the two weeks before Christmas, and cheapest from April to mid-June. The cheapest published **scheduled fares** start at around £600 return during low season (though special offers can go as low as £480), rising to around £1000 return at peak periods – to stand a chance of getting one of the cheaper tickets at these times, aim to book anything up to six months in advance. Flights with Qantas from Aberdeen, Belfast, Edinburgh, Glasgow, Manchester or Newcastle via Frankfurt, Rome or Paris are around £50 cheaper than those routed via Heathrow. Lauda

Air, Garuda, Emirates Airlines and Malaysia Airlines all offer competitive rates, though in the first instance it's always worth checking with the **discount flight agents** listed on p.6, who have many discounted ticket offers, particularly for students and under-26s. In addition, Britannia Airways offer cheap **charter fares** from London Gatwick (Nov–Feb only) at around £550 return, the only restriction being a maximum stay of eight weeks. UK and Australian **departure taxes** (£27 and £16 respectively) are normally included in ticket prices.

Flying **from Ireland**, most of the cheaper routings involve a stopover in London, but from Dublin there are often good deals on Olympic via Athens. Singapore Airlines have flights from Dublin, Shannon or Cork via London, Singapore and Sydney, while Malaysia Airlines also go from the same three Irish airports via Kuala Lumpur. Fares start at around IR£680 for an open one-year return in low season, increasing to around IR£1600 over Christmas. From Belfast, Malaysia Airlines have return tickets from £666 (low season), £950 (high).

## Stopovers and RTW tickets

Making one or more **stopovers** en route is one way of breaking up the long flight to Australia. You'll usually have to pay a supplement, although with Thai Airways and Singapore Airlines, stopovers in Bangkok and Singapore are

---

**The Australian Tourist Commission Office is at Gemini House, 10–18 Putney Hill, London SW15 6AA; brochure line ✆0906/807 0707 (calls charged at 60p/min); www.australia.com. Tourism Victoria is at The Australia Centre, Melbourne Place, Strand, London WC2B 4LG (✆0171/240 7176).**

---

included in the price of the ticket. Alternatively, **round-the-world** tickets offer a good way of including Australia as part of a longer journey. The routing permutations are endless, but fares normally reflect the length of the route chosen and the number of stops to be made; London–Bangkok–Melbourne–Los Angeles–London, for example, would cost around £900.

## Airlines and discount agents

### Airlines

**Air New Zealand** ℂ0181/741 2299; *www.airnz.com*. Daily from London Heathrow via Los Angeles.

**Britannia Airways** c/o Austravel ℂ0171/734 7755. Charter flights from London Gatwick (Nov–Feb only).

**British Airways** ℂ0345/222 111, Dublin ℂ01/874 7747; *www.british-airways.com*. Daily from London Heathrow.

**Emirates Airlines** ℂ0171/808 0808; *www.emirates.com*. Daily from London Gatwick and Manchester via Dubai.

**Garuda** ℂ0171/486 3011; *www.garuda.co.id*.Three times weekly from London Gatwick.

**KLM Royal Dutch Airlines** ℂ08705/074 074; *www.klm.com*. Daily from most major British airports via Amsterdam and Singapore/Bangkok.

**Lauda Air** ℂ0171/630 5924. Three flights a week via Vienna and Kuala Lumpur.

**Malaysia Airlines** ℂ0171/341 2020, Dublin ℂ01/676 1561; *www.malaysiaairlines.com*. Daily from London Heathrow to Kuala Lumpur with four weekly onward connections to Melbourne.

**Olympic Airways** ℂ0171/409 3400, Dublin ℂ01/608 0090. Twice weekly from Dublin and London Heathrow via Athens and Bangkok.

**Qantas** ℂ0345/747 767, Dublin ℂ01/874 7747; *www.qantas.com.au*. Daily from London Heathrow via either Singapore, Kuala Lumpur or Bangkok.

**Singapore Airlines** ℃0181/747 0007, Manchester ℃0161/830 8888, Dublin ℃01/671 0722; *www.singaporeair.com.* Twice-daily from Heathrow and five times weekly from Manchester via Singapore.

**Thai Airways** ℃0171/499 9113; *www.thaiair.com.* Daily from Heathrow via Bangkok.

**United Airlines** ℃0845/8444777; *www.ual.com.* Daily from Heathrow via Los Angeles or SanFrancisco.

## Discount agents

**UK Austravel** London ℃0171/734 7755, plus branches in Bristol, Manchester, Leeds and Bournemouth; *www.austravel.net.* Australia travel specialists. Also issue ETAs (see p.13) and traditional visas (£16).

**Bridge the World** ℃0171/734 7447. RTW ticket specialists.

**Campus Travel** ℃0171/730 8111, branches nationwide; *www.campustravel.co.uk.* Student travel specialists.

**Flightbookers** ℃0171/757 2468; *www.flightbookers.net.* Discounted fares on scheduled flights..

**London Flight Centre** ℃0171/244 6411. Discounted flights; can also arrange Australian visas.

**North South Travel** ℃01245/492 882. Discounted flights – profits support projects in the developing world.

**Quest Worldwide** ℃0181/547 3322. Specialists in RTW tickets and Australian discount fares.

**STA Travel** ℃0171/361 6262, branches nationwide; *www.statravel.co.uk.* Specialists in student/youth travel.

**Trailfinders** ℃0171/938 3366, branches nationwide. Multi-stop and RTW tickets; visa service also available.

**Travel Bag** ℃0171/287 5556. Direct and RTW flights.

**Travel Bug** London ℃0171/835 2000, Manchester ℃0161/721 4000; *www.travel-bug.co.uk.* Discounted tickets.

**Travelmood** London ℃0171/258 0280. Direct and RTW flights.

**IRELAND Australia Travel Centre** Dublin ℃01/874 7747. Good deals on Qantas tickets.

**Thomas Cook** Dublin ℂ01/677 1721, Belfast ℂ01232/550 232.
Mainstream package-holiday and flight agent.
**Trailfinders** Dublin ℂ01/677 7888. Multi-stop and RTW tickets.
**Unijet Belfast** ℂ01232/314 656. Discounted fares.
**Usit NOW** Dublin ℂ01/602 1700, Belfast ℂ01232/324 073, plus
branches nationwide; *www.usitnow.ie*. Student and youth travel
specialist.

# Getting there from North America

There are no non-stop flights from North America to
Melbourne, but plenty of one-stop services, usually routed
via Sydney. The **flying time** to Melbourne, excluding
stopovers, is approximately fifteen hours from Los Angeles;
twenty hours from New York or Chicago. From Canada,
most flights connect through Los Angeles. Flying time from
Vancouver to Melbourne is approximately eighteen hours;
from Toronto or Montréal its about twenty.

## Fares

Fares are highest from December to February; lowest from
April to August. Typical **scheduled fares** to Melbourne
from the west coast of the US are around $1000–1500 (high

season), $800-1200 (low); from the east coast, add $200–300. From Vancouver, expect to pay CDN$2200/1700 (high/low season); add an extra CDN$200–300 from Montréal or Toronto. Fares depend upon how far in advance you purchase your tickets, as well as how many seats are available on a particular flight. Booking through a **discount travel agent** (see list opposite) can knock $100 or so off published fares. Another possibility are the **charter flights** offered by companies such as Jetset (*www.jetset.com.au*). Fares are usually slightly cheaper than on scheduled flights, but generally come with various restrictions – check conditions carefully before booking. Charter flights can only be booked through a travel agent, not directly with the airline.

## Circle-Pacific and RTW tickets

**Circle-Pacific tickets** allow for a certain number of stopovers and are usually valid for one year. Booked through a discount agent or consolidator, a typical itinerary from Los Angeles via Tokyo, Hong Kong, Bangkok, Singapore, Jakarta, Bali, Cairns and Melbourne costs about $2600. A sample **round-the-world (RTW) ticket** from Los Angeles via Melbourne, Bangkok, Delhi, Bombay and London will cost in the region of $2000.

.............................................................................

**US visitors should contact the "Aussie Helpline" (℀847/296 4900) for tour information.**

.............................................................................

Airlines, discount agents and consolidators

### Airlines

**Air New Zealand** US ℀1-800/262-1234, Canada ℀1-800/563-5494; *www.airnz.com*. Daily from Los Angeles via Sydney.

**Canadian Airlines** US ✆1-800/426-7000, Canada ✆1-800/665-1177; *www.cdnair.ca*. Daily from Vancouver and Toronto via Honolulu and Sydney.

**Cathay Pacific** ✆1-800/233-2742; *www.cathay-usa.com*. Daily from Los Angeles, San Francisco and Vancouver via Hong Kong and Sydney.

**Japan Airlines** ✆1-800/525-3663; *www.jal.co.jp*. Daily from New York, Chicago, Los Angeles, San Francisco and Vancouver via Tokyo.

**Malaysia Airlines** ✆1-800/552-9264; *www.malaysiaairlines.com*. Daily from Los Angeles and New York via Kuala Lumpur and Sydney.

**Qantas** ✆1-800/227-4500; *www.qantas.com.au*. Daily from Los Angeles via Sydney.

**Singapore Airlines** ✆1-800/742-3333; *www.singaporeair.com*. Daily from Los Angeles and San Francisco via Sydney, and New York via Singapore.

**United Airlines** ✆1-800/538-2929; *www.ual.com*. Daily from Los Angeles and San Francisco via Sydney.

## Discount agents and consolidators

**Air Brokers International** ✆1-800/883-3273 or 415/397-1383; *www.airbrokers.com*. Consolidator.

**Air Courier Association** ✆1-800/282-1202 or 303/215-0900; *www.aircourier.org*. Courier-flight broker.

**Airtech** ✆1-800/575-8324 or 212/219-7000; *www.airtech.com*. Courier-flight broker.

**Austravel** ✆1-800/633-3404; *www.australia -online.com/austravel*. Flights and customized tours.

**Council Travel** ✆1-800/226-8624 or 212/822-2700; *www.counciltravel.com*. Student travel specialists.

**Educational Travel Center** ✆1-800/747-5551 or 608/256-5551; *www.edtrav.com*. Student and consolidator fares.

**High Adventure Travel** ✆1-800/350-0612 or 415/912-5600; *www.highadv.com*. RTW and Circle-Pacific tickets. Web site allows you to design and price your own RTW itinerary.

**Moment's Notice** ©1-718/234-6295; *www.moments-notice. com*. Discount travel club.

**Now Voyager** ©212/431-1616; *www.nowvoyagertravel.com*. Consolidator.

**Skylink** ©1-800/AIR-ONLY. Consolidator.

**STA Travel** ©1-800/777-0112; *www.statravel.com*. Specialist in student/youth fares.

**TFI Tours International** ©1-800/745-8000 or 212/736-1140. Worldwide consolidator.

**Ticket Planet** ©1-800/799-8888 or 415/288-9999. Worldwide consolidator.

**Travel Avenue** ©1-800/333-3335 or 312/876-6866; *www.travelavenue.com*. Discount travel company.

**Travel Cuts** ©1-800/667-2887; *www.travelcuts.com*. Canadian discount travel organization.

**Traveler's Advantage** ©1-800/548-1116; *www. travelersadvantage.com*. Discount travel club.

**Worldtek Travel** ©1-800/243-1723; *www.worldtek.com*. Discount travel agency for worldwide travel.

# Getting there from New Zealand

There's a good choice of flights to Melbourne **from New Zealand**: routes are busy and competition is fierce, resulting in an ever-changing range of deals and special offers. It's a relatively short hop across the Tasman Sea, with a flying time from Auckland to Melbourne of around three and a half hours.

## Flights and fares

Qantas and Air New Zealand have regular flights from Auckland, Wellington and Christchurch to Melbourne; United Airlines, Malaysia Airlines, Thai Airways and Ansett also have services from Auckland. **Fares** depend on how much flexibility you want: many of the cheapest deals are hedged with restrictions – typically, they must be booked at least seven days in advance, with a maximum stay of thirty days. Return fares run at around NZ$700 for a thirty-day ticket, NZ$800 for a longer stay of up to six months. Flying at peak times (primarily December to mid-January) can add substantially to the prices quoted above, while flying from Wellington or Christchurch also adds an extra NZ$150–200.

**The Australian Tourist Commission is at Level 13, 44–48 Emily Place, Auckland 1 ☏09/379 9594.**

Whatever kind of ticket you're after, your first call should be to one of the **specialist travel agents** listed below; staff can fill you in on all the latest fares and special offers.

## Airlines and discount agents

### Airlines

**Air New Zealand** ℂ09/366 2400; *www.airnz.com*.
**Ansett Australia** ℂ09/309 6235; *www.ansett.com*.
**Ansett New Zealand** ℂ09/307 6950; *www.ansett.co.nz*.
**Malaysia Airlines** ℂ09/373 2741; *www.malaysiaairlines.com*.
**Qantas** ℂ09/357 8900; *www.qantas.com.au*.
**Thai Airways** ℂ09/377 3886; *www.thaiair.com*.
**United Airlines** ℂ09/307 9500; *www.ual.com*.

### Travel agents

**Adventure World** ℂ09/524 5118.
**Budget Travel** ℂ0800/808 040 for nearest branch.
**Destinations Unlimited** ℂ09/373 4033.
**Flight Centres** Auckland ℂ09/309 6171, Wellington ℂ04/472 8101, Christchurch ℂ03/379 7145; *www.flightcentre.com*.
**STA Travel** Auckland ℂ09/309 0458, Wellington ℂ04/385 0561, Christchurch ℂ03/379 9098, plus branches countrywide; *www.statravel.com.au*.
**Thomas Cook** ℂ09/379 3920; *www.thomascook.com.au*.

# Packages and tours

**Package deals** can be a hassle-free way of getting a taste of Melbourne. There's a huge variety of holidays and tours to Australia available in New Zealand; call any of the travel agents listed above. Subsidiaries of airlines such as Air New Zealand, Ansett and Qantas package short city-breaks (flight and accommodation) and fly-drive deals for little more than the cost of the regular airfare.

# Visas and red tape

All visitors to Australia require a **visa and a valid passport**, except New Zealanders, who need only a passport. You can get visa application forms from the Australian High Commissions, embassies or consulates listed on p.14. **Three-month tourist visas** (valid for multiple entries over one year) are issued free and either processed over the counter or returned within three weeks by mail. You may be asked to show proof that you have **sufficient funds** – at least $1000 per month – to support yourself during your stay. A new computerized system, the **Electronic Travel Authority** (ETA), is gradually doing away with the three-month visa. Passengers' details are transmitted to Australia by their airline or travel agent, with the ETA usually being issued in only a few minutes. Passengers use the ETA in their passport in place of a visa.

Having a visa is not an absolute guarantee that you'll be allowed into Australia – immigration officials sometimes check to see if you have sufficient funds and that you have a return or onward ticket out of Australia. In extreme cases, they may **refuse entry**, or restrict your visit to a shorter period.

**Six-month visas** incur a fee (£18 in the UK, $30 in the US). If you think you might stay more than three months, it's best to get the six-month visa in advance, since once you're in Australia **extensions** cost A$145, and are non-refundable. Once issued, a visa usually allows multiple entries so long as your passport remains valid.

.............................................................................................

> **To extend your visa in Melbourne, contact the Department of Immigration and Multicultural Affairs at 2 Lonsdale Street (℡13/1881). Make sure to apply at least a month before your visa expires, as the process can take some time.**

.............................................................................................

Citizens of the UK, Canada, Holland, Japan and Korea aged between 18 and 25 (and in some cases 30), can apply for a **working holiday visa**, which grants a twelve-month stay and allows the holder to work for up to three months with the same employer. You'll need to apply in your home country several months in advance and be able to show evidence of sufficient funds. For further information, contact your local embassy or consulate (see below).

## Australian embassies and consulates

**CANADA**, Australian High Commission, Suite 710, 50 O'Connor St, Ottawa, Ontario K1P 6L2 ℡613/236-0841, fax 236-4376; Australian Consulate-General, Suite 316, 175 Bloor St East, Toronto, Ontario M4W 3R8 ℡416/323 1155, fax 323 3910; Australian Consulate, World Trade Center Complex, Suite 602-999, Canada Place, Vancouver, BC V6C 3E1 ℡604/684 1177, fax 684 1856.

**IRELAND**, Australian Embassy, Fitzwilton House, Wilton Terrace, Dublin 2 ℡01/676 1517, fax 678 5185.

**NEW ZEALAND**, Australian High Commission, 72–78 Hobson St, Thorndon, Wellington ℡04/473 6411, fax 498 7135; Australian Consulate-General, 8th Floor, Union House, 32–38 Quay St, Auckland 1 ℡09/303 2429, fax 377 0798.

**UK**, Australian High Commission, Australia House, Strand, London WC2B 4LA ℡0171/379 4334, fax 240 5333; Australian Consulate, Chatsworth House, Lever St, Manchester M1 2DL ℡0161/228 1344, fax 236 4074.

**US**, Australian Embassy, 1601 Massachusetts Ave NW, Washington DC 20036–2273 ℡202/797-3000, fax 797-3168;

Australian Consulate-General, Century Plaza Towers, 19th Floor, 2049 Century Park East, Los Angeles, CA 90067 ☏310/229-4800, fax 277-2258; Australian Consulate-General; Australian Consulate-General, International Building, 150 East 42nd St, 34th Floor, New York, NY 10117-5612 ☏212/351-6500, fax 351-6501; Australian Consulate-General, 1 Bush St, 7th Floor, San Francisco, CA 94104-4413 ☏415/362-6160, fax 986-5440.

## Customs

Those aged over 18 have a **duty-free allowance** on entry of 1125ml of alcohol and 250 cigarettes/250g of tobacco. Australia has strict quarantine laws that apply to fruit, vegetables, fresh and packaged food, seeds and some animal products, among other things. As well as drugs and firearms, Australian custom officials are strict about steroids, pornographic material, protected wildlife and associated products.

# Money and costs

If you've arrived from Asia you'll find Melbourne expensive on a day-to-day basis, but fresh from Europe or the USA you'll discover prices on a par or somewhat cheaper. By planning carefully, it's relatively easy to manage on a modest budget.

## Currency

The Australian currency is the **Australian dollar**, which is divided into 100 cents. Notes are available in denominations of $100, $50, $20, $10 and $5, while coins come in values of $2, $1, 50c, 20c, 10c and 5c. Exchange rates fluctuate at around A$2.50 for £1; A$1.60 for US$1; and A$0.84 for NZ$1.

## Costs

The absolute minimum **daily budget** is around $30–40 a day for food, board and transport if you stay in hostels, travel on buses and eat and drink frugally. On the other hand, if you're staying in hotels or B&Bs, and eating out regularly, reckon on $70–90; extras such as clubbing, car rental and tours will all add to your costs.

## Travellers' cheques and plastic

**Travellers' cheques** are the best way to bring your funds into Australia (remember to keep a list of the serial numbers separate from the cheques). The most widely accepted brands are American Express and Thomas Cook, denominated in US or Australian dollars, or sterling.

**Credit cards** come in handy as a back-up source of funds, and can also save on bank commissions; the most useful are Visa, Mastercard and American Express, followed by Bankcard and Diners Club. ATMs are generally open 24 hours and allow international access for cards in the Cirrus-Maestro network (including Visa and Mastercard).

## Banks and exchange

**Banking hours** are Monday to Thursday 9.30am–4pm and Friday 9.30am–5pm, although some branches of the Bank of Melbourne open on Saturday from 9am to noon. The major banks, with branches countrywide, are Westpac, ANZ, Commonwealth and National. You can also **exchange foreign currency** at the airport, or at Thomas Cook or American Express offices in town (see p.210).

## Emergency cash

In an emergency, **wiring money** is the quickest option. International money transfers can be made to any nominated bank in Australia and cost approximately A$25. Transfers can take anywhere from a few days to several months. Alternatively, you can use MoneyGram, where you receive money via a MoneyGram agent such as American Express (℗1800/230 100); charges vary according to the amount, but can be up to ten percent.

MONEY AND COSTS

# THE GUIDE

# Introducing the city

**M**elbourne's **Central Business District (CBD)** is a large, flat rectangle, with wide blocks laid out on a grid pattern, making navigation easy. The main north–south artery is **Swanston Street**, and the most important east–west streets are **Collins** and **Bourke streets**.

The half of the CBD **east of Swanston Street** is an attractive legacy of the riches borne from the goldrush era, when Melbourne enjoyed its period of greatest prosperity. From this period date many of the city's finest civic buildings, including the mammoth **Parliament House** and the magnificent cathedrals of **St Patrick's** and **St Paul's**. At the eastern edge of the district, the fashionable shops and cafés of the **"Paris End"** of Collins Street offer style and culture of a more contemporary kind, as does atmospheric **Chinatown**, still home to the longest established of the city's many ethnic communities.

**West of Swanston Street**, the other half of the CBD is home to bustling **Bourke Street Mall**, a pedestrian-only strip flanked by arcades, department stores and the classical General Post Office. Southwest on Collins Street is Melbourne's tallest building, the **Rialto Towers**, while to the north, **Queen Victoria Market** is a popular venue for shopping and socializing.

Running along the southern edge of the CBD, the **Yarra** river provides the city's principal axis, dividing the greater metropolitan area in two. Along its southern bank are arranged many of Melbourne's newest and glitziest buildings, including the enormous leisure complexes of **Southgate** and the **Crown Casino**, the **Melbourne Exhibition Centre** and the **Victorian Arts Centre**, with its distinctive spire.

Just north of the CBD, the inner suburbs of **Carlton** and **Fitzroy** are at the heart of Melbourne's vibrant ethnic and alternative cultures. South of the CBD, the main thoroughfare is St Kilda Road, a busy, tree-lined boulevard which runs past the exclusive suburbs of **South Yarra**, **Prahran** and **Toorak** before reaching the seafront at **St Kilda**, 3km south of the city centre. Beyond these, the city's sprawling **outer suburbs** hold fewer points of interest for the visitor, although **Williamstown**, on a promontory southwest of the city, warrants a visit for its maritime leanings and lively weekend coffee trade. Further afield, in the northeastern suburbs of Bulleen and Eltham, the artist retreats of the **Museum of Modern Art at Heide** and **Montsalvat** are well worth the trek to see two notable places of bohemian creativity.

...........................................................................................

**The telephone code for the Melbourne area is ℗03.**

...........................................................................................

# Arrival

Despite its urban sprawl, **arrival** in Melbourne should prove a relatively uncomplicated experience. Most visitors are likely to arrive either at Tullamarine Airport, 22km northwest of the city, or at one of the two main bus terminals, both conveniently located in the CBD.

# By air

Melbourne's main point of arrival is **Tullamarine Airport**, a thirty-minute drive northwest of the city. The airport's international terminal (the domestic terminal is next door) has baggage lockers (24hr; $4–8), a 24-hour Thomas Cook **foreign exchange** desk with reasonable rates, and various ATMs. There are also two **travellers information service desks** on the ground and first floors (daily 6am–last flight), which can help you with **accommodation** – you can also book a room through the interactive video unit on the ground floor.

**Buses** into the city leave from just outside the ground-floor level of the international terminal. The Skybus service (6.40am–11.40pm every 30min; 11.40pm-6.40am hourly; $10) runs to the Melbourne Transit Centre, Spencer Street Station and Bus Terminal, Melbourne Town Hall and Exhibition Street (the night service between 11.40pm and 6.40am goes to Melbourne Town Hall only). On weekdays (7.15am–4.15pm), Saturday (8.30am–1.30pm) and Sunday (1–5.30pm), the bus driver will drop you off at most city hotels on request. Tickets can be purchased on board, or from the travellers information service desks. A **taxi** to the city should cost about $30. **Car rental** desks are located in the car park opposite the airport.

The drive into town carries visitors on the western section of the CityLink tollway and through a dramatic new entrance to the city: on exiting the Tullamarine Freeway towards the Yarra bridge you approach a long orange concrete wall, then a massive yellow tilted beam (nicknamed "the Cheesestick") suspended over the freeway, followed on the right by thirty-metre-high red pillars.

## By bus

The **Melbourne Transit Centre** is just north of the city centre at 58 Franklin Street. Greyhound Pioneer Australia and Skybuses arrive here. Other interstate operators, including McCafferty's and Firefly, use the **Spencer Street Bus Terminal** on the western side of the city, just north of the Spencer Street train station. This terminal is also served by V/Line buses, which operate mostly within Victoria.

## By ferry

Visitors arriving from Tasmania **by ferry** dock at Station Pier in Port Melbourne, about 4km southwest of the city centre. The ferry terminal is served by tram #109 to Collins Street in the CBD. On Wednesday, Friday and Sunday, Skybus also run a service from the ferry to the Melbourne Transit Centre in the city.

## By train

**Spencer Street Station**, about 100m south of the Spencer Street Bus Terminal, is the terminus for country and inter-state trains. Facilities are limited, although there is a left-luggage office (daily 6am–10pm).

.....................................................................................

**Some hostels offer a free pick-up service from bus, train or ferry terminals on request.**

.....................................................................................

# Information

Melbourne's main tourist centre, the **Victorian Visitor Information Centre**, is housed in the Melbourne Town Hall on Swanston Street, at the corner of Little Collins Street (Mon–Fri 9am–6pm, Sat & Sun 9am–5pm; ✆9650 7721). The centre can help book accommodation, tours and travel, and also has an **AusRes booking desk** (✆9650 1522), providing accommodation and tour services. Next door, the **City Experience Centre** (CEC) (Mon–Fri 9am–7pm, Sat & Sun 10am–5pm) has more information, multilingual touchscreens and permanent displays. It also organizes a free "Greeter Service", whereby visitors are matched up with local volunteers according to language and interests (book at least three days in advance on ✆9658 9524, fax 9654 1054). Nearby, at 360 Bourke Street, the **Royal Automobile Club of Victoria** also has a free accommodation booking service (Mon–Fri 9am–5.30pm, Sat 9am–2pm; ✆9790 2121), while **Information Victoria** at 356 Collins Street (Mon–Fri 8.30am–5.30pm; ✆1300/366 356) has brochures, books and a large range of local maps. There are also volunteer-staffed **visitor information booths** at Bourke Street Mall and Flinders Street Station (Mon–Thurs 9am–5pm, Fri 9am–7pm, Sat 10am–4pm, Sun 11am–4pm), and **VISITS information terminals** – interactive touchscreen machines where you can look up anything from a cab phone number to a Chinese restaurant – at Melbourne Town Hall, 230 Collins Street and outside Melbourne Central, opposite the State Library of Victoria. Other sources of information include **Parks Victoria** at Level 2, 35 Whitehorse Road in Kew (Mon–Fri 9am–5pm; ✆13/1963), which has information on national parks and conservation areas in Victoria; the **National Trust**

INFORMATION

**25**

# Melbourne on the Internet

**AFL** *www.afl.com.au* Comprehensive footy site including player profiles, loads of statistics, and news and features by football writers from *The Age*.

**The Age** *www.theage.com.au* Online edition of Melbourne's prestigious daily, *The Age* has breaking news, business and sports info, special reports, and weather and flight details.

**Beat** *www.beat.com.au* Updated each week, *Beat* is the modish online magazine of the free street paper of the same name. Focusing on Melbourne's music and entertainment scene, it has profiles of upcoming bands, reviews, gig and club guides, and links to music and arts sites.

**CitySearch Melbourne** *www.melbourne.citysearch.com.au* Easily digestible Melbourne guide produced in conjunction with *The Age* newspaper. Covers a wide range of topics, including entertainment, events, eating, drinking, shopping, sports, travel and recreation.

**Festivale** *www.festivale.webcentral.com.au* Webzine filled with arts and entertainment information. Includes film, theatre and book sections, as well as a pictorial guide to Melbourne's attractions, with clickable maps and instructions on how to get to them by public transport.

**TISM** *www.tism.wanker.com* Explores the rapid and bizarre rise to fame of legendary Melbourne band TISM (This Is Serious Mum). Includes a hilarious biography, music links, downloadable videos and lyrics to many of their ruthlessly satiric songs. Gained national fame in 1995 when their *Machiavelli and the Four Seasons* album, featuring the hit song "I'm On The Drug That Killed River Phoenix", went gold.

**Tourism Victoria** *www.tourism.vic.gov.au* Informative Web site containing details on Melbourne and Victoria's key attractions, accommodation, shopping, sports, arts, events, food and drinking, plus a search facility and links to related sites.

**What's On In Victoria** *www.whatson.vic.gov.au* Detailed information covering cultural activities, sporting and entertainment events, kids' activities, how to book tickets, and even where to pa

Tasma-Terrace, 6 Parliament Place (Mon–Fri 9am–5pm; ©9654 4711), where you can buy guides for walking tours and National Trust properties; and the **Melbourne Information Line** (©1300/655 452), which has details of exhibitions, children's activities, and transport and parking.

> The Victorian Visitor Information Centre has seven colour-coded *Heritage Walk* pamphlets describing walking tours in the city and surrounding areas, as well as the *Another View* brochure, a guided Koori walking trail to seventeen Aboriginal sites.

In most of the information centres you can pick up a copy of the monthly *Melbourne Events*, a particularly good source of city-wide information. Daily cinema and theatre **listings** appear in *The Age*, Melbourne's leading daily newspaper; the Friday edition also contains an excellent pull-out entertainment section, "EG", which has music listings, as does "Hit", the Thursday insert of Melbourne's other daily, the *Herald Sun*. Music listings are also included in *Beat* and *Inpress* magazines, available free from record shops, bars and fashion outlets.

Melbourne's best **street directory** is *Melway*, available from bookshops and newsagents.

**INFORMATION**

# City transport

Melbourne's integrated transport system of trams, trains and buses is called **The Met**, and a range of tickets valid on all forms of transport is available through the new **Metcard** automated ticketing system. Unless you're going on a day-trip to the outer suburbs, you can get anywhere you need to, including St Kilda and Williamstown, on a **zone 1 ticket**. An ordinary zone 1 ticket costs $2.30 and is valid for unlimited travel within the zone for two hours (or all night if bought after 7pm) on any form of transport. A day-ticket ($4.40) is better value if you're making several trips, while for longer stays a weekly ticket ($19.10) is even more economical. You can also buy **short-trip tickets** ($1.50), which allow travel on a particular section of the bus or tram route.

...................................................................................................

**Long regarded as synonymous with Melbourne, tram conductors ("connies") were phased out in May 1998 and replaced by machines, resulting in plummeting revenue, widespread fare evasion and vandalism.**

...................................................................................................

Tickets (including day and weekly tickets) can be bought on board trams and buses (but not on trains) or from widely loathed ticketing machines in train stations or retail outlets. To avoid queuing in front of the machines (which usually only accept coins, although machines in larger train stations sometimes give change for $10 notes and accept credit cards), it's better to buy tickets in advance at milk bars (grocery stores), newsagents, train stations or the City Met Shop at 103 Elizabeth Street. These outlets are also the source of some **discounted tickets**, such as a five-pack of two-hour tickets and the "Short Trip 10", which gives ten short rides for $12.50. Tickets must be validated in the machines at train stations prior to travelling, or on board trams and buses as you enter.

Services operate Monday to Saturday from 5am until midnight, and Sunday from 8am until 11pm, supplemented in the early hours of Saturday and Sunday by NightRider buses (see p.30). For further information, call the **Met Information Centre** (daily 7am–8.55pm; ℃13/1638), or the **Metcard Help Line** (℃1800/652 313).

## Trams

Melbourne's **trams** run down the centre of the road, and can be boarded through either the front or middle doors. Stops are signposted, and there are often central islands where you can wait – if not, take care crossing the road. The colour map at the back of the book shows the main routes.

## Trains

**Trains** are the fastest way to reach the outer suburbs. An underground loop system connects the city centre's five train stations: **Spencer Street**, which also serves as the station for interstate and country buses and trains; **Flagstaff**, on the corner of La Trobe and William streets; **Melbourne Central**, on the corner of Swanston and La Trobe streets; **Parliament**, on Spring Street; and **Flinders Street**, the main suburban station, at the junction of Flinders and Swanston streets. Bicycles can be carried free except during rush hours (Mon–Fri 7–9.30am & 4–6pm), when an extra adult concession fee has to be paid. Surfboards can also be carried on payment of a concession fee.

## Buses

**Buses** often run on the same routes as trams, as well as filling

# Useful tram routes

In the **city centre**, useful trams include the **#1** and **#22**, which travel north–south along Swanston Street, and the **#19**, **#57** and **#59**, which run along Elizabeth Street. Trams **#11** and **#12** run east–west along Collins Street; **#86** and **#96**, along Bourke Street. A free and particularly convenient way to get around town are the burgundy-and-cream **City Circle Trams**, which run in a loop (look for the specially marked stops) around Flinders, Spring, La Trobe and Spencer streets.

Routes **#1** and **#22** continue **north of the city centre** to Carlton; route **#11** to Fitzroy. Other useful services include **#57** for North Melbourne and **#86** for Collingwood. East of the city centre, tram **#75** serves East Melbourne, Richmond and Hawthorn.

Heading **south of city**, tram **#8** runs from Swanston Street via South Yarra to Toorak; tram **#6** to Prahran. Tram **#1** runs through South Melbourne and Albert Park, while tram **#96** runs from Bourke Street through South Melbourne and Albert Park to St Kilda – the latter is served by a number of other routes. See p.80 for details.

gaps where no train or tram services exist, but they are generally the least useful mode of public transport for visitors apart from the special **NightRider** buses, which go to the outer suburbs on Saturday and Sunday mornings, departing from City Square hourly between 12.30am and

**London Transport Bus Tours (©9557 8100) have a number of competitively priced daily tours ($20–45), which range from city-centre sights to night-time excursions to Melbourne's inner suburbs.**

4.30am ($5). Each bus is equipped with a mobile phone so the driver can book a taxi to meet you at a bus stop (free call), or you can call a friend ($1) to meet you.

## Car

**Driving** requires some care, mainly because of the trams, though recent findings in *The Age* also revealed that Melbourne has the most reckless drivers in Australia. You can **overtake a tram** only on the left and must stop and wait behind it while passengers are getting off, as they usually step directly into the road (there's no need to stop, however, if there's a central pedestrian island). There is also a peculiar road rule known as the **"hook turn"**, which accommodates trams at major intersections in the city centre: when turning right, you pull over to the left-hand lane (leaving the right-hand lane free for through-traffic and the tram tracks clear for trams) and wait for the lights to change to amber before turning. Black-and-white signs overhead indicate when this rule applies. For more information on road rules, the *Victorian Road Traffic Handbook* is available from bookshops and Vic Roads offices (call ✆13/1171 for the nearest office).

> **For car and campervan rentals and information on parking, see p.211 and p.214.**

## Taxis

Melbourne's **taxis** wait in ranks at central locations like the *Hotel Sofitel* in Collins Street, Flinders and Spencer Street stations, and the Myer department store in Lonsdale Street. Alternatively, call Arrow Taxi Services (✆13/2211), Black Cabs Combined (✆13/2227), Embassy Taxis (✆13/1755),

# Melbourne's public toilets

Mid-nineteenth-century Melbourne was a famously filthy town. Satirists called it "Shit Melbourne" and "Marvellous Smellbourne", and the paucity of **public toilets** was so severe that townspeople were forced to relieve themselves in the city's busy streets and lanes. In response, the authorities set about introducing urinals and sewer systems until, by the turn of the century, the city's toilets were the most advanced in Australia.

The following selection isn't exhaustive, but should give you an idea of what's on offer. "M" and "W" denote men's and women's toilets respectively.

**Hotel Sofitel**, 25 Collins St. M & W: The toilets on the 36th Floor, affording vertiginous city vistas, are known as the "loos with the views". Hygienic cubicles, soft toilet paper and clean mirrors will have you whizzing back for more.

**Melbourne Central**, 30 Lonsdale St. M: Pleasantly fitted-out toilet on the second floor with a single cubicle, urinal and basin. Small, so be prepared to wait. W: Well-ventilated, ground-floor loo with clean facilities and good lighting.

**Melbourne Town Hall**, Collins St entrance. M: Large, tiled restroom, excellently lit and with secure locks on the cubicle doors. W: Similar to the men's convenience – well appointed, with soft uplighting and lots of cubicles.

**Public Toilet**, Elizabeth St, outside the GPO. M & W: Nineteenth-century underground amenities, displaying delicate wrought-iron lacework at street level, are hardly flushed with comfort, and would make even the most desperate soul think twice before entering.

**Spencer Street Station**, Spencer St. M: Spacious facility on the mezzanine, with a disabled unit. W: A dozen mostly clean cubicles, a disabled toilet and nappy-change area.

or the Silver Top Taxi Service (✆13/1008), or hail one on the street when the rooftop light is illuminated. For wheelchair-accessible cabs, call Central Booking Service (✆1300/364 050) at least one day in advance. Finding a taxi late at night is difficult, especially at weekends, so if you know you'll need one, book it.

# The Eastside

T he **Eastside** – the area of the city centre bounded by Swanston, Flinders, Spring and Victoria streets – impressively captures the "Marvellous Melbourne" era which followed the discovery of gold in 1851. Replete with nineteenth-century civic landmarks, it also buzzes with designer shops and elegant watering holes, and continues to serve as the focal point of much of Melbourne's cultural and political life.

Many of Melbourne's best-known buildings were constructed in the three decades after gold was discovered in 1851, including the imposing **Parliament House** on Spring Street, book-ended by small and tranquil gardens to the north and south, and the handsome **Old Treasury Building** nearby. Melbourne's short but bounteous history is also reflected in two magnificent nineteenth-century cathedrals, **St Patrick's** and **St Paul's**, built to administer spiritual salvation to a rapidly expanding and increasingly diverse population, while to the north is probably the most worthwhile of all the city's sights, the **Old Melbourne Gaol**, which captures in grisly detail the fates of some of the early city's less fortunate souls. Civic monuments apart, there is plenty to enjoy, from the well-heeled boutiques and cafés at the **"Paris End"** of Collins Street to the characterful restaurants and stores of **Chinatown**, home to the large

Chinese community that established itself in Melbourne in the 1880s and which – later augmented by waves of post-war Greek and Italian immigrants – has done much to give the Eastside precincts their cosmopolitan accent.

........................................................................................

**The area covered by this chapter is shown in detail on colour map 4.**

........................................................................................

# FLINDERS STREET STATION AND AROUND

**Map 4, G5.** Tram #1, #16, #22, #48 or #75.

Located in the heart of the city on the corner of Flinders Street and St Kilda Road, the neoclassical **Flinders Street Station** (1910) is the traditional gateway to the city for the 100,000-plus commuters who pass through it every day. The station's imposing bulk – complete with dome and clock tower – is reasonably eye-friendly, while the entrance acts as a landmark-cum-meeting place (Ava Gardner and Gregory Peck had a gloriously prolonged goodbye here in the film *On the Beach*), where people gather under the famous clocks, each of which indicates the next scheduled departure on a different suburban line.

Opposite the station, on the corner of Swanston and Flinders streets, **St Paul's Cathedral** (Mon–Fri 7am–5.45pm, Sat 8am–5pm, Sun 7.30am–7.30pm) was built between 1880 and 1891 on the site where the colony's first settlers had held ecumenical services in a tent pitched under a gum tree. Constructed to the Gothic Revival design of noted English architect William Butterfield – who never actually visited Australia – the cathedral's spire is the second-largest Anglican structure of its kind in the world, after England's Salisbury Cathedral. Inside, intricate tiled floors compete with carved woodwork, magnificent stained-glass windows and a beautiful pulpit bearing a representation of the head of Nellie Cain, daughter of lay canon William Cain, chairman of the committee which organized the building of the church.

Running up from the cathedral is central Melbourne's main north–south axis: **Swanston Street**. It's an unremarkable stretch of low-rent shops and fast-food joints, but if you need a recharging drink the historic **Young & Jackson's** pub is on the corner of Swanston and Flinders streets. The land on which the hotel stands was originally purchased by John Batman for £100, then used as a butcher's shop until licensed as a watering hole in 1861. Upstairs, patrons drink pots under the portrait of **Chloe**, a full-length nude by French artist Jules Lefebre (her lover) that seems tame today, but which drew thin-lipped disapproval from Melbourne society when first exhibited at Melbourne's International Exhibition in 1880.

# MELBOURNE TOWN HALL

**Map 4, G4.** Tours Tues–Thurs 10.30am & 2.30pm, and on the third Sat of the month hourly 10am–3pm; free. Tram #1 or #22 from Swanston St; tram #9, #11 or #12 from Collins St.

Two blocks north of the cathedral is another civic icon: **Melbourne Town Hall**, dating from 1870 (the portico was added in 1887; an adjacent administrative block in 1908). It's best known as the place where Australia's famous operatic soprano Dame Nellie Melba made her debut in 1884, but it's also played host to everything from public debates and waltzes to poultry shows and wrestling. Here the Queen sipped tea in the stately Melbourne Room in 1954; here, ten years later, the Beatles waved to their adoring fans from the balcony; and here, in 1997, Germaine Greer kicked off the annual Melbourne Writers' Festival by launching a stinging attack against "penetration culture" (old-fogey Melburnians are still recovering). The Town

Hall can only be seen by tour, when you can roam through rooms mired in syrupy nostalgia. There's also an excellent collection of rustic paintings by early Melbourne artists Tom Roberts and George Folingsby.

Facing Melbourne Town Hall, **City Square** was created during the 1960s by clearing a number of nineteenth-century buildings and has been dogged by controversy ever since – it's currently an enormous hole in the ground which will eventually be filled by a car park with a five-star hotel on top. In the meantime you can still see the forty-ton statue of a bewhiskered Burke and Willis, two of Australia's best-known explorers who perished on a transcontinental expedition in 1860. Also worth a look from here is the neo-Gothic **Manchester Unity Building** (1932), on the corner of Collins and Swanston streets, inspired by the Chicago Tribune Building.

# THE "PARIS END"

**Map 4, I4.** Tram #9, #11 or #12 from Collins St.

From City Square, **Collins Street** rises up past the pompous Melbourne Athenaeum and the lovingly restored Regent Theatre (see p.171) to **Scots Church**, whose Gothic Revival design merits a quick peek, though it's famous mainly as the place where Dame Nellie Melba first sang in the choir. Further up, the towering, I.M. Pei-designed *Hotel Sofitel* dominates the upper part of the street, known as the **"Paris End"** (or "Top End"): a strip of exclusive boutiques and cafés where metropolitan movers unwind over lattes before their next boardroom meeting. At **no. 101** is one of Melbourne's more daring modern commercial buildings, inventively combining erotic sculptures with freestanding columns, while nearby Collins Place plays host to a dreary **arts-and-crafts market** every Sunday (9am–5pm). Opposite, at no. 36, is one of

Australia's last bastions of male chauvinism, the toffy, men-only **Melbourne Club** (1858).

At the top of Collins Street, on the junction with Spring and Macarthur streets, the superb **Old Treasury Building** (Mon–Fri 9am–5pm, Sat & Sun 10am–4pm; $5) is emblematic of Melbourne's goldrush prosperity, combining elegance with unbridled opulence in its graceful balconies and high-ceilinged rooms. Completed in 1862 to a design by 19-year-old John James Clark, its basement once held fortunes in gold, though today it houses nothing more valuable than an exhibition on the social and architectural history of Melbourne. The building is also used for special events like exhibitions and live performances.

Adjoining the building are the small and beautiful **Treasury Gardens**, packed most weekdays with public servants from nearby offices.

# FITZROY GARDENS

**Map 4, L3–L4.** Tram #9, #11 or #12 from Collins St.

A stone's throw east, **Fitzroy Gardens** stand on what was a swamp until the 1860s, when the land was reclaimed and turned into a garden laid out in the shape of the Union Jack – a jingoistic conceit later abandoned in favour of a more free-flowing design. They're best appreciated on weekdays, as weekends tend to attract cavalcades of bridal parties having their photographs taken. The gardens' main attraction is **Captain Cook's Cottage**, the family home of English navigator Captain James Cook (daily: April–Sept 9am–5pm; Nov–March 9am–5.30pm; $3). The cottage was purchased in 1933 by Russell Grimwade, a wealthy Melbourne businessman, who had it shipped over piece by piece from its original location in Whitby, Yorkshire, and presented as a gift to the state of Victoria for its 1934 centenary. Kitsch abounds in the red-brick and creeper-covered cottage with period fittings, which attempts to re-create the atmosphere of eighteenth-century England, reinforced by worthy displays about the explorer himself. Elsewhere in the gardens, a tacky model Tudor village continues the olde-worlde theme, while the conservatory's flower displays (daily 9am–5pm; free) and the Fairies' Tree – an old gum tree sculpted with fairies, dwarfs, gnomes and koalas – are popular with visitors of all ages.

# PARLIAMENT HOUSE AND AROUND

**Map 4, J3.** 40min tours Mon–Fri 10am, 11am, noon, 2pm, 3pm & 3.45pm on days when parliament is not sitting (ring ©9651 8911 for dates); free. Tram #96 from Bourke St.

Returning to the Old Treasury Building and heading up Spring Street brings you to **Eastern Hill**, the area selected by Charles La Trobe, Victoria's first governor, for state use in the 1840s. Oozing authority at its summit is the colossal **Parliament House**, built in stages between 1856 and 1930 on a grassy knoll known as Lovers' Lane. Following the federation of Australia's six colonies in 1901, the first Federal Parliament of Australia took over the building, forcing the Victorian Government to find alternative accommodation in the Royal Exhibition Building (see p.68), where it remained until 1927, when the Federal Parliament shifted to Canberra, allowing the Victorian Government to reclaim its original home.

Through the main doors a vestibule leads into the elaborate Queen's Hall, used mainly for formal state functions, while doors to the right and left connect with the chambers of the Legislative Council and Legislative Assembly. Don't miss **Question Time** (2pm; arrive early to claim a seat), when you can sit in the Public Gallery and – depending on the importance of the debate – listen either to the members' heated exchanges or count the number who have fallen asleep.

Opposite Parliament House, the immaculately preserved **Windsor Hotel** began life as the Grand Hotel in 1883, before being taken over three years later by future Victorian premier James Munro, who established his moral credentials by immediately declaring the establishment teetotal. Check out the palatial interior, its rooms resonating with the hum of well-bred conversation, or indulge in a posh afternoon tea (daily 3.30–5.30pm) of tarts and lamingtons in the hotel's restaurant, *111 Spring Street*. Just north on the same side of the street, the **Princess Theatre** is a sparky piece of nineteenth-century chic which was transformed into one of Melbourne's most extravagant buildings when tarted up in recognition of Queen Victoria's Jubilee Year in 1887.

To the northeast looms **St Patrick's Cathedral**, designed by William Wardell, the architect responsible for some of Melbourne's finest nineteenth-century churches (Mon–Fri 8am–6pm, Sat 8am–7.30pm, Sun 8am–8pm). A more modest church stood on the site until 1850, when the Reverend J.A. Goold, Bishop of Melbourne, decided it was too small for the city's burgeoning population and had it demolished. Its replacement was still under construction when, in 1858, the ambitious Goold declared that a still grander cathedral was required, to be constructed on the proceeds of Victoria's booming pastoral industries. Work proceeded slowly, however, and was frequently suspended as labour vanished to the goldfields. Finally consecrated in 1897, the cathedral boasts one of the city's finest collections of stained-glass windows, and the finely proportioned interior is graced by an enormous marble crucifix.

# CHINATOWN

**Map 4, G3.** Tram #1 or #22 from Swanston St.

Heading back towards the city centre, Melbourne's small but lively **Chinatown** revolves around the section of Little

Bourke Street between Swanston and Exhibition streets. Australia's oldest permanent Chinese settlement, the area began as a few boarding houses in the 1850s, when the gold-rushes attracted Chinese prospectors (mainly from the Pearl River Delta near Hong Kong), then grew as gold petered out and Chinese fortune-seekers returned from the backbreaking work of prospecting to settle in the city. Despite being spruced up in 1974 as a tourist attraction, Chinatown retains a low-rise, narrow-laned, nineteenth-century character, with atmospheric cafés and restaurants lined cheek by jowl. Jackie Chan, the famous Hong Kong actor and director, made good use of the location when he shot several scenes here for his Cantonese-language flick *Mr Nice Guy*, in which he played the part of a Melbourne TV chef.

........................................................................................

**For details on the places to eat in Chinatown, see
"Eating", p.122. Chinatown is also close to some of
Melbourne's best Italian restaurants like *Pellegrini's*
(p.120) and the *Florentino Restaurant and Cellar Bar* (p.117).**

........................................................................................

Established in 1985 in an old warehouse on Cohen Place, the **Chinese Museum** (Mon–Fri & Sun 10am–4.30pm, Sat noon–4.30pm; $5) traces the experience of Chinese immigrants in Australia during the mid-nineteenth century, especially their role in the development of Melbourne. The museum is worth a visit for the 92-metre-long Dai Loong dragon alone, which is paraded each Chinese New Year and during the Moomba Festival (see p.177). There's also a good collection of antiques and artefacts relating to Chinatown's social history, together with an exhibition gallery on the top floor showcasing Chinese artists from Melbourne and elsewhere. The museum organizes guided tours ($15, or $28 including lunch; ℗9662 2888) of the building and Chinatown; these require a minimum of four people, and should be booked two or three days in advance.

CHINATOWN

**41**

# STATE LIBRARY OF VICTORIA

**Map 4, G2.** Mon & Wed 10am–9pm, Tues & Thurs–Sun 10am–6pm; ℗9669 9888. Introductory tours Mon–Fri and first and third Sat of the month 2pm; free. Tram #1 or #22 from Swanston St.

North of Chinatown along Swanston Street, the **State Library of Victoria**, one of Victoria's grandest civic monuments, was completed in 1856 under the direction of the library's founder and well-known Melbourne philanthropist Sir Redmond Barry, the judge who sentenced Australia's notorious bushranger Ned Kelly to hang (see p.44), although construction of the portico, dome and reading room wasn't finished until 1913. The library houses a trove of rare and antiquarian books, along with material such as the diaries of Charles La Trobe and John Pascoe Fawkner, and the deed of land purchase by John Batman from the Dugitalla Aborigines.

........................................................................

> **Just south of the State Library along Lonsdale Street, Melbourne's Greek precinct has cake shops and travel agencies, and restaurants such as** *Stalactites* **(p.120) and** *Tsindos* **(p.121).**

........................................................................

The library is currently being restored – work is due to continue until 2004. It's also the temporary home until 2001 of the **National Gallery of Victoria** (daily 10am–5pm; free), where you can see classic Australian and European works.

# RMIT

**Map 4, F1–G2.** Tram #1 or #22 from Swanston St.

The **Royal Melbourne Institute of Technology (RMIT)**, just across La Trobe Street, is a scene-stealer that mixes the shock of the new with style and proportion from the old days. Constructed from the shell of an original Victorian building embellished with striking modernist facades, its architectural surprises include Building 8, with its playful combination of colour, shapes and perforations, and Storey Hall's pick'n'mix facade of livid green and purple patterns, loosely arranged according to the principles of chaos theory. The interest continues inside Storey Hall, with terrific installations, including a copy of *Vault* (see p.59) and an auditorium in which the original Victorian fittings have been immersed in great panels of pink, purple, green and white. There's also a serene 1990s minimalist gallery (Mon–Fri 11am–5pm, Sat 2–5pm; free) and a subterranean café.

Immediately north are the congenial red-brick **Melbourne City Baths** (1860), where Melburnians had their weekly wash at the turn of the century. Relax here in inviting lounges and open-air terraces after a swim, workout or sauna (see p.185).

# OLD MELBOURNE GAOL

**Map 4, G1.** Daily 9.30am–4.30pm; $7; ℗9663 7228. Tram #1 or #22 from Swanston St.

Behind the RMIT on Russell Street, the massive **Old Melbourne Gaol** is the city's most popular sight, largely on account of its associations with Victorian bushranger Ned Kelly, who was hanged here on November 11, 1880. Opened in 1854, the gaol was modelled on Joshua Jebb's Pentonville Prison in London, with high-ceilinged brick cells and observation towers to prevent escape. Melbourne's general state of lawlessness during the goldrushes caused such overcrowding that the jail was continually expanded – later additions included the thick outer wall where, in 1880, thousands gathered to hear that Kelly had shuffled off this mortal coil. A mix of condemned men and women (segre-

OLD MELBOURNE GAOL

# Ned Kelly

Even before Ned Kelly became widely known, folklore and ballads were popularizing the free-ranging bush outlaws as potent symbols of freedom and resistance to authority. By the time he was 11, **Ned Kelly**, son of an alcoholic rustler and a mother who sold illicit liquor, was already in constant trouble with the police, who considered the whole family troublemakers.

Ned became the accomplice of the established bushranger Harry Power, and by his mid-teens had a string of warrants to his name. Ned's brother Dan was also wanted by the police and, hearing that he had turned up at his mother's, a policeman set out, drunk and without a warrant, to arrest him. A scuffle ensued and the unsteady constable fell to the floor, hitting his head and allowing Dan to escape. The following day warrants were issued for the arrest of Ned (who was in New South Wales at the time) and Dan for attempted murder; their mother was sentenced to three years' imprisonment.

From this point on, the **Kelly gang**'s crime spree accelerated and, following the death of three constables in a shoot-out at Stringybark Creek, the biggest manhunt in Australia's history began, with a £1000 reward offered for the gang's apprehension. On December 9, 1878, they robbed the bank at Euroa in Victoria's northeast, taking £2000, before moving on to Jerilderie in New South Wales.

After a year on the run, the gang formulated a grand plan: they executed Aaron Sherritt, a police informer, in Sebastopol, thus attracting a train-bound posse from nearby Beechworth. It was planned to derail this train at Glenrowan with as much bloodshed as possible before moving on to rob the bank at Benalla and barter hostages for the release of Kelly's mother. In the event, having already sabotaged the tracks, the gang commandeered the Glenrowan Inn and, in a moment of drunken candour, Kelly detailed his ambush to a schoolteacher who escaped, managing to save the special train. As the armed troopers approached the inn, the outlaws donned the home-made **iron armour** that has since become their motif. In the ensuing gunfight Kelly's comrades were either killed or they commited suicide as the inn was torched, while Ned himself was taken alive, tried by the same judge who had incarcerated his mother, and sentenced to hang.

Public sympathies lay strongly with Ned Kelly, and a crowd of five thousand gathered outside Melbourne Gaol on November 11, 1880 for his execution, believing that the 25-year-old bushranger would "die game". True to form, his last words are said to have been "Such is life."

gation didn't exist until 1864), remand and short-sentence prisoners, and "lunatics" (often, in fact, drunks) were housed here; long-term prisoners languished in hulks moored at Williamstown, or at the Pentridge Stockade. The jail was recommended for closure in 1870, but it wasn't until 1929 that it was shut for good, although it served as a detention barracks for AWOL soldiers during World War II. Much has been torn down since its closure, but the entrance and outer wall still survive, and it's worth walking round the outside of the building to take a look at the formidable arched brick portal on Franklin Street.

......................................................................................

**Night tours (Wed & Sun: April–Oct 7.30pm; Nov–March 8.30pm; $17; advance bookings through Ticketmaster ℡13/6100)** use the spooky atmosphere of the prison to full effect.

......................................................................................

The gruesome collection of **death masks** on show in the tiny cells bears witness to the nineteenth-century obsession

**OLD MELBOURNE GAOL**

with phrenology, a wobbly branch of science which studied how people's characters were related to the size and shape of their skulls. Accompanying the masks are compelling case histories of the murderers and their victims. Most fascinating are the women: Martha Needle, who poisoned her husband and daughters (among others) with arsenic, and young Martha Knorr, the notorious "baby farmer", who advertised herself as a "kind motherly person, willing to adopt a child". After receiving a few dollars per child, she killed and buried them in her backyard. The jail serves up other macabre memorabilia, including a scaffold still in working order, various nooses, and a triangle where malcontents were strapped to receive lashes by the cat-o'-nine-tails. Perhaps the ultimate rite of visitor passage is the "Art of Hanging", an interpretive display that's part educational tool and part setting for a medieval snuff movie. Linger long enough and everyone will think you're hard.

# The Westside

**T**he **Westside** – bounded by Spencer Street to the west, Flinders Street to the south, Swanston Street to the east and Victoria Street to the north – was for centuries a favoured hunting ground for the local Aboriginal people, and later the area where John Pascoe Fawkner and John Batman founded the settlement of Melbourne in 1835. Docks were built, marshlands drained, and slaughterhouses and gasworks introduced, but development only really took off once vast numbers of fortune-seekers began pouring into Melbourne during the goldrush of the 1850s, when it became the centre of the city's daily life, its commercial heart, and the hub of its sea and rail transport.

Much has changed since the area's heyday, and it now has few obvious attractions, save for the **Rialto Towers** to the west and the multicultural melee of the **Queen Victoria Market** to the north. Here and there, however, are examples of goldrush architecture, glorious gardens and interesting museums, while a fascinating network of historical arcades, laneways and passageways conceals some of the city's finest cafés and speciality shops.

The area covered in this chapter is shown in detail on colour map 4.

# QUEEN VICTORIA MARKET

**Map 4, D1.** April–Oct Tues & Thurs 6am–2pm, Fri 6am–6pm, Sat 6am–3pm, Sun 9am–4pm; Nov–March same hours plus Wed 6.30–10.30pm. Tram #19, #57 or #59 from Elizabeth St.

On the corner of Victoria and Elizabeth streets, the **Queen Victoria Market** is at once historic landmark, popular shopping destination and much-loved city institution. Built on the site of Melbourne's first general cemetery, the market was officially opened in 1878. Its collection of huge, decorative sheds and high-roofed halls – regarded as only temporary when first built – remains, fronted along Victoria Street by restored shops, their original awnings held up by decorative iron posts.

Although quaint and tourist-friendly, the real appeal of the Queen Victoria Market lies in its rowdy, down-to-earth qualities. A stroll through the market, from the dozen stalls selling nothing but blood-red tomatoes to another dozen plying dodgy leather goods and souvenirs, is much more fun than loafing around the city's expensive designer shops. Amidst the potpourri of people and produce are food and deli halls – great for sampling Middle Eastern, Italian, Asian and seafood dishes – while vans outside dispense hot dogs, pies and ice cream. Saturday morning marks a weekly social ritual as Melbourne's foodies turn out for their groceries; Sunday is for clothing and shoe shopping; while Wednesday night's focus in summer is on

A guided "Foodies' Dream Tour" (Tues & Thurs–Sun 10am; $18 including food tasting; ☏9320 5822) explores the market's culinary delights, while heritage tours (same days 10.30am; $12 including coffee and pastries; ☏9320 5822) acquaint visitors with its history and the canny traders on the stalls.

QUEEN VICTORIA MARKET

live music, jugglers, alfresco eating and drinking, and shopping for jewellery and furniture.

Abutting Queen Victoria Market to the southwest are **Flagstaff Gardens**, the site of one of Melbourne's earliest burial grounds (a Gothic monument marks the graves of some of the town's pioneers). In 1840, an observatory incorporating a flagstaff and signal house was built, complete with a cannon which was fired to announce the arrival of important vessels in Port Phillip Bay. From this vantage point, the townsfolk would watch as passengers were ferried up the Yarra to the wharf at the foot of William Street. By the 1880s most of the structures had been torn down for the planting of shade trees, lawns and flowerbeds, which today provide a welcome antidote to the hurly-burly of the city.

# MELBOURNE CENTRAL

**Map 4, F2.** Mon–Thurs & Sat 10am–6pm, Fri 10am–9pm, Sun 11am–6pm. Tram #1 or #22 from Swanston St.

A couple of blocks east of Flagstaff Gardens, **Melbourne Central** shopping complex was opened in 1991 as a fillip to Melbourne's moribund retail scene. Inside the 55-storey steel-and-glass building is a Minotauran maze containing over 160 shops, including the upmarket Japanese department store Daimaru (see p.199). The complex is also home to an ingenious cone-shaped glass dome enclosing a historic brick **shot tower** built on this site in 1889–90. Suspended from the dome is a hot-air balloon and a large fob watch that lets loose every hour with fascinatingly grotesque renditions of Australian songs. Avoid the complex at midday, when there's a jam of office workers, students from the nearby RMIT, and commuters surfacing from the Melbourne Central train station below.

# BOURKE STREET MALL

**Map 4, E4–F4.** Tram #1 or #22 from Swanston St.

The corner of Swanston and Bourke streets marks the start of **Bourke Street Mall**, Melbourne's bustling retail hub, which extends west to Elizabeth Street. The mall has been closed to traffic since 1972, although the odd tram trundling through makes for rather anarchic interactions with pedestrians. Here you'll find an entrance to the lovely old Royal Arcade (see p.52), some of the city's major department stores (including David Jones and Myer – see p.200), and sundry food and clothing shops.

The mall's western end is dominated by the **General Post Office** (GPO), a solid, porticoed pile with Doric, Ionic and Corinthian styles represented in the ground, first and second storeys respectively. Work began on the present GPO in 1859, taking twenty years to complete – the distinctive clock tower was added shortly afterwards. For most Melburnians, however, the GPO's most important architectural feature is its broad bluestone steps, which are at their most useful during the Melbourne International Comedy Festival (see p.178), when they provide an excellent podium for watching clowns on unicycles or avant-garde troupes flailing themselves into insensibility. If the comics don't convulse you, Melbourne's stab at public sculpture – a giant brown purse at the foot of the steps – will.

# THE BLOCK

**Map 4, G4.** Tram #19, #57 or #59 from Elizabeth St.

The area south of Bourke Street Mall to Collins Street – known as **The Block** – was made fashionable in the 1890s by the young milords and miladies who came here to promenade or ride about in their carriages. It's still a draw for dedicated boulevardiers, lured by exclusive shops and cappuccino.

# Small wonders

Honeycombing the area bordered by Swanston, Queen, Lonsdale and Flinders streets is one of the city's highlights – a large and labyrinthine network of **arcades and passageways**, perfect for serendipitous exploring. The following selection is only an introduction – the "Arcades and Laneways" pamphlet, part of the *Heritage Walk* series available at the Victorian Visitor Information Centre (see p.25), has full details.

**Block Place** (Little Collins Street, between Swanston and Elizabeth streets). Narrow, dimly lit warren, where Asian take-aways and clothing stores jostle for space with umpteen cafés – some little more than holes in the wall – specializing in excellent coffee and pastries.

**Degraves Street** (Flinders Lane, between Swanston and Elizabeth streets). Cosmopolitan walkway that throbs with office workers at lunchtime. The tables down the middle are great for people-watching, while Vespas anchored at kerbside provide a nice Italian touch.

**Hardware Street** (Bourke Street, between Queen and Elizabeth streets). Home to the *Campari* restaurant and the very spiffy *Segafredo*, where the coffee is exemplary even by Melbourne standards. Ranged around the street are old-fashioned barbershops, camping and ski stores. In summer, the laid-back bustle, colourful awnings and footpath tables lend the street an ersatz Mediterranean ambience.

**Howey Place** (Little Collins Street, between Swanston and Elizabeth streets). Small but capacious arcade dotted with expensive women's boutiques and cosy cafés.

**McKillop Street** (Bourke Street, between Queen and Elizabeth streets). Opposite Hardware Street, this laneway oozes Victorian charm with browsable music, antique and second-hand stores amidst the quaint streetlamps and benches.

Running off Elizabeth Street (there are other entrances at Little Collins Street and Bourke Street Mall), the **Royal Arcade**, Melbourne's oldest, was opened in 1869 to connect Collins and Bourke streets. It's worth taking a look to see the haphazard mix of cafés and secondhand emporiums flanking the sunlit passageways. Perched at the arcade's entrance on Little Collins Street is a clock with two creepy, larger-than-life wooden figures – Gog and Magog – who strike the time each hour, while a dusty Father Time watches over the arcade's entrance at Bourke Street Mall.

Across Little Collins Street and through Block Place is Melbourne's most illustrious arcade. Constructed in 1892 in emulation of Milan's Galleria Vittorio Emmanuele, the **Block Arcade** features intricate mosaic-tiled flooring, an enormous glass-domed roof and an eye-catching selection of shops and cafés. You can take a spin through the arcade's ground floor and upper rooms on an organized tour (Tues & Thurs 1pm; $5; ©9654 5244), which winds up over free afternoon tea at the historic *Hopetoun Tea Rooms* (see p.118).

# WEST ALONG COLLINS STREET

**Map 4, D5–F5.** Tram #11 or #12.

Leaving the Block and heading south down Elizabeth Street brings you back to **Collins Street**. West of here, at the intersection with Queen Street, the **English, Scottish and Australian Bank** (1887), designed by William Wardell, houses a sumptuous banking chamber, as well as the churchy Cathedral Room, which often hosts exhibitions and performances. Below street level, a small museum (Mon–Fri 9am–4.30pm; free) has displays of weights, scales, safes and adding machines.

Just before reaching the Rialto Towers, it's worth a diversion to the recently opened **Immigration Museum** (daily 10am–5pm; $7), situated on the corner of Flinders and

William streets in the Old Customs House. Inside, a poignant collection of images and displays includes dolls brought by children from their home countries, and a detailed cross-section of a ship used to transport immigrants to Australia. On the second floor, the **Hellenic Antiquities Museum** (same hours and admission price) has temporary exhibitions of ancient Greek culture, while out front a plaque marks the spot where John Batman founded Melbourne, with his famous words: "This will be the place for a village".

# RIALTO TOWERS

**Map 4, D5.** Mon–Thurs & Sun 10am–10pm, Fri & Sat 10am–11pm; $7.50. Tram #9, #11 or #12 from Collins St.

On Collins Street, between King and William streets, the **Rialto Block** juxtaposes stylish nineteenth-century buildings, born from the easy times of the 1880s land boom, and sleek modern office blocks, including the vertiginous **Rialto Towers**, Melbourne's tallest building. In the 1980s, the block was at the centre of a storm of vituperation as conservationists and developers fought over the planned Rialto Towers development. Part of the controversy stemmed from the proposal to make it the tallest building in the city (a fact which invoked change, something Melburnians have always been divided about); part was caused by the planned demolition of some of the older sites fronting Collins Street to make way for the development. After protracted discussions, the heritage properties were spared, and construction of the new towers began.

The result is a skyscraper that has permanently broken up Melbourne's skyline – hairily high at 253m, covered with more than 13,000 windows reflecting a glassy, gridded city. On a clear day, take an elevator ride to the **observation deck** on the 55th floor. As you make your way to the windows, a warts-and-all view awaits: Melbourne, both the city and its flat, limitless suburbs; the railyards with their spaghetti of tracks, grimy goods sheds and engineless carriages; the Melbourne Cricket Ground, near at hand, a perfect truncated doughnut; the higher and more distant ridge of the Dandenong Ranges; the ant-like life below. There's also a bird's-eye view of *Le Meridien at Rialto* next door, a late nineteenth-century wool store that's now a five-star hotel, while the night view is equally spectacular. Pity that the food from the licensed café doesn't match the view, or that Melbourne's answer to New York's Empire State Building is a notorious magnet for young lovers. Back on street level and just to the right of the elevator, the **Rialto Vision Theatre** screens "Melbourne the Living City" (free with observation-deck admission), an audiovisual presentation that skilfully stretches two minutes of worthwhile material over twenty.

The **West End**, hugging the edges of the CBD around the Rialto Towers, is where Melbourne was first settled, and where the city's earliest industrial and commercial interests began. Its proximity to the Yarra meant it was the principal gateway to town: in the wake of the goldrush, the area heaved with merchant stores, seedy hotels, pawnshops and brothels. It's now rather subdued, consisting mostly of unkempt warehouses and wool stores from the 1850s – forlorn reminders of what happened when Melbourne expanded to the east – and newer office blocks of should-be-outlawed dreariness.

# The River District

Nowhere is the giddy transformation of Melbourne's urban spaces more apparent than in the **River District**, the area on either side of the Yarra from the Docklands in the west to the Melbourne Cricket Ground in the east. The current $10-billion building boom – driven by a demand for inner-city accommodation and offices – is on a scale not seen since the goldrush and "Marvellous Melbourne" era. As the city centre becomes ever more congested, so development has swept towards the river and the vast waterways of the Docklands, which is set to become Melbourne's next major commercial, residential and entertainment precinct, doubling the size of the CBD in the process.

Cranes and scaffolding are everywhere, yet visitors still flock here despite the upheaval to enjoy some of the city's best cafés, shops, gardens and museums. The Yarra itself, once the lifeblood of the infant settlement, is now a popular focus of leisure activities, and the majority of the district's attractions stretch along its south bank and down St Kilda Road. Principal among them is the **Victorian Arts Centre**, home to some of Australia's leading performing-arts companies, while further west along the river are the two enormous leisure complexes of **Southgate** and **Crown Casino** and the inventively designed **Melbourne Exhibition Centre**, which offers a possible clue as to what the future city will look like. Stretching down St Kilda Road beyond the Arts Centre are the expansive parklands and gracious nineteenth-century buildings of **Kings Domain** and the **Royal Botanic Gardens**, while on the opposite bank of the river lies the city's sporting precinct, **Yarra Park**, with its various stadiums, principal among them the legendary **MCG**.

········································································

**The area covered in this chapter is shown in detail on colour map 4.**

········································································

# THE YARRA RIVER

Now quiet and orderly, the **Yarra** was formerly an unruly river "choked with the trunks and branches of trees". In the nineteenth century, tidal movements of up to 2m often menaced the city with floods, a problem which wasn't solved until 1888, when the river was deepened and widened to allow for the upgrading of Melbourne's port facilities, and its embankments raised.

Long reviled by Sydneysiders as the "the river that flows upside down" (the mud is on the top), the Yarra is still nevertheless an essential part of Melbourne, its banks now dotted with barbecues and beautified by tree-lined boulevards and paths. A **boat cruise** is the best way to see the river (see box opposite), but it can also be explored on foot or by bike on the **cycle paths** which run along both riverbanks. Bikes can be rented from Hire a Bicycle (✆9758 7811) on the south side of Princes Bridge; prices range from $5 for thirty minutes to $14 for three hours.

# Yarra cruises

**Cruising** on the Yarra has been a popular pastime since Melbourne's earliest days, when steamers plied regularly up and down the river and out to the resorts of Queenscliff and Sorrento. Nowadays the choice of vessels on offer ranges from quaint sailing boats and steamships to gondolas and hi-tech motor launches.

**Gondola Cruises** (℃0411/114 736) Recline in a Venetian-style gondola with a glass of bubbly in one hand and a drumstick in the other. Prices range from $55 (food additional) per person for a one-hour lunch or dinner cruise to $75 per boat (up to four people) for a forty-minute champagne cruise (price includes champagne). Departures by appointment only from Southgate.

**Melbourne River Cruises** (℃9629 7233) Excursions upriver to Herring Island or downriver to Westgate Bridge departing every thirty minutes daily from Princes Walk, below the northern end of Princes Bridge. Cruises (1hr 15min) cost $13 each, or you can take a combined upstream and downriver cruise for $25.

**Penguin Waters Cruises** (℃015/311 922) Two-hour sunset cruises leaving at 6pm from Berth 2 at Southgate to Melbourne's penguin colony. The price ($40) includes champagne and barbecued prawns.

**Southgate River Tours** (℃9682 5711) Trips daily at 2pm, 3.30pm and thirty minutes prior to sunset up- or downriver. A meal at either *Planet Hollywood* or the *Official All Star Café* at the Crown Casino is thrown in with the price ($25).

**Williamstown Bay & River Cruises** (℃9682 9555) Daily departures from Berth 7 at Southgate for scenic boat trips down the Yarra to Williamstown and back (11am, 1pm, 3pm & 5pm; return trips noon, 2pm, 4pm & 6pm; $10 one way, $18 return).

# VICTORIAN ARTS CENTRE

**Map 4, H6–H7.** Tram #8 from Swanston St.

At the southern end of Princes Bridge is the **Victorian Arts Centre** – home to Opera Australia, the Australian Ballet, the Melbourne Symphony Orchestra and the Melbourne Theatre Company. The centre comprises three main buildings: the National Gallery of Victoria, the Melbourne Concert Hall and the Theatres Building, which is topped by one of Melbourne's most blatant landmarks: a 162-metre-high lattice spire which inspires love, hatred and every degree of feeling in between. Dull by day, by night it's transformed into a powerful rod of purple light.

Designed by Roy Grounds and completed in 1968, the **National Gallery of Victoria** is a resolutely grey slab of 1960s formalism. It's currently undergoing a $136-million redevelopment due for completion in late 2001 (see "Coming soon" box, p.62); until then, part of its collection is on display in the State Library (see p.42).

The **Melbourne Concert Hall** and the **Theatres Building** have worthwhile guided tours, during which you can view the permanent art collection (front of house tour: Mon–Fri noon & 2.30pm, Sat 10.30am & noon; $9; backstage tour: Sun 12.15pm & 2.15pm; $12). The highlight is the fun and accessible **Performing Arts Museum** in the Theatres Building (daily 10am–11pm; free), which covers everything from opera to rock'n'roll: you can see the hand-painted jackets worn by Neil and Tim Finn during Crowded House's *Woodface* tour, and Dame Edna Everage's frocks and spectacles. It also has splendid temporary exhibitions, normally focusing on popular culture.

On Sunday, a good **arts-and-crafts market** (10am–5.30pm) is held outside the Arts Centre on the paved promenade under Princes Bridge.

# SOUTHGATE AND CROWN CASINO

**Map 4, D3–G6.** Tram #8 from Swanston St.

Awash with swanky cafés, bars and shops, **Southgate,** the city's flashest food, drink and shopping complex, lies on the Yarra's riverbank opposite Flinders Street Station (to which it is linked by a beautifully engineered pedestrian bridge affording grand views of the river). Built on former industrial wasteland in the early 1990s, Southgate's three levels fizz with life, especially at lunchtimes and weekends, when it attracts hordes soaking up the views across the river.

West of Southgate, the enormous **Crown Casino**, stretching across 600m of riverfront, provides the focal point for the Yarra as it flows through the city centre. Australia's largest gambling and entertainment palace, the casino is crammed with a grim assortment of tacky gaming rooms, theme restaurants, cafés, bars, nightclubs, cinemas, designer shops and the luxury *Crown Towers* hotel. Equally egregious is the five-storey, black-marble atrium, which features "Seasons of Fortune", a sound-and-light show set amidst a waterworld of fountains and ponds. Outside the only distinguishing feature, apart from eight granite-columned towers which belch fire at night, is the promenade fountain, which provides a kind of assault course for children dodging the jets of water.

Visible from the Crown Casino on the opposite riverbank is Ron Robertson-Swann's 1980s abstract sculpture **Vault**, one of Australia's most maligned public artworks. Looking like a wall that's collapsed and been hurriedly put back together again, it was formerly the focal point of the City Square (incredibly, it was thought to harbour sex offenders and cause people to urinate), until being unceremoniously ripped from its home and plonked in ankle-deep mud next to the Yarra, where it's now used as a crash pad at night by the city's homeless.

# The Crown Casino

The **Crown Casino** is reputedly the most visited tourist destination in Victoria, offering gambling and glitzy entertainment on a breathtaking scale. The vast and ostentatious complex, the largest casino outside North America, boasts 350 table games (chips cover denominations from 25c to a $1-million plaque) and over 2500 gaming and slot machines, themed areas like "The Monte Carlo Room" and betting facilities, all of them open around the clock. Apart from shiny lights and jackpot signs, the casino has dozens of cafés and restaurants, a 24-hour cinema complex with fourteen auditoriums, plenty of watering holes and nightclubs, designer stores and ballrooms.

Ostensibly built to make money by wooing rich punters from Asia, Crown's stocks have recently taken a dive due to the Asian economic meltdown. In an attempt to reinvent itself, Crown has set its sights squarely on **local gamblers**, who come disproportionately from Melbourne's poorer western suburbs. The disturbing reality is that this targeting, coupled with the concentration of poker machines in municipalities across Melbourne (again, most noticeably in socially disadvantaged suburbs), is taking its toll – family breakdown, domestic violence, theft, unemployment, mental illness and even suicide have been just some of the more unpleasant side effects. In response, the Federal Government announced an inquiry in 1998 into Australia's $80-billion gambling industry, much to the chagrin of premier Jeff Kennett, whose government has a large stake in its success: gambling represents over fifteen percent of state tax and, after payroll tax and property taxes, is the most important source of revenue to the state budget.

# MELBOURNE EXHIBITION CENTRE

**Map 4, C8.** Mon–Fri 8.30am–6pm, Sat & Sun 9am–1pm; free.
Tram #96 from Bourke St; tram #12 or #109 from Collins St.

Directly across Clarendon Street, the striking **Melbourne Exhibition Centre** (known locally as "Jeff's Shed", a reference to Jeff Kennett, the state premier behind its construction) is a whimsical example of the city's dynamic new architectural style. Opened in 1996, it was designed by Melbourne's hottest architectural practice, Denton, Corker and Marshall, the team behind the distinctive Tullamarine Freeway gateway, the Museum of Victoria and just about every other construction project of note in Melbourne during the last five years. Facing the river is an immense, 450-metre-long glass wall, while the street entrance has an awning resembling a ski jump propped up by wafer-thin "blades and sticks" (as they're known in fashionable Melbourne architectural parlance), amongst which yellow and purple colours are craftily concealed. Inside, display spaces host everything from trucking and technology displays to Melbourne's annual Sexpo, featuring condom collections, adult videos and the like. Gliding over the water between here and the recently revamped Melbourne Convention Centre on the opposite side of the Yarra, a covered steel-and-glass footbridge provides pedestrians with an elegant, weatherproof route across the river.

Berthed in the wooden-walled Duke and Orr's dock next to the Melbourne Exhibition Centre, the **Polly Woodside** (daily 10am–4pm; $7) is a small barque-rigged sailing ship built in 1885 and described as "the prettiest vessel ever launched in Belfast". After a working life, most of it spent carrying coal and nitrate between Europe and South America, she was acquired by the National Trust in 1968. Now faithfully restored under her original name, you can climb on board and take the ropes, or explore the captain's

# Coming soon

For the new millennium, the River District is emerging from its massive **building programme** with several high-profile developments appearing from the chaos – from flashy new stadiums to the serenely modern Federation Square and the revamped National Gallery of Victoria.

**The Docklands**, Melbourne's old railway and port area, is poised to reopen in 2000. This historic precinct will include the Colonial Stadium, which will host AFL matches and other sporting events, a Paramount theme park, a movie megaplex, TV studios and a residential district with space for 15,000 people. The potential highlight of the project is the planned 560-metre-high, 113-storey **Grollo Tower**, intended to be the world's tallest skyscraper, although complete funding for its construction has still to be found.

Occupying the railyards opposite Flinders Street Station, the $220-million **Federation Square** will combine riverside parkland with a loose assemblage of buildings, including a cinemedia centre, civic square, countless cafés and restaurants, and the new **Museum of Australian Art** (due to open in late 2000) which will provide a home for the Australian paintings formerly held by the **National Gallery of Victoria** (this, too, is currently being redeveloped, with a planned reopening in late 2001).

Also due for completion in 2001, the **Melbourne Aquarium**, on the corner of King and Flinders streets, will boast around two hundred marine species, mostly from the Southern Ocean. Visitors will move among the exhibits on a specially designed conveyor belt in a plastic viewing "tube".

The **Multi-Purpose Venue (MPV)**, due to be finished in early 2000, is being built just south of the MCG and will come complete with a velodrome, tennis and basketball facilities, moveable seating and a retractable roof.

quarters and storage holds below. Adjoining the ship are historic cargo sheds containing pumping engines and a museum of shipping relics relating to the history of the docks and Port Melbourne.

# KINGS DOMAIN

**Map 4, I7–J9.** Tram #8 from Swanston St.

Returning to the Victorian Arts Centre and heading down St Kilda Road brings you to the grassy open spaces of **Kings Domain**. At the northern end of the domain lies the Sidney Myer Music Bowl, an outdoor shell which serves as a music arena for the Victorian Arts Centre, while further south is the palatial **Government House**, official residence of the Governor of Victoria. The National Trust runs guided tours (Mon & Wed 10am–3pm, Sat 11am; closed Dec 16–Jan 25; $8; booking compulsory on ©9654 4711) of the formal gardens and several of the rooms. Most spectacular is the enormous state ballroom, which includes a velvet-hung and -canopied throne, brocade-covered benches and gilded chairs, all brilliantly lit by three massive crystal chandeliers.

Immediately south of Government House, the **Observatory Gate** complex includes a number of Italianate buildings, painstakingly restored. The visitor centre (Mon–Fri 9am–5pm, Sat & Sun 10am–5.30pm; guided walks daily except Sat 2pm; $4) has a café and garden shop, where you can buy botanical books, maps and brochures. Around the time of the new moon, stargazing tours ($10 bookings ©9252 2300) allow visitors to track and chart the darkest reaches of space through huge old telescopes.

Across Birdwood Avenue, **La Trobe's Cottage** (Mon, Wed, Sat & Sun 11am–4.30pm; $2) was bought in London by Victoria's first lieutenant governor, Charles La Trobe, who had it shipped over to Melbourne in 1863. The remains of the humble prefabricated house were re-erected on the present site in 1998. Small but elegantly furnished, it features the first governor's furniture and possessions, plus historical displays on the early days of the colony. Next door, the **Australian Centre for Contemporary Art** (Tues–Fri 11am–5pm; Sat & Sun 2–5pm; free) presents top-notch installations and multimedia exhibitions.

The **Shrine of Remembrance** (daily 10am–5pm: free), in the southwestern corner of the domain, was built in 1934 to commemorate those who served their country during various conflicts. It's a rather menacingly stolid mass whose architectural style is part Greek Classical, part Aztec pyramid. The strangeness continues when a disembodied voice booms out and calls you within to see the symbolic "Ray of Light", a shaft of sunlight that strikes the memorial stone each year at 11am on Remembrance Day (November 11) – an effect that's conveniently simulated every thirty minutes by an electric light. In the **Garden of Appreciation**, next to the Shrine, a bronzed statue carrying the words "Homage" and "Remembrance" commemorates the care given to the widows and children of soldiers killed in action.

**West from the bottom of Kings Domain across St Kilda Road, the suburb of South Melbourne has a thriving café and restaurant scene and value-for-money accommodation – see p.132 and p.110 for details.**

Heading east across Kings Domain from the Shrine of Remembrance brings you to the **Royal Botanic Gardens** (daily: April–Oct 7.30am–5.30pm; Nov–March 7.30am–8.30pm). Established in 1846, the gardens now contain ten thousand types of plant and over fifty species of bird, not to mention great clumps of big bushy trees, rockeries, waterfalls, flowerbeds and pavilions. Highlights include the herbarium, shady walks through native rainforests, and a large ornamental lake where you can feed the swans and eels.

# MELBOURNE CRICKET GROUND (MCG)

**Map 4, M6.** Tram #75 from Wellington Parade or the Epping line train from Flinders St Station to Jolimont Station.

Opposite Kings Domain on the north bank of the Yarra (and connected to it by Swan Street Bridge) lies Melbourne's sporting precinct: **Yarra Park**. Within its wide, open spaces are an abundance of venues including the Melbourne Park National Tennis Centre (home of the Australian Open tennis championship), the "Glasshouse", or Melbourne Sports & Entertainment Centre, Olympic Park (where the Melbourne Storm rugby league team play their matches) and, especially, the venerable **Melbourne Cricket Ground (MCG)**. Originally built in 1838, but transformed to host the 1956 Olympic Games, the MCG (affectionately known as "the G") is Australia's oldest cricket ground and the country's biggest and most popular stadium. As well as being the spiritual home of AFL football, the arena accommodates cricket, international soccer and rugby union, state-of-origin rugby league, music concerts and other major events.

The present-day MCG has a capacity of 100,000 spectators (the attendance record is held by American evangelist Billy Graham, who in 1959 drew a crowd of 130,000 to his Melbourne crusade). It really comes to life during the AFL season, when it regularly packs in footballing crowds for club games involving Melbourne sides, plus the AFL Grand Final itself. Despite potential competition from new venues such as the Colonial Stadium and the Olympic Stadium in Sydney, the MCG's place as an icon among Australia's sporting stadiums is assured – annual pilgrimages to the AFL Grand Final continue to take place there as they have done since the last century, while the Boxing Day cricket test match at the MCG is a tradition synonymous with Australia's Christmas since 1968.

**East of Yarra Park, the suburbs of Richmond and Hawthorn have good eating and accommodation possibilities – see p.130 and p.106 for details.**

For a greater understanding of the MCG's resonant place in Australia's sporting history, there are one-hour **tours** of the stadium (daily 10am–3pm on the hour; $9.50; ✆9657 8879), when you can walk onto the hallowed turf. Included in the price is admission to a number of sporting museums including the Australian Gallery of Sport, the Olympic Museum, the Cricket Hall of Fame, the Aussie Rules Exhibition, and the stately Members Pavilion and Long Room.

MELBOURNE CRICKET GROUND (MCG)

# Carlton and Fitzroy

**W**ith the goldrush of the 1850s, the settlement of Melbourne began to spread outwards, and by the decade's end prosperous suburbs such as Carlton and Fitzroy had taken root. **Carlton** is still home to the city's thriving middle classes, who stock up on chic clothing and authentic victuals from the Italian food-and-café strip of **Lygon Street**. Southwest of here is the late nineteenth-century **Royal Exhibition Building**, home of Australia's first parliament, and the new **Museum of Victoria**, while flanking Carlton's northwestern reaches, the small enclave of **Parkville** is home to the city's **university** and the popular **Melbourne Zoo**.

Bordering Carlton to the east, **Fitzroy** is now famed for its alternative and bohemian mood. In **Brunswick Street** it has one of the city's most colourful arteries, with engagingly rakish eating places and lifestyle stores. As for outstanding examples of residential colonial buildings, Fitzroy has them in spades.

.......................................................................

The area covered in this chapter is shown in detail on colour map 5.

.......................................................................

# CARLTON

**Map 5, D3–F7.** Tram #1 or #22 from Swanston St.

**Carlton** lies just north of the city, but in terms of looks and feel it could be a million miles away, with its café society based around the fashionable trattorias of **Lygon Street**. It was here, in the 1950s, that Melburnians sipped their first espressos and tasted their first spaghetti from exotic spots like the *University Café* (see p.130), *La Cacciatora* and *Toto's*, opened by some of the Italian immigrants who flooded into Melbourne in the postwar years. Lygon Street held an unconventional allure in staid Anglo-Saxon Melbourne, attracting the city's intelligentsia, who soon made the pretty, kilometre-long strip their second home.

--------

**For the best places cafés and restaurants in Carlton,
see "Eating", p.123.**

--------

These days, however, Carlton's relevance as an intellectual and culinary milieu is on the wane. Its former bohemians have either left or aged embarrassingly, while Lygon Street has gone upmarket, although the encroaching designer stores and tourist restaurants haven't yet completely displaced the arts centres, old-fashioned grocers and bookshops. Sustaining the street's heart and soul are a smattering of unpretentious ethnic cafés and restaurants, where students still congregate over tiny cups of bitter existential coffee.

## Royal Exhibition Building and Museum of Victoria

**Map 5, E6–E7.** City Circle tram.

The picturesque Carlton Gardens, at Carlton's southeastern corner, are the setting for the **Royal Exhibition**

**Building**. Built in 1879 for the International Exhibition of the following year, it later housed the first Federal Parliament and then, from 1901 to 1927, the Victorian Government. In its prime, the Exhibition Building was a perfect symbol of Melbourne's vaulting ambition, with a dome higher than London's St Paul's Cathedral. Sadly, all the buildings were demolished apart from magnificently restored Neoclassical Main Hall – although this is still big enough to host the annual Melbourne International Flower and Garden Show (see p.178), plus everything from bridal shows to alpaca-lassoing exhibitions.

---

**Guided tours of the Royal Exhibition Building (minimum of ten people) can be booked on ℂ9270 5000; $4.50.**

---

Next door, the **Museum of Victoria** is scheduled to reopen in mid-2000 in a new $250-million building by architects Denton, Corker and Marshall, designers of the Melbourne Exhibition Centre (see p.61), with which it shares some of its most striking architectural feature. These include the "ski-jump" awnings and gigantic "blades" – concrete slabs used as walls and roof – which will house the Gallery of Life, an indoor rainforest that's planned to contain over six thousand plants and trees, and a zoo. Flanking the forest will be a children's museum, the Bunjilaka Aboriginal Centre (with objects and images illustrating the recent history of Aboriginal peoples), social and natural history exhibits, cafés and restaurants. Some of the museum's science and technology collection is currently on view at Scienceworks in Spotswood (see p.87). Also part of the museum, at the Rathdowne Street entrance, is the 480-seater **IMAX Theatre** (see p.174).

# Melbourne University

**Map 5, B2–C5.** Tram #1 or #22 from Swanston St.

Just west of Lygon Street in the adjacent suburb of Parkville, **Melbourne University** is worth a visit for its formidable **art collection** (Tues, Wed & Fri–Sun 10am–5pm, Thurs 10am–9pm; free). This is housed in **The Potter**, near the corner of Elgin and Swanston streets, a small but striking building adorned with Classical busts and reliefs and containing drawings, archeological exhibits, and nineteenth- and twentieth-century Australian art by the likes of Norman Lindsay, Joy Hester and Rupert Bunny. The life of Percy Grainger – composer, linguist, fashion maverick – is captured in the **Percy Grainger Museum** (Mon 10am–1pm, Tues 10am–4pm, Wed 10am–5pm; free) at Gate 13, Royal Parade, in the south-western corner of the university. Opened in 1938, Grainger designed the museum and stocked it with over 250,000 of his personal effects, including musical instruments and Bibles collected from his travels around the world. His provocative and thoroughly interesting life – he regularly wore outfits made from terry towelling, favoured sadomasochistic sex and was unusually close to his mother, Rose (all major no-nos in the prim and proper Melbourne of the time) – was recently captured in the film *Passion* by Australian director Peter Duncan. Least known of the university's attractions is the **underground car park** beneath the South Lawn, a Gothic netherworld of concrete arches and columns which was used for the police garage scenes in the film *Mad Max*.

---

**The National Trust** organize full-moon tours of the Melbourne General Cemetery: April–Sept $15; bookings essential on ©9654 4711.

---

Just north of the university, the **Melbourne General Cemetery**, established in 1853, is the oldest in the city, although most of its fine examples of funerary architecture have disappeared or fallen apart. Here are buried over half a million people, including Melbourne founder John Batman, explorers Burke and Wills, and Australian Prime Minister Sir Robert Menzies.

## Melbourne Zoo

**Map 3, C2–C3.** Daily 9am–5pm; $14. Tram #55 or #56 from William St; tram #68 from Elizabeth St.

West from the cemetery, the green plenitude of Royal Park is home to the **Melbourne Zoo**, opened in 1862 and the oldest in Australia. Some of its original features are still in evidence, including the landscaped gardens with their Australian and foreign trees, and a few restored Victorian-era cages, but almost all the animals have now been rehoused in more sympathetic enclosures.

........................................................................................

**During January (Thurs–Sun) and February (Fri–Sun) the zoo stays open until 9.30pm for meals, jazz concerts and twilight tours.**

........................................................................................

The new **Australian bush habitat**, densely planted with more than twenty thousand native plants, contains wombats, koalas, echidnas, monitor lizards and cockatoos, while a maze of underground enclosures allows you to observe dozing groups of wombats and includes a small tunnel where you can experience the burrowing lifestyle of these animals. The **Great Flight Aviary** (daily 10.30am–4.30pm) has areas of rainforest, wetland and a patch of scrub with a huge gum tree where many birds like the blue crane and bower bird nest, while the dark **Platypus Habitat** (daily 9.30am–4.30pm) is also worth a visit to see these notoriously elusive mammals. Other highlights include the Butterfly House (daily 9.30am–4.30pm); the gorilla and small-ape enclosures; and the popular meerkats, to the right of the main entrance. For sustenance, there's the *Lakeside Bistro* (daily 11am–4pm), and plenty of other takeaway facilities.

# FITZROY

**Map 5, G3–H6.** Tram #11 from Collins St.

Melbourne's first and Australia's smallest suburb, **Fitzroy** has had a varied and fluctuating history. In the early years of European settlement it was considered eminently desirable – high, dry and conveniently north of the city. Many colonial buildings remain intact; apart from the CBD, Fitzroy houses the city's finest collection of mid-nineteenth-century bluestone buildings (the best examples, like Royal Terrace, are in Nicholson Street opposite the Royal Exhibition Building, or on Victoria Parade further south). Gradually, however, the area's fortunes declined, and by the turn of the century Fitzroy was providing land and cheap labour for noxious trades such as tanning and soap and candle manufacturing. By the 1930s, even the factories had moved to the suburbs and Fitzroy had become a slum. Gradually, the suburb's fortunes were revived: first by the arrival of a mix of European, Middle Eastern and Asian immigrants; later by the young and sophisticated suburbanites who stumbled upon the area during the early 1970s, setting the fashion ever since for terrace-style living and louche gentility.

Fitzroy's focal point is **Brunswick Street**, where, in the shadow of Housing Commission high-rises, you can pick up clothes and accessories from funky shops at knock-down prices, eat at the area's plethora of ethnic restaurants, drink decaff with artists and actors, bury your head in Aussie "grunge" literature in one of the street's late-night bookshops, or down a VB at the many bars and live music venues sprinkling the strip. The fires of anti-fashion raging through the area have also left the street full of hotels with "raw" paint jobs and deliberately half-finished decor inside.

For details of the best places to eat in Brunswick Street, see p.123; for pubs and bars, see p.149; for music venues, see p.157.

Running at right angles across Brunswick Streeet is the centre of Melbourne's Spanish community, **Johnston Street**, a lively stretch of tapas bars and flamenco restaurants. Nearby, Fitzroy's fringe-art leanings are embodied in a number of local **galleries**, in particular the New York-style Tolarno Galleries (Tues–Sat 11am–6pm) at 121 Victoria Street and 200 Gertrude Street (Tues–Sat 10am–5.30pm), a converted warehouse which is now a state-funded gallery and studio space for emerging artists.

FITZROY

# South Yarra, Prahran and Toorak

The trio of suburbs southeast of the city centre is one of Melbourne's premier destinations for food, shopping and promenading. Just south of the river, **South Yarra** has long been the haunt of fashion-minded Melburnians, centred on exclusive **Chapel Street**, with its painfully cool cafés and shops of label-proud arrogance. Also in South Yarra, stately **Como House** provides an insight in the luxurious life of a nineteenth-century landowner.

Chapel Street continues south to the less salubrious but infinitely funkier environs of **Prahran**, boasting switched-on **Greville Street** and its surrounding markets. The gay strip of **Commercial Road** separates the two suburbs, combining bookshops, gift and clothes stores with gyms, cafés and restaurants.

For a real blue-blood experience, head east from Prahran to the rich heart of **Toorak**, which boasts even glitzier designer boutiques than South Yarra, but few tourist attractions.

The area covered in this chapter is shown in detail on colour map 6.

# SOUTH YARRA

**Map 6, D3–E5.** Tram #8 or #72 from Swanston St or the Sandringham line train to South Yarra Station.

A magnet for the svelte and well-heeled, **South Yarra** is home to Melbourne's smart set, who comb the racks at designer stores, stuff themselves at chic hangouts, then boogie at nightclubs to work it all off. Heart of the district is the strip of **Chapel Street** between Toorak and Commercial roads – the so-called "Golden Mile", or "right" end. Halfway down is the **Jam Factory**. Jam-making began here in 1885 and continued until the factory's closure in 1973. Six years later the building was overhauled and reopened as a monster cinema-and-entertainment centre. The brick-and-bluestone complex is quite comely, for a former factory, and still has quaint machinery on display, but you'll have to look hard for it among kitsch Hollywood effigies of Marilyn Monroe, James Dean and R2-D2.

......................................................................................

For details of the best places to shop in Chapel Street and South Yarra, see p.191; for places to eat, see p.133; for bars and clubs, see p.143.

......................................................................................

## Como House

**Map 6, G3.** Tours daily every 30mins from 10.15am to 4.15pm; $9; ©9827 2500. Tram #8 from Swanston St.

Overlooking the river from Como Avenue is **Como House**, a fine example of the townhouses built by the city's well-to-do nineteenth-century landowners. The site was originally bought by George and Alfred Langhorne in 1837 from the Woiworung Aboriginal people and used as a stock run. Nine years later, a single-storey villa was built on the banks of the Yarra for the barrister Edward Eyre Williams, who named it after Lake Como in Italy, where he supposedly proposed to his wife. The house then enjoyed a succession of wealthy owners, including wine merchant John Brown (who added a second storey) and prominent graziers and Melbourne citizens the Armytage family, who extended the house by adding a ballroom wing in 1874. Now beautifully restored by the National Trust, many of the house's original furnishings remain intact, while the surrounding landscape of landscaped gardens, and pine and cypress glades is an ideal spot for a picnic.

**Twilight tours ($25 including champagne supper) of Como House are held on the first Saturday of each month.**

# PRAHRAN

**Map 6, A7–B8.** Tram #6 from Swanston St or the Sandringham line train to Prahran Station.

Chapel Street continues south to **Commercial Road**, renowned for its large gay and lesbian community (see "Gay Melbourne", p.165), then into **Prahran** proper, an area given an interesting dimension by the influx of newcomers – shopkeepers, students, and emigrants from Italy and Greece – who settled here in the 1950s. The further south you go, the more the fashion boutiques and upmarket cafés give way to secondhand clothing stores, tattooists and fish-and-chip shops. Forget South Yarra's antiseptic superficiality; here, street cred generally means the whiff of body odour, shaved heads of chartreuse pink and nose rings.

Just off Chapel Street in the heart of Prahran, **Greville Street** is a fantastic pocket of eccentric bohemia – young, brash and full of freewheeling brio. These days, it's taken over from Chapel Street as the corridor of cutting-edge cool, with retro and designer boutiques, trendy gift shops, music outlets, and bijou nightspots like the *Continental* (see p.134). Things really hot up over the weekend, and every Sunday the small **Greville Street Market** has arts, crafts and secondhand clothes and jewellery on the corner of Gratton Street in Gratton Park (noon–5pm).

# TOORAK

Map 6, F5–G6. Tram #8 from Swanston St.

East of South Yarra, **Toorak** is synonymous with money and born-to-rule pedigree. When Melbourne was founded, the wealthy chose to build their homes here, high on the banks of the Yarra, while the cottages of the poor were confined to narrow streets on the flood-prone areas below. During the 1950s and 1960s, old Melbourne money was joined by new, when an influx of European Jews – who had arrived penniless in Australia – celebrated their hard-earned wealth by moving to Toorak.

Snobbish and conservative, Toorak has little to see or do, apart from wandering around leafy streets full of homes with vast gardens and box hedges. On Toorak Road, you can window-shop at the wickedly expensive **Toorak Village**, a higgledy-piggledy mock-Tudor mess that seems to have rewritten the book on bad 1970s architecture. Alternatively, pavement-café tables are unrivalled spots for watching streams of late-model Range Rovers (known locally as "Toorak Tractors") idling past, or cliques of charity gala-attending matrons making their way to and from the hairdressers. Those interested in early woodcarvings of Australian flora and fauna should make a pilgrimage to **St John's Church** (daily 8am–6pm), on the corner of Toorak and Clendon roads. Ornamental reliefs by the sculptor E.

TOORAK

Prenzil of kangaroos, dingos, wattles and ferns can be found on the arm ends and heads of pews on both the north and south side of the church. St John's also hosts high-class weddings, usually involving either a local footy star or a scion of Melbourne society.

# St Kilda

**W**hen the wealthy merchants and legislators of goldrush-era Melbourne sought refuge from the congested and polluted city, they settled upon a green bayside area 5km to the southeast. Within a decade the beach suburb of **St Kilda** had become the address of choice for Melbourne's monied. Then, in 1857, Victoria's second train line – running from the city to St Kilda – was opened, and suddenly the suburb's briny pleasures were accessible to the great unwashed. St Kilda's grandeur went to seed as the wealthy took flight to more exclusive areas like South Yarra and Toorak, while in the 1930s its substantial mansions were either demolished or converted into a crumbling sea of dosshouses, apartment blocks, dance halls and tacky amusements.

Rejuvenation and renovation occurred in the early 1990s, which marked a turnaround in St Kilda's fortunes. Since then, property values have skyrocketed and new cafés and bars seem to open daily. The downside is that many of those who gave the suburb its raffish character – artists, actors, musicians and eccentrics – have been forced out by rising rents and gentrification. Even so, there's still plenty to explore. Starting in **Fitzroy Street**, with its landmark hotels and eateries, it's only a short distance to the **Upper Esplanade** and **foreshore**, favourite places for

atting, seeing and being seen. Continuing
'll come to the Jewish enclave of **Acland**
.ed nowadays for its cake shops and sharp cafés,
ond St Kilda are the excellent **Jewish Museum**
**,on Lea**, one of Melbourne's grand nineteenth-
estates.

Tra. s no longer run to St Kilda, but the suburb is easily
reached by any of three **tram routes**: the quickest routes
are trams #96 from Bourke Street in the city to Barkly
Street; #15 or #16 from Swanston Street to Barkly Street;
or #10 or #12 from Collins Street to the intersection of
Park and Fitzroy streets.

The best time to visit St Kilda is in February, when the
**Midsumma Gay Festival** and the **St Kilda Festival** take
place; both feature music, outdoor performances, exhibitions and dancing.

**The area covered in this chapter is shown in detail on
colour map 7.**

# FITZROY STREET

**Map 7, C6–F4.**

For years, **Fitzroy Street** was the focus of St Kilda's often
overblown reputation as Melbourne's epicentre of drugs and
sleaze. Recently, however, it has gone decidedly upmarket:
most of the pawnshops, hamburger joints and adult bookstores have given way to cafés and bars, although Grey
Street is still home to prostitutes, drug addicts and down-
and-outs.

On the corner of Grey and Fitzroy streets, **The George
Hotel** has been the barometer of St Kilda's fortunes since
the days in the nineteenth century when it was one of

Australia's finest hotels. By the end of the 1940s, the Depression and two world wars had taken their toll, but despite the chipped crockery and peeling paint, the hotel's permanent residents clung to the genteel rituals of its glory days. The writer Hal Porter, who worked as the hotel's assistant manager in 1949, described it as "the Titanic that missed the iceberg". By the late 1970s, the *George* had become seriously run-down, with the hotel's Seaview Ballroom a venue for Melbourne's punk rock explosion. Eventually, after years of colourful neglect, the hotel was transformed in the early 1990s into a slick wine bar and restaurant, with adjoining gallery, cinema and apartment complex.

# UPPER ESPLANADE AND FORESHORE

Map 7, B6–D8.

Running from the western end of Fitzroy Street, the palm-lined **Upper Esplanade** is the work of a committee set up in 1906 to provide municipal entertainment that did not offend "good taste or sound morals". The European-style, split-level boulevard with its foreshore parkland is still pretty tame, even if the iced confections and sea baths have been replaced by rollerbladers, *gelatis* and the odd topless bather.

Taking pride of place on the Upper Esplanade is the **Esplanade Hotel** (or "Espy"), a famously beer-soaked corner of the city and one of Australia's best-known band venues, with fantastic views overlooking Port Phillip Bay. Each Sunday, the Upper Esplanade hosts the popular **St Kilda Arts and Craft Market** (see p.201).

For more on the *Esplanade Hotel,* see "Pubs, bars and clubs" (p.156) and "Live music" (p.161).

Across Jacka Boulevard (the Lower Esplanade), **St Kilda Pier** (1904) doubles both as a café and as the departure point for **boat trips** across the bay to Williamstown (Sat & Sun 11.30am–3.30pm; $10 return; ℂ9397 2255). Penguin-watching cruises also depart from here daily at 4.30pm ($20–30; ℂ0412/187 202) – a less crowded alternative to Phillip Island.

Dominating the southern end of the Upper Esplanade, the magnificent Rococo **Palais Theatre** hosts touring bands, while nearby is "Mr Moon", a laughing face whose gaping mouth serves as an entrance to St Kilda's most famous icon: **Luna Park**. Despite a couple of new attractions, there's nothing very hi-tech about this 1912 amusement park: the Scenic Railway (the world's oldest operating roller coaster) runs along wooden trestles, the dodgem cars could do with a lick of paint and the Ghost Train wouldn't spook a toddler, but that's half the fun. Most rides cost around $3.

# ACLAND STREET AND AROUND

Map 7, C6–E8.

St Kilda has long had a strong Jewish presence. Following World War II, Western European Jews introduced **Acland Street** to *kugelhöpfs*, Wiener schnitzels and early-morning get-togethers, while Eastern European Jews have added their mark since the collapse of the former Soviet Union, particularly in the section of Carlisle Street east of St Kilda Road. The leafy northern end of Acland Street is predominantly residential, although there are a few cafés and bars. At no. 26, occupying a National Trust-listed mansion, **Linden** is probably the best community gallery in Australia (daily except Mon 1–6pm; free; ℂ9209 6560), with contemporary art exhibitions year round. The southern end of Acland Street – a melange of continental cake shops, book-

shops, Jewish restaurants, bars, cafés, florists and gi<
is St Kilda's cosmopolitan hub; on sunny weekends
crowds can be unbearable. To escape the visiting hordes,
head for the **St Kilda Botanical Gardens** – across Barkly
Street and up nearby Blessington Street (sunrise–sunset;
free) – which include a huge rose garden, an indigenous
plant section, a duck pond and a conservatory.

# AROUND ST KILDA

North of here, the rewarding **Jewish Museum** at 26 Alma
Road (Tues–Thurs 10am–4pm, Sun 11am–5pm; $5; tram
#67 from Swanston St to stop no. 32) was opened in 1995,
with permanent and temporary exhibitions displaying thousands of pieces of Judaica.

**Rippon Lea**, at 192 Hotham Street in Elsternwick (daily
except Mon 10am–5pm; $9; tours on the half hour from
10.30am, and estate tours every day at 2pm), is several kilometres southeast of St Kilda. Work on this nineteenth-
century Romanesque mansion and its "pleasure gardens"
was begun by Frederick Sargood, who made his fortune
during the goldrush. The 33-room mansion has magnificent
grounds complete with ornamental lake and fernery, and a
way-over-the-top interior that combines opulent Victoriana
with cod silent-era Hollywood style. The grounds are also
popular for picnics at weekends. To get there, take a
Sandringham-line train from Flinders Street Station in the
city and get off at nearby Rippon Lea Station, or catch tram
#67 from Swanston Street to stop no. 42.

# Williamstown

Until the Yarra was widened in the 1880s to allow for the upgrading of Melbourne's port facilities, **Williamstown** was Port Phillip Bay's major seaport. Established in 1835, it saw scores of vessels unloading convicts, gold-diggers and pastoralists bound for the open plains of central Victoria. But as Melbourne's port facilities improved, Williamstown's maritime significance waned. Eventually, a band of industrial suburbs to the west of the centre isolated Williamstown from the city and the small seaside settlement withdrew into itself.

Then, with the opening of the Westgate Bridge near the mouth of the Yarra in 1978, "Willy" became more accessible, and its charms were rediscovered. On weekends it's every bit as frantic as St Kilda or Southgate, yet on weekdays it could be just another quiet country town. Most visitors beat a path to **Nelson Place**, Williamstown's historic precinct, ringed by stately bluestone buildings, cafés, pubs and galleries. From here it's a short stroll to the picturesque waterfront park of **Commonwealth Reserve** and **Gem Pier**, while further east, **Port Gellibrand** is where convicts from Britain were shipped ashore. There are also three small but excellent rail and maritime museums and some popular beaches. In the adjacent suburb of Spotswood, **Scienceworks** deserves a visit for its fascinating array of interactive displays and exhibits.

..................................................................................................................

**For Williamstown restaurant reviews, see p.141.**

..................................................................................................................

As the crow flies, Williamstown is only 5km southwest of the city. The easiest way to get there is to catch a Williamstown **train** from Flinders Street Station to the end of the line, from where it's a short walk along Ann Street to Nelson Place, the suburb's busy hub. By **boat**, Williamstown is connected to St Kilda Pier by the Williamstown Bay & River Cruises' *John Batman* ferry (see p.82), and to Southgate by the same company's *Williamstown Seeker* (see p.57).

If you're feeling energetic, you could always **cycle** to Williamstown: a bicycle path runs along the St Kilda foreshore to Port Melbourne and Eastbridge Park (under the Westgate Bridge), from where you can catch a punt (Mon & Fri–Sun; $3 one way, $5 return) across the mouth of the Yarra to join up with the track, which then winds through Riverside Park and on to Williamstown, a total of around 10km each way.

# AROUND NELSON PLACE

**Map 3, A6–A7.**
Ferries berth at **Gem Pier** and, as they pull in, you'd almost think you were coming ashore at a naval shipyard. The HMAS *Castlemaine*, a decommissioned World War II minesweeper, is permanently docked at the pier, and now houses an interesting **maritime museum** (Sat & Sun noon–5pm; $4). Also here, the three-masted topsail schooner *Alma Doepel* runs two-hour cruises around the bay most weekends and public holidays ($25; ✆9646 5211).

Next to Gem Pier, the small park of **Commonwealth Reserve** affords panoramic views of Melbourne's city skyline and houses a tourist office (Mon–Fri 11am–3.30pm, Sat & Sun 11am–5pm), bandstand, tide-gauge house and a water fountain donated by one Reverend John Wilkinson to deter sailors from hitting the grog. Across the park is displayed an anchor from the nineteenth-century British warship HMVS *Nelson*, the first vessel to enter the nearby dockyards. On the first and third Sunday of each month, the popular **Williamstown Craft Market** is held in the reserve (9am–5pm).

The section of **Nelson Place** opposite is lined with cafés, restaurants, bookshops, ice-cream parlours and one of the highest concentrations of pubs anywhere in the southern hemisphere (hence the Reverend Wilkinson's water fountain). On the corner of Nelson Place and Symes Street (which runs down to Gem Pier), the **Customs Wharf Gallery** (daily 10am–6pm) is a National Trust-listed building housing tacky galleries and handicrafts shops.

# POINT GELLIBRAND

**Map 3, A7.**

Continuing along Nelson Place past the piers, dockyards and storage tanks brings you to **Point Gellibrand**. Plans are afoot to turn a large chunk of this area into a public park and medium-density housing – a move that has outraged locals, who are increasingly concerned that Willy is being imperilled by unrestrained development. Nearby, a copper ball in the convict-built **Timeball Tower** is lowered each day at 1pm – a time-check by which shipmasters used to calibrate their chronometers before taking to sea. Further southwest of the tower are the remains of **Fort Gellibrand**, a former defence battery that saw plenty of mock battles but never fired a shot in anger. Just behind here, and below an old railway embankment, mutineering convicts stoned the Inspector-General of Penal Establishments, John Price, to death in 1857. In the nineteenth century, convicts were carried by barge ashore from prison hulks moored at sea and employed on public works, including the building of **Breakwater Pier** on the south-eastern tip from bluestone extracted from quarries on Point Gellibrand. For a time, Ned Kelly (see p.44) languished in a yellow-daubed prison hulk anchored offshore.

Around the point and beyond the cricket ground, **Williamstown Beach** is one of Melbourne's best bayside swimming spots, while the lush **botanical gardens**, just back from the beach, are a good spot for a picnic. Following Giffard Street along the eastern side of the Botanical Gardens as far as Electra Street to no. 5 brings you to the small **Williamstown Museum** (Sun 2–5pm; $2), a repository for a fine collection of maritime displays and some interesting artefacts from the suburb's early development, including antique furnishings and detailed models of ships. Williamstown's other museum is trainspotter heaven: the **Railway Historical Society Museum** (Sat & Sun noon–5pm; $5) on Champion Road, which has an impressive collection of beautifully restored steam and diesel engines. The museum is next to North Williamstown Station, the second-to-last stop on the Williamstown line.

# SCIENCEWORKS

**Map 3, A5.** Daily 10am–4.30pm; $8; ☏9392 4800. Williamstown and Werribee lines to Spotswood Station, then a 15min walk.

**Scienceworks**, at 2 Booker Street in Spotswood, is an excellent hands-on museum that takes the geekiness out of science and technology. Inside the space-age building, set in appropriately desolate wasteland, the tactile displays, hi-tech exhibits and touring shows on themes such as *Star Trek* are ingenious, fun and highly interactive. There's also an enormous planetarium, where you can learn about the night sky. Part of the exhibition consists of the original Spotswood Pumping Station, an unusually attractive early industrial complex with working steam pumps.

..............................................................................................

**If you're cycling from the city, Scienceworks is just off the bicycle route west of Riverside Park.**

..............................................................................................

# The outskirts

A visit to Melbourne's spacious, leafy **outer suburbs** will give you a feel for what life here is really all about. Many have quite distinct characters and personalities, whether as enclaves of café society or self-styled artists' communities. The **northeast** of the city, spread out around the Yarra as it meanders inland, boasts the charming artistic retreats of the Museum of Modern Art at Heide, and Montsalvat in the adjacent suburb of Eltham. Melbourne's **western** outskirts also deserve a visit for the opulent mansion and grounds of Werribee Park, Victoria's Open Range Zoo, with its mix of African and Australian animals, and the delightful You Yangs Regional Park.

Apart from the You Yangs, all of these places are accessible by **public transport**, although probably the most enjoyable way of getting around is by tram or bicycle, or a combination of both.

## NORTHEAST ALONG THE YARRA

One of the best ways to explore Melbourne's **northeast** is by bicycle (see p.211 for information on bike rental). A **bicycle path** runs beside the Yarra all the way from the city centre to Eltham, 24km inland. Starting at Southgate it passes through South Yarra and Toorak before reaching

Yarra Bend and Studley parks, with their prime riverside frontage, sandstone escarpments, golf courses, boathouses, playing fields and untouched bushland. From here there are great views of the city skyline and the massive CUB Brewery.

After passing Collingwood Children's Farm (see p.207) and then riding under the Johnston Street Bridge, you'll catch a glimpse of Dight's Falls, the remains of an 1840s flourmill. Just beyond here is the junction of the Yarra with Merri Creek, from where you can continue along the river to Fairfield Boathouse or take the walking track to Kane's Bridge, which leads back to Studley Park Boathouse. Both have cafés and rent out boats for around $10–18 per hour.

If you're feeling energetic, you can continue on from Fairfield Boathouse to **Banksia Park**. In the late 1880s and 1890s this area was a magnet for a group of artists known as the Heidelberg School, who broke with European landscape conventions and charted a distinctive and more naturalistic depiction of Australian conditions. For more information, contact the Banyule City Council (✆9490 4222) or the Museum of Modern Art at Heide (see below), who can also provide details on the **Heidelberg Artists Trail**, a six-kilometre path of information panels and reproductions located at the sites where Arthur Streeton, Tom Roberts and Frederick McCubbin once set up their easels beside the river.

## Museum of Modern Art at Heide

Tues–Fri 10am–5pm, Sat & Sun noon–5pm; $5; ✆9850 1500.
Hurstbridge line to Heidelberg Station, then bus #291;
alternatively, catch bus #200 from Market St, which will drop you at the front gate.

Adjoining Banksia Park, the **Museum of Modern Art at Heide** is set in bush property at 7 Templestowe Road in

Bulleen. Heide was the home of urbane art patrons John and Sunday Reed, who bought this former dairy farm in 1934; it was also where the modernism movement gained a stronghold in Australia during the 1930s and 1940s. A volatile collection of artists such as Sidney Nolan, Joy Hester, Albert Tucker and Arthur Boyd flourished here with support from the Reeds. The property has numerous sculptures by artists such as Bruce Armstrong, Anthony Caro and Anishka Kapoor, and an exquisite kitchen garden, while the gallery holds a collection of modern Australian art from the 1920s to the 1980s, plus temporary exhibitions of contemporary art. If you're **driving**, Heide is well marked off the Eastern Freeway (take the Bulleen Road turn-off).

## Montsalvat

Daily sunrise–sunset; $5. Hurstbridge line to Eltham Station, then a 2km walk.

Eltham, just east of Heide, cemented its reputation as a crafts centre in 1935 when the painter and architect Justus Jorgensen founded **Montsalvat**, a European-style artists' colony complete with rustic buildings, tranquil gardens, galleries and studios. Built with the help of his students and followers, the colony's eclectic design was inspired by medieval European buildings, with wonderfully quirky results. Jorgensen died before it was completed, and it has deliberately been left unfinished, although he did live long enough to oversee the completion of the mud-brick Great Hall, whose influence is evident in other similar buildings around Eltham. Today the colony is still home to assorted painters, potters and craftspeople, while the galleries and grounds are often used for visual and performing arts, exhibitions, and jazz and classical concerts.

# WEST TO WERRIBEE PARK AND BEYOND

Map 2, F4.

Beyond Melbourne the western outskirts lapse into drab suburbia until you approach Werribee. Here, stately **Werribee Park** adjoins the grassy plains of Victoria's Open Range Zoo, while further west, the **You Yangs Regional Park** makes for a picturesque detour.

## Werribee Park and around

Daily 10am–5pm; $10; ©9741 2444. Werribee line to Werribee Station, then bus #439 to the park entrance.

Thirty kilometres west of Melbourne on K. Road in Werribee, **Werribee Park** is an award-winning estate and sixty-room Italianate mansion – the largest private residence in Victoria – built from goldmining riches between 1874 and 1877. Guides in period costume can show you inside the homestead, or around the Victorian-era lawns (a great place for a picnic) and adjoining Victoria State Rose Garden; alternatively, free headsets providing a self-guiding commentary are available at the entrance.

Next door to Werribee Park, **Victoria's Open Range Zoo** (daily 10am–5pm; $14; ©9731 9600) is home to Australian and African herbivores including rhinos, hippos, giraffes, zebras and meerkats. The savannah-like conditions are designed to resemble as closely as possible the natural habitats of the animals, which roam freely and can be seen by bus safari tour (the first at 10.30am, the last at 3.40pm; free).

## You Yangs Regional Park

Some 15km west of Werribee, the **You Yangs Regional Park** is a small volcanic range with several walks around the central Flinders Peak, which is well worth climbing for the views across the bay and down towards Geelong. Within the park, rock hollows have been enlarged by Aborigines to ensure water was available during the driest spells. The You Yangs are inaccessible by public transport; driving, take the marked turn-off on the Melbourne–Geelong Freeway at Little River.

# LISTINGS

# Accommodation

Melbourne has a range of accommodation options, from first-class hotels to dormitories. The only time you're likely to have problems **finding a room** is during major sporting events such as the Grand Prix or AFL Grand Final (see "Sport", p.187 and 182), when rooms are often booked out a long time in advance – it's best at these times to reserve a couple of months ahead. Hostels, particularly those in St Kilda, also fill up quickly over December and January. Again, plan on making a reservation, preferably not less than a week in advance.

---

The telephone code for the Melbourne area is ℗03. Calling Melbourne from abroad, dial ℗0011 61 3, followed by the number.

---

If you fly in without a reservation, head for the **travellers information service desks** (daily 6am–last flight; ℗9297 1814) at Melbourne's Tullamarine Airport. Located on the ground and first floors of the international terminal, they provide a free booking service for all types of accommodation throughout the city and suburbs. You can also use the interactive accommodation board near the information service desk on the ground floor. Bookings can be made downtown at the **Victorian Visitor Information Centre**

# Accommodation prices

All accommodation listed in this book has been categorized according to the following **price codes**, which represent the **cheapest rate for a double or twin room available** (excluding special offers). Note that rates generally increase during major sporting and cultural events, summer months (Dec–March) and peak holiday periods such as Christmas and Easter. For hostels providing dormitory accommodation, the code represents the per-person charge for a bed.

| | | |
|---|---|---|
| ① under $20 | ② $20–30 | ③ $30–45 |
| ④ $45–60 | ⑤ $60–75 | ⑥ $75–100 |
| ⑦ $100–$150 | ⑧ $150–200 | ⑨ over $200 |

(Mon–Fri 9am–6pm, Sat & Sun 9am–5pm; ✆9650 7721, fax 9650 3314) in the Melbourne Town Hall on Swanston Street. Again, there's no booking fee. For **gay and lesbian accommodation**, ring Gay Share (✆9650 0200), which arranges house shares.

When deciding which **area** to stay in, your basic choice is between the CBD, adjacent inner-city suburbs, and St Kilda. The **city centre** (particularly Collins Street) and the leisure precincts of Southgate and the Crown Casino are the domain of upmarket hotels, while a number of mid-range joints cluster around Spencer Street Station, although unfortunately the area is rather noisy and unattractive. For cheaper rooms, there's plenty of backpacker accommodation, especially along Elizabeth Street. **Inner-city suburbs** such as North and East Melbourne, Carlton, Richmond, South Yarra and South Melbourne offer good alternatives to the CBD in all price ranges, while **St Kilda** has perhaps the best-value accommodation in Melbourne, with hostels by the bucketload and plenty of inexpensive hotels and motels.

Our listings are grouped by **area**, subdivided into **type of accommodation** (hotels and motels, B&Bs, and hostels). The majority are easily accessible by tram, train or bus.

# CITY CENTRE

## Adelphi Hotel

**Map 4, H4.** 187 Flinders Lane ✆9650 7555, fax 9650 2710.
Boutique hotel *par excellence*, the 34-room *Adelphi Hotel* has slick service and an even slicker design. The ultramodern, minimalist interior extends to the large rooms and bars, and is topped off with a glass-bottomed rooftop pool suspended above the street. ⑧.

## Astoria City Travel Inn

**Map 4, B4.** 288 Spencer St ✆9670 6801, fax 9670 3034.
Pleasant motel three blocks north of Spencer Street Station, conveniently located on the City Circle Tram route. Units are spacious and bright, and amenities include free videos, swimming pool, laundry (at a nominal charge) and a licensed restaurant. ⑥.

## Batmans Hill

**Map 4, C6.** 66 Spencer St ✆9614 6344, fax 9614 1189.
Handy to Spencer Street Station, *Batmans Hill* has an elegant Edwardian facade that belies a functional and modern interior. A wide range of facilities includes bars, a restaurant and 24hr room service. ⑦.

## City Centre Private Hotel

**Map 4, I3.** 22 Little Collins St ☎9654 5401, fax 9650 7256.

Good position on a quiet street 100m from Parliament Station. Rooms are serviced daily; most have fridges and all share bathrooms. Facilities include small and basic kitchens, a TV lounge and laundry. **③**.

## Crown Towers Hotel

**Map 4, E7.** Level 2, Crown Casino, 8 Whiteman St, Southbank ☎9685 4300, fax 9292 6299.

This luxurious five-star in Australia's largest casino is far and away the most opulent place to stay in Melbourne. Combining a central location with spacious and beautifully appointed rooms, it's the ideal destination for high-rollers and cashed-up travellers, although the glitzy tat surrounding the hotel is a real downer. **⑨**.

## Hotel Enterprize

**Map 4, C6.** 44 Spencer St ☎9629 6991, fax 9614 7963.

Opposite Spencer Street Station, this solid, old-fashioned hotel has reasonably plush en suite rooms and a good restaurant downstairs. Room service and undercover parking available. **⑦**.

## Grand Hyatt

**Map 4, H4.** 123 Collins St ☎9657 1234, fax 9650 3491.

This over-the-top hotel has 547 rooms, eighteen executive suites and a lobby big enough to land a plane in. If you're really flush, you can upgrade to the hotel's "Regency Club", where there's a butler on call and free breakfast and drinks. **⑨**.

## Kingsgate Hotel

**Map 4, D5.** 131 King St ☎9629 4171, fax 9629 7110.

Huge hotel with averagely plush en suite rooms with TV, air-conditioning, bar-fridges and telephones, while the budget rooms with shared facilities have recently been upgraded.

There's a 24hr reception, but no kitchen facilities. Budget ③,
en suite ④.

## Le Meridien at Rialto

**Map 4, D5.** 495 Collins St ℂ9620 9111, fax 9614 1219.
In *Le Meridien* brochurese, this hotel is "the soul of Europe in
the heart of Melbourne", and once inside you'll see why.
Behind an Italian Gothic facade and beneath the vertiginous
Rialto Towers are 242 rooms stacked with romantic French
furnishings and decor, while the hotel's eateries have excellent
food prepared by some of Melbourne's finest chefs. ⑨.

## Miami Hostel and Motor Inn

**Map 4, A1.** 13 Hawke St ℂ9329 8499, fax 9328 1820.
Mostly motel-style accommodation, although it dabbles as a
lodging house for international students. Standard rooms are
simple but clean; en suite and larger family rooms with TV,
wardrobe and ceiling fan are particularly good value, as are the
weekly rates, which include dinner Monday to Friday. Standard
③, en suite ⑥.

## Pacific International Terrace Inn

**Map 4, C6.** 16 Spencer St ℂ9621 3333, fax 9621 1922.
Popular with business types, and close to the Melbourne
Exhibition Centre. Pleasant and well maintained, it offers en
suite rooms, complimentary breakfasts, loads of tourist information and friendly, unstuffy staff. ⑦.

## Premier Grand Hotel

**Map 4, C6.** 33 Spencer St ℂ9611 4567, fax 9611 4655.
Originally the head office for the Victorian Railways, "the
Grand" has been redeveloped into an expensive hotel with
large loft-style suites. Facilities include a fully contained
kitchen in each room, swimming pool, spa, gym, valet parking
and 24hr room service. ⑧.

## Sheraton Towers Southgate

**Map 4, G6.** 1 Southgate Ave ℘9696 3100, fax 9690 5889.

Large, reasonable rooms, but the advantage of this hotel is its height, affording great views over Southgate, the Yarra and the city centre. Includes a good fitness centre, while the elegant Tisane Lounge serves high tea (daily 2.30–5pm) and posh cocktails at night. ⑨.

## Sofitel Hotel

**Map 4, I4.** 25 Collins St ℘9653 0000, fax 9650 4261.

I.M. Pei-designed hotel with marvellous views across Melbourne and surrounds. Gloriously comfortable rooms, which begin on the 36th floor, as well as a good spread of cafés and restaurants, including the airy and reasonably cheap *Café La* and *Le Restaurant* (see p.119), a formal dining place with sensational vistas. ⑨.

## Stork Hotel

**Map 4, E1.** 504 Elizabeth St ℘9663 6237, fax 9663 8895.

Small goldrush-era hotel with simple but pleasant rooms and shared facilities. Central location opposite Queen Victoria Market. ③.

## Victoria Vista Hotel

**Map 4, G4.** 215 Little Collins St ℘9653 0441, fax 9650 9678.

Old but refurbished hotel. En suite rooms have TV, telephone, and tea- and coffee-making facilities. There's also a café and bar, and undercover parking. ⑥.

## Windsor Hotel

**Map 4, I3.** 103 Spring St ℘9653 0653, fax 9633 6001.

Built in 1883 opposite Parliament House, this grand colonial pile has played host to Sir Laurence Olivier, Vivien Leigh and Muhammad Ali, as well as legions of silverhairs who just can't seem to keep away. The prestigious suites are pure nineteenth-century opulence. Service is understated but excellent, and don't leave without taking afternoon tea at the hotel's *111 Spring Street* restaurant. ⑨.

## Backpackers City Inn
**Map 4, H3.** 197 Bourke St ℰ9650 2734, fax 9650 5474.
Reasonable accommodation, given the price. Non-dorm rooms have TVs and bar-fridges; shared toilets and showers. Dorms ①, rooms ③.

## Hotel Bakpak
**Map 4, E1.** 167 Franklin St ℰ9329 7525, fax 9326 7667.
Gargantuan hostel (formerly known as *Downtown Backpackers*) in an old school building. Standard facilities and services include a simple and mostly clean kitchen, café, travel shop, free airport pick-up, gym, bar, in-house backpacker employment agency and a 10ft TV screen that's used for regular movie nights. Dorms have four to sixteen beds (separate men's and women's dorms available on request), fans and lockers; the double rooms are spartan affairs affording little privacy. Dorms ①, rooms ③.

## Exford Hostel
**Map 4, G3.** 199 Russell St ℰ9663 2697, fax 9663 2248.
In an extremely central position above a pub, this hostel is secure and clean, and has a tiny courtyard with barbecue. Twins and doubles are well worth the money. Dorms ①, rooms ③.

## Flinders Street Station Hotel
**Map 4, G5.** 35 Elizabeth St ℰ9620 5100, fax 9620 5101.
Newly opened, bright and spacious backpacker accommodation above a bar and bottle shop and close to Flinders Street Station. Twin-share, doubles, four-bed dorms and rooms with en suite, plus TV, Internet and reading rooms. Dorms ①, rooms ③.

CITY CENTRE: HOSTELS

## The Friendly Backpacker

**Map 4, E6.** 2 William St ℡9670 1111, fax 9670 9911.
Well-run backpacker lodge with mixed- and single-sex dorm
rooms, a self-catering kitchen, foreign currency exchange, pool
tables, jukebox, two TV lounges and an excellent noticeboard.
A full-time cleaner ensures all rooms are given a determined
dose of hygiene. Close to the Skybus route to the airport. ①.

## The Hotel Y

**Map 4, E1.** 489 Elizabeth St ℡9329 5188, fax 9329 1469.
Mostly en suite rooms with fridge, telephone and air-conditioning (TVs in the de luxe rooms), although the few dorm
beds are expensive at $25. Also has a small kitchen, laundry, a
sinfully cheap but excellent licensed café, undercover parking
and a swimming pool (currently in the throes of renovation).
Near the Melbourne Transit Centre and Queen Victoria
Market. Dorms ②, rooms ⑤.

## Queensberry Hill YHA

**Map 4, C1.** 78–86 Howard St ℡9329 8599, fax 9326 8427.
Excellent value, purpose-built hostel with dorms, single, dou-
ble and family rooms, plus apartment-style accommodation.
Facilities include a cafeteria and a huge, well-equipped kitchen.
It's a 10min walk from the Melbourne Transit Centre, or the
Skybus will drop you off on request. Dorms ①, rooms ④.

## Toad Hall Guesthouse

**Map 4, E1.** 441 Elizabeth St ℡9600 9010, fax 9600 9013.
Historic Victorian building close to the Melbourne Transit
Centre providing friendly, cosy, secure and clean facilities. Car
parking available. Dorms ①, rooms ④.

## Victoria Hall

**Map 4, G1.** 380 Russell St ℡9662 3888, fax 9639 0101.
International student accommodation that accepts budget trav-

ellers when rooms (no dorms) are available. Top value, especially for single rooms, and great location near the Old Melbourne Gaol and Lygon Street. Breakfast and cheap dinner available on request. Book in advance. ②.

# CARLTON, FITZROY AND NORTH MELBOURNE

## HOTELS AND MOTELS

### Downtowner on Lygon
**Map 5, C7.** 66 Lygon St, Carlton ℂ9663 5555, fax 9662 3308. Attractively refurbished en suite rooms, some with spas, plus a restaurant and undercover parking. ⑦.

### Lygon Lodge
**Map 5, D6.** 220 Lygon St, Carlton ℂ9663 6633, fax 9663 7297. Good drive-in motel in terrific location. Rooms are clean and attractive, and some have small kitchenettes. ⑤.

## HOSTELS

### Carlton College
**Map 5, D7.** 101 Drummond St, Carlton ℂ9663 1644, fax 9639 2165. Student accommodation that turns into a backpackers' hostel from mid-December to mid-February. The small dorms, singles, twins and doubles are simple but good. Plenty of communal facilities like a games room, TV lounge, laundry and a kitchen-cum-breakfast area. Rate includes breakfast. Dorms ①, rooms ②.

### Chapman Gardens YHA
**Map 5, A2.** 76 Chapman St, North Melbourne ℂ9328 3595, fax 9329 7863.
Mainly twin-share rooms, self-catering kitchen, free car park-

ing, free bike rental and personal lockers. Leafy setting and very friendly atmosphere. Dorms ①, rooms ③.

------

**To reach North Melbourne, take tram #57.**

------

## City Scene
**Map 5, A7.** 361 Queensberry St, North Melbourne ☏9348 9525, fax 9427 9001.
Large, relatively new hostel close to Queen Victoria Market. Mixed and segregated four- and six-bed dorms, as well as twin rooms; free access to the Melbourne City Baths' (see p.185) pool and gym included. Dorms ①, rooms ③.

## The Nunnery
**Map 5, F6.** 116 Nicholson St, Fitzroy ☏9419 8637, fax 9417 7736.
This attractive guesthouse, housed in a former convent, is Fitzroy's only budget accommodation option. A small court-yard and a tiny rooftop are the only outdoor sitting areas, and the dorms are rather cramped, but the atmosphere is busy and friendly, and there's also a big, cosy TV lounge and a kitchen. Dorms ①, rooms ④.

# EAST MELBOURNE AND RICHMOND

### HOTELS AND MOTELS

## East Melbourne Hotel
**Map 4, N4.** 2 Hotham St, East Melbourne ☏9419 2040, fax 9417 3733.
Clean and comfortable budget rooms with heating and shared facilities above a pub at the Punt Road end of the street. Cheap meals and pool table at the café-bar downstairs. ④.

## Hilton on the Park

**Map 4, M4.** 192 Wellington Parade, East Melbourne ©9419 2000, fax 9419 2001.

Opposite the MCG, and popular with football and cricketing enthusiasts, facilities include the Hepburn Day spa (massages from $37.50 for 30min), sauna, pool and second telephone lines that allow you to surf the Internet or handle email. ⑧.

## Magnolia Court Boutique Hotel

**Map 4, N3.** 101 Powlett St, East Melbourne ©9419 4222, fax 9416 0841.

Elegant, small hotel in a quiet residential street. Tastefully furnished rooms with all facilities in two older, lovingly restored buildings and a newish motel section. Excellent breakfasts available in an airy room overlooking a courtyard garden. ⑦.

---

**To reach East Melbourne and Richmond, take tram #75 or the Belgrave and Alamein line from Flinders Street Station.**

---

**B&BS**

## Georgian Court Guesthouse

**Map 4, N4.** 21–25 George St, East Melbourne ©9419 6353, fax 9416 0895.

Cosy B&B with standard rooms and shared facilities, plus en suite rooms equipped with TV, fridge and radio; all bright, tastefully furnished and serviced daily. Quiet, but very central to the CBD, MCG and Richmond. ⑤.

## Palm Court B&B

**Map 3, F4.** 2 Grattan Place, Richmond © & fax 9427 7365.

Spacious rooms and open fireplaces set in restored Victorian grandeur. Much favoured by gay and lesbian visitors to

Melbourne. It's one block directly east of the Richmond Cricket Ground in Yarra Park (Map 4, N6), across Punt Road. ③.

## Central Accommodation

**Map 3, F3.** 21 Bromham Place, Richmond ©9427 9826, no fax. Small, friendly place with four- and six-bed dorms (one women-only) plus a few double rooms, ideally located close to the main drags of Church Street and Bridge Road. Rate includes free access to the Melbourne City Baths (see p.185). Walk a block north from the corner of Bridge Road and Church Street, then turn left down Highett Street. Bromham Place is on your right. ①.

## Richmond Hill Hotel

**Map 3, F4.** 353 Church St, Richmond ©9428 6501, fax 9427 0128. Clean and well-run ex-YWCA in a refurbished old mansion with cosy sitting rooms, large shared kitchen, courtyard, bar and off-street parking. Accommodation consists of dorms (some women-only), single, double and family rooms; the more expensive ones include a buffet breakfast. Dorms ①, rooms ③.

# SOUTH YARRA, PRAHRAN AND TOORAK

## Hotel Como

**Map 6, D4.** 630 Chapel St, South Yarra ©9824 0400, fax 9824 1263. Melbourne's checkpoint for glitz and glamour is a favourite haunt of supermodels and celebs like Kylie Minogue. Suites and studios are individually themed, stylish and very chic. Check in, and then check out the king-size beds, Swedish-style furniture and free toiletries, then catch a movie at the Como Centre in the same complex, or step outside for coffee and shopping. ⑨.

## South Yarra Hill Suites Hotel

**Map 6, B3.** 14 Murphy St, South Yarra ℂ9688 8222, fax 9820 1724. Clean, comfortable and spacious one- and two-bedroom apartments, serviced daily. Rates are high but offer good value, including an excellent complimentary breakfast. One-bedroom ⑧, two-bedroom ⑨.

### B&BS

## Tilba Hotel

**Map 6, A4.** 30 Toorak Rd, South Yarra ℂ9867 8844, fax 9867 6567. Small and beautiful hotel in a sumptuous nineteenth-century mansion. Rooms of all different shapes and sizes abound; other features include a grand staircase, a conservatory housing a giant wooden birdcage, and plenty of antique furnishings. ⑦.

## Toorak Manor Boutique Hotel

**Map 6, G6.** 220 Williams Rd, Toorak ℂ9827 2689, fax 9824 2830. Close to Chapel Street, this lovely old establishment has eighteen rooms replete with opulent Victoriana. A silver-service breakfast is included in the price. ⑦.

## West End Hotel

**Map 3, E5.** 76 Toorak Rd West, South Yarra ℂ9866 3135, no fax. Reasonable value, old-fashioned B&B in the heart of exclusive South Yarra and near the Royal Botanic Gardens. ③–④.

### HOSTELS

## Chapel Street Backpackers

**Map 6, C9.** 22 Chapel St, Windsor ℂ9533 6855, fax 9533 6866. Offers small dorms, security, an Internet service and 24hr

SOUTH YARRA, PRAHRAN AND TOORAK: B&BS, HOSTELS

**109**

access. Breakfast is included with the rate, and they'll pick up mornings and evenings from Spencer Street Station. To get there, take the Sandringham line train from Flinders Street Station to Windsor Station; the hostel is across the road. Dorms ①, rooms ④.

### Lords Lodge Backpackers

**Map 3, F5.** 204 Punt Rd, Prahran ✆9510 5658, fax 9533 6663. Small, non-smoking hostel near the bars, cafés and retro shops of groovy Greville Street. Basic but reasonably clean singles and double rooms (all with heating), and medium-sized dorms (some women-only) with fridge and lockers. Dorms ①, rooms ②.

# SOUTH MELBOURNE AND ALBERT PARK

## HOTELS AND MOTELS

### Bleak House Hotel

**Map 3, C5.** 97 Beaconsfield Parade, Albert Park ✆9690 4642, fax 9690 4062.
Excellent pub accommodation in bright, clean rooms with shared facilities. Front rooms have great views over the beach and Port Phillip Bay. Close to the Tasmanian ferry terminal. ②.

### Hotel Victoria

**Map 3, C5.** 123 Beaconsfield Parade, South Melbourne ✆9690 3666, fax 9699 9570.
Seafront hotel with comfortable, modern-style accommodation. All rooms are en suite; the more expensive have spas and views across the bay. En suite without spa ⑥, en suite with spa ⑦.

--------------------------------------------------------

**To reach South Melbourne and Albert Park, take tram #1 or #96.**

--------------------------------------------------------

## Nomads Market Inn

**Map 3, D5.** 115 Cecil St, South Melbourne ℗9690 2220, fax 9690 2544.

Dorms and twin rooms with complimentary breakfast and free beer at check-in. Free bike rental and transport to and from train and bus stations; also has a licensed bar and kitchen. Close to the South Melbourne Market and Melbourne Sports and Aquatic Centre (see p.189). Dorms ①, rooms ③.

# ST KILDA

**HOTELS AND MOTELS**

## Bayside Motel

**Map 7, D5.** 63 Fitzroy St ℗9525 3833, fax 9534 1831.

Value-for-money triples have all the mod cons, although rooms facing the street can get a bit noisy (ask for one at the back). Secure car park at the rear. ④.

## Charnwood Motor Inn

**Map 7, G5.** 3 Charnwood Rd ℗9525 4199, fax 9525 4587.

Secluded, quiet location 5–10min walk from Fitzroy Street. Rooms are simple but clean, with en suite, TV, and tea- and coffee-making facilities. ⑤.

## Novotel Bayside Melbourne

**Map 7, C7.** 16 The Esplanade ℗9525 5522, fax 9525 5678.

Apricot-coloured eyesore with a bird's-eye view of the beach and Sunday market, plus heated pool, gym, spa, sauna, café and restaurant. Convenient for both Acland and Fitzroy streets. ⑧.

ST KILDA: HOTELS AND MOTELS

## Warwick Beachside St Kilda

**Map 7, C5.** 363 Beaconsfield Parade ℂ9525 4800, fax 9537 1056.
Close to the cafés and pubs of Fitzroy Street, these 1950s-style brick buildings contain nicely refurbished one- and two-bedroom units, all with TV, telephone and kitchen facilities. Good weekly rates. ⑤.

**B&BS**

## Olembia Bed and Breakfast

**Map 7, F7.** 96 Barkly St ℂ9537 1412, fax 9537 1600.
Old Edwardian building in a leafy setting provides a peaceful, non-smoking retreat from the bustle of Barkly Street. Smallish singles, twins and doubles are spotlessly clean and appealing affairs, as are the dorms (some women-only). Book in advance. Dorms ①, rooms ④.

## Robinsons by the Sea

**Map 7, B4.** 335 Beaconsfield Parade ℂ & fax 9534 2683.
One of Melbourne's best B&Bs, *Robinsons* has five cosy rooms (sharing three bathrooms), a downstairs sitting room and meals area, where the breakfasts are truly memorable. Ask for one of the balcony rooms, which have views overlooking the sea and terrific features such as canopied beds and open fireplaces. ⑦.

**HOSTELS**

## Enfield House

**Map 7, E5.** 2 Enfield St ℂ9534 8159, fax 9534 5579.
Stately Victorian-era mansion and annexe with basic dorms and rooms with refurbished bathrooms but very little else. Services are minimal, although pluses include organized Friday-night pub-crawls and inter-hostel soccer matches. Transport to train and bus stations, ferry terminal and airport is also provided. Rates include pancake breakfast. Non-smoking.

ST KILDA: B&BS, HOSTELS

Walk up Grey Street from the junction with Fitzroy Street and take the first right (Jackson St). Enfield Street is on your left. Dorms ①, rooms ②.

## Leopard House

**Map 7, E5.** 27 Grey St ⓒ & fax 9534 1200.
One of St Kilda's better budget options, this large old house has lockable dorms (segregated or mixed), a good noticeboard, free weekly BBQs and a courtyard kitted out with comfortable furniture. Friendly atmosphere with knowledgeable staff. One of the few places to refund if you cancel a booking. ①.

## Ritz for Backpackers

**Map 7, F4.** 169 Fitzroy St ⓒ9525 3501, fax 9525 3863.
Well-furnished and friendly hostel above the English-style *Elephant and Wheelbarrow* pub. Rooms are simple and generally clean, and there are two TV lounges, pool table, dining room, tiny kitchen and Internet kiosk. Dorms ①, rooms ③.

## St Kilda Coffee Palace

**Map 7, E5.** 24 Grey St ⓒ9534 5283, fax 9593 9166.
Bustling hostel in large and rambling building popular with ravers. Some of the spacious dorms are women-only, and there's plenty of super-clean motel-style accommodation on the top floor with en suite bathrooms. Nice rooftop garden, plus good travel shop and work centre. Pick-up service from the bus terminals and Tasmanian ferry. Dorms ①, rooms ③.

ST KILDA: HOSTELS

# Eating

The rivalry between Melbourne and Sydney for the title of **food capital** of Australia is taken very seriously by both cities, although in truth the two are so different that each can be said to have its own distinctive style. Where Sydney is brash, fast-paced, alfresco and Asian-inspired, Melbourne is more relaxed and considered – café life is seen as a cultural activity, while dining out tends to be a serious, more classical affair driven by French and Italian influences. During the 1970s and early 1980s, Melbourne's restaurants lagged behind Sydney and Adelaide's more innovative approaches, but in the last decade a handful of newly arrived French and British chefs (brought, legend has it, to Melbourne by their homesick Australian girlfriends), along with locals such as Mietta O'Donnell and Stephanie Alexander, have been responsible for the development of a new wave of cooking in the city.

If you want to make your own meals, see p.201 for details of some of Melbourne's best places to shop for food.

There are more than five hundred restaurants and cafés in the CBD, and the city council wants more. However, many of Melbourne's best eating spots are to be found outside the city centre in **suburbs** such as Fitzroy, South Melbourne, South Yarra, St Kilda, and the Vietnamese enclave of Richmond – affectionately known as "Little Saigon". In the past, the Italian eateries of Lygon Street in Carlton were among the city's culinary highlights – unfortunately, they've become something of a tourist trap and are now best avoided. Of course, there are always **fast-food** outlets, with branches of *McDonald's*, *KFC*, *Pizza Hut* and Australian chains such as *Hungry Jacks* and *Sizzlers* in virtually every neighbourhood. There's even *Kosher Express*, a fast-food restaurant in Carlisle Street, Balaclava, where orthodox Jews munch on "McDavid" burgers or sip "koshercino".

The other major difference in dining between Melbourne and Sydney is **price**, with a main course at a top Melbourne restaurant costing around $10–15 less than its Sydney counterpart. Most restaurants and upmarket cafés offer special **lunchtime** set menus of three courses with wine for about half the cost of an equivalent evening meal. **Pubs** are also good value, and nowadays offer interesting food and beverages at reasonable prices, as do the **food halls** in major department stores, Southgate and the Crown Casino. In addition, many Melbourne eateries are **bring your own** (BYO), allowing you to supply your own drink – this generally includes even licensed restaurants (though it pays to check first). Note, however, that a corkage fee ($1–2 per person) often applies. Most places listed also accept payment by **credit card**.

---

Two indispensable guides to the city's restaurants are
*The Age Cheap Eats in Melbourne* and *The Age Good Food Guide*, available from bookshops and major
newsagents.

EATING

## Restaurant prices

In the following listings, prices are indicated by the terms
**cheap** (under $15), **inexpensive** ($15–25), **moderate** ($25–40),
**expensive** ($40–60) and **very expensive** (over $60). These
refer to the cost of a starter, main course and dessert for one
person. Drinks are *not* included in these estimates.

# CITY CENTRE

### Becco
**Map 4, I3.** 11–25 Crossley St ✆9663 3000.
Daily noon–11pm. Expensive.
If the pleasing Italian-style fare and interesting wine selection
from the formal dining area doesn't whet your appetite, perhaps a quick drink, dessert or late supper at the bar will, or you
can pick up a takeaway from the produce store (see p.201).

### Blakes
**Map 4, G6.** Ground Level, Southgate ✆9699 4100.
Daily noon–11pm. Expensive.
Innovative, sophisticated food mixing Asian, Mediterranean and
European flavours to great effect. The brisk and intelligent ser-
vice, quality wine list and city views simply add to the appeal.

### Blue Train Café
**Map 4, G6.** Level 3, Southgate ✆9696 0111.
Mon–Fri 7am–1am, Sat 7am–2am, Sun 7am–midnight. Cheap to
inexpensive.
Attracts a young, hip crowd and dishes out basic meals like
wood-fired pizzas, pasta and salad. There's also full bar service
and plenty of reading material if you're dining solo.

## Box

**Map 4, G4.** 189 Collins St ℂ9663 0411.

Mon noon–3pm, Tues–Sat noon–late. Expensive.

Next to the Regent Theatre, *Box* is a small space split over two levels, with a formal though cosy restaurant offering imaginative food one flight up. If you're not looking to spend too much, there's also an affordable café serving light snacks and a bar downstairs (inexpensive).

## Cafe L'Incontro

**Map 4, G4.** Cnr Little Collins & Swanston streets ℂ9650 9603.

Daily 24hr. Cheap.

The food from this smart-looking licensed café (mostly nachos, pasta and sweets) plays second fiddle to the alfresco setting in a prime location overlooking busy Swanston Street.

## Florentino Restaurant and Cellar Bar

**Map 4, I3.** 80 Bourke St ℂ9662 1811.

Mon–Sat 7.30pm–11pm. Inexpensive to expensive.

One of Melbourne's finest places for good coffee, the *Florentino Cellar Bar* (inexpensive) also has cheap wines and pasta. Upstairs is Melbourne institution *Florentino* (Mon–Sat noon–11pm; expensive), the pricier Italian-French restaurant that's been synonymous with fine dining for many years.

## Food Court

**Map 4, D7.** Ground Level, Crown Casino, 8 Whiteman St, Southbank.

Daily 7am–late. Cheap.

Hugely popular food court, hawking everything from Singaporean noodles, Mexican nachos, salads and sandwiches to fish and chips. Some stalls are licensed, others aren't.

## Gopals

**Map 4, G5.** 39 Swanston St ℂ9650 1578.

Tues–Fri noon–8.30pm, Sat 5–8.30pm. Cheap.
Typically wholesome, vegetarian food from the Hare Krishna organization. Even cheaper is their *Crossways Food for Life* at 123 Swanston Street, which has all-you-can-eat deals for next to nothing.

## Hopetoun Tea Rooms

**Map 4, F4.** Shop 2, Block Arcade, off Elizabeth St ✆9650 2777.
Mon–Thurs 9am–5pm, Fri 9am–6pm, Sat 10am–4pm. Cheap.
Food and drink have been served in these elegant surroundings for more than a century. Times change, but the scones and cakes, as well as newfangled delicacies like focaccia with pesto sauce, are still delicious.

## Il Bacaro

**Map 4, H4.** 168–170 Little Collins St ✆9654 6778.
Mon–Sat noon–11pm. Expensive to very expensive.
Charges like a wounded bull and sometimes disinterested service mar an otherwise interesting menu and intimate ambience. An award-winner when first started, *Il Bacaro's* backward slide seems to suggest it is simply coasting. But it's nice coasting, mind.

## Kenzan

**Map 4, I4.** 45 Collins St ✆9654 8933.
Mon–Sat noon–10pm. Moderate to expensive.
Epitome of Japanese food and style: great sushi selection and cool, elegant surroundings in the basement of the *Sofitel Hotel*.

## Koko

**Map 4, D7.** Level 3, Crown Casino, 8 Whiteman St, Southbank ✆9292 6886.
Daily noon–3pm & 6.30–11pm. Expensive to very expensive.
Melbourne's premier Japanese restaurant, *Koko* inhabits a large and decorative space fitted out with tables, myriad grills, a tran-

quil water garden and, in one corner, a sushi-sashimi bar perfect for a pre-dinner drink.

## Langtons

**Map 4, I4.** 61 Flinders Lane ✆9663 0222.
Mon–Sat 7am–11pm. Moderate to expensive.
Excellent place for breakfast or dinner in the French style, with some of the best regional wines and service in Melbourne. No expense has been spared on the minimalist decor, which includes parquet floors, polished brass columns and a theatrical open kitchen dominated by a copper Bonnet stove.

## Le Restaurant

**Map 4, I4.** Sofitel Hotel, 25 Collins St ✆9653 0000.
Tues–Sat 7–11pm. Expensive.
Luxurious restaurant serving carefully prepared seasonal dishes. Apart from the food and superb table settings, you can admire the sublime views over Melbourne from the comfort of your chair. For a cheaper alternative, try the hotel's *Café La* (moderate).

## Lounge

**Map 4, G3.** 243 Swanston St ✆9663 2916.
Mon & Tues 10am–1am, Wed–Sun 10am–6am. Cheap.
Standard student fare like rolls, pizza, rice dishes and salads, with lots of fashionable young things snuggling at well-spaced tables and around the pool tables.

## Melbourne RSL Duckboard Club

**Map 4, I4.** 91 Flinders Lane ✆9654 5576.
Tues–Fri noon–2pm. Cheap to inexpensive.
Good, honest tucker like sausages, eggs and chips served with a can-do, no-prob Aussie attitude.

## Nudel Bar

**Map 4, I3.** 76 Bourke St ✆9662 9100.

CITY CENTRE

Daily 11am–11pm. Cheap to inexpensive.

Wide-ranging menu covering mostly Asian and European dishes such as *mee goreng* and Hungarian goulash, with benches downstairs for quick meals when you're seriously pressed for time. The *tom yum* is a blinder.

## Pellegrini's Espresso Bar
**Map 4, I3.** 66 Bourke St ℗9662 1885.

Mon–Sat 8am–11.30pm, Sun noon–8.30pm. Cheap.

A Melbourne institution, *Pellegrini's* has hardly changed since it first opened in the 1950s, with its time-warp decor of chequered floors and mirrored walls. It's just the ticket for hearty Italian fare (risotto, meatballs, spag bol) presented with blinding speed. Also good for coffee and scrummy home-made cakes.

## Punch Lane
**Map 4, I2.** 43 Little Bourke St ℗9639 4944.

Mon–Thurs noon–midnight, Fri & Sat noon–2am, Sun 5pm–midnight. Moderate.

An eclectic menu spanning antipasto to curries, comfortable seating in solid red leather chairs, late suppers and good wines from the bar make this a classy haunt for Melbourne urbanites.

## Stalactites
**Map 4, G3.** 177 Lonsdale St ℗9663 3316.

Daily 24hr. Cheap to inexpensive.

Operating for twenty years, *Stalactites* serves so-so *giros*, souvlaki, moussaka and *saganaki*, all dished up in a dimly lit dining area. For more upmarket Greek cuisine, try *Antipodes* (inexpensive to moderate) a few doors down.

## Stella
**Map 4, I2.** 159 Spring St ℗9639 1555.

Mon–Fri noon–11pm, Sat 5.30pm–11pm. Moderate to expensive.

Striking interior design and excellent East-meets-West cuisine (aka "modern Australian"), plus a long and discursive wine list. The crowd is young and groovy, although the hug-hug, kiss-kiss behaviour might put you off your meal.

## Travellers' Aid Society Tearooms
**Map 4, G4.** 169 Swanston St ℃9654 2081.

Mon–Fri 8am–5pm. Cheap.

Located on the second floor, these tearooms are like a blast from the past: naff 1950s decor, Devonshire teas, crumpets, muffins, hearty quiches and classic milkshakes in big plastic cups straight out of grandma's parlour.

## Tsindos
**Map 4, G3.** 197 Lonsdale St ℃9663 3194.

Mon–Fri noon–3pm & 5–10pm, Sat & Sun 5–11pm. Cheap to inexpensive.

Established Greek café with all the classics, including tara-masalata, moussaka and souvlaki. Leave some space for the incredibly sweet desserts.

## Vis
**Map 4, G3.** 243 Swanston St ℃9662 9995.

Mon–Fri 10am–1am, Sat 2pm–1am. Inexpensive to moderate.

Sleek, pleasurable eating spot with reasonably priced, stylishly presented Asian and Italian food in a retro setting.

## Walter's Wine Bar
**Map 4, G6.** Level 3, Southgate ℃9690 9211.

Daily 11am–1am. Moderate.

Award-winning restaurant-cum-wine bar, *Walter's* prepares excellent contemporary bistro food, and has knowledgeable staff, good Australian wines by the glass and superb views across the Yarra to the city. Opposite here, *Walter's Wine and Food Store* (daily 8am–8pm; inexpensive) is an affordable deli where you can sit down over a glass of wine and sandwich.

CITY CENTRE

# CHINATOWN

### Bamboo House
**Map 4, I2.** 47 Little Bourke St ℂ9662 1565.
Mon–Fri noon–11pm, Sat & Sun 5.30–11pm. Moderate.
Much favoured by businessfolk and politicians, who come for
the scampi, spicy Sichuan beef and tea-smoked duck, and the
deal-making and point-scoring that usually accompanies the
meal.

### Chine on Paramount
**Map 4, H3.** Shops 9 & 10, 101 Little Bourke St ℂ9663 6565.
Daily noon–late. Moderate to expensive.
Located in the Paramount Centre, *Chine* is a formal restaurant-
cum-café with tables, booths and the ubiquitous fish tank.
Mainly Cantonese dishes, including delicious soups, and has a
good sprinkling of local and imported wines.

### Flower Drum
**Map 4, H3.** 17 Market Lane, off Bourke St ℂ9662 3655.
Mon–Sat noon–late, Sun 6pm–late. Expensive.
Quite simply the finest Chinese restaurant in Melbourne – if
not Australia. Its capacious space, sophisticated cuisine (Peking
duck, dumplings, Hainanese pork, *yi-meen* noodles) and
discreet service from an army of waiting staff has garnered it
a clutch of top awards. An essential Melbourne dining
experience.

### Kun Ming Cafe
**Map 4, G3.** 212 Little Bourke St ℂ9663 1851.
Mon, Fri & Sat noon–3pm & 5–10pm, Sun 5–9pm. Cheap to
inexpensive.
No-frills cooking, with food such as short soup and sweet-
and-sour pork served on laminex tables with knives and forks.

A bustling café, and you certainly can't quibble with the prices.

## Mask of China

**Map 4, H3.** 115–117 Little Bourke St ©9662 2116.

Mon–Fri & Sun noon–late, Sat 6pm–late. Expensive.

Extensive menu and wine list with emphasis on seafood, poultry and fresh produce with no gluggy sauces in sight. Service is also good. Try the banquet, which changes every few weeks.

## Shark Fin House

**Map 4, H3.** 131 Little Bourke St ©9663 1555.

Daily 11am–11pm. Cheap to inexpensive.

*Yum cha* specialists located in a converted three-storey warehouse that is the quintessential Chinese eating experience: preposterously loud, closely stood tables, adrenaline-charged waiters and queues of people waiting to be seated.

## West Lake

**Map 4, G3.** 189 Little Bourke St ©9662 2048.

Daily noon–2am. Cheap.

This noisy and often messy restaurant speeds good *yum cha* and delicious desserts to your table.

# CARLTON AND FITZROY

## Akari 177

**Map 5, G6.** 177 Brunswick St, Fitzroy ©9419 3786.

Mon & Sat 6–10.30pm, Tues–Fri noon–3pm & 6–10.30pm. Cheap to inexpensive.

A mainstay on Brunswick Street for many years, *Akari 177* has a deluge of Japanese-style goodies, with wonderful beef sushi (regular sushi too) and recommended daily specials. The owner also sells wonderful Japanese ceramics.

# Café culture

In Sydney the talk is all about real estate, but in Melbourne the
passion is **coffee**. Cafés of every shape and size can be found
throughout the CBD, from shoeboxes in Block Place to the
wide-open spaces of *Lounge* (see p.119), which can seat over
a hundred. The new emphasis on inner-city living, combined
with a natural reaction to large corporate enterprises like
Southgate and the Crown Casino, has seen a coterie of cafés
spring up, showing that with little more than an idea, a coffee
machine and a place to put it, anything is possible. Human and
intimate, these cafés are the perfect accompaniment to the
European architectural style and feel of the area. And, judging
by their popularity and Melbourne's clamour for coffee, there's
plenty of scope for more.

It's almost impossible to be objective when talking about
cafés, and everyone feels strongly about their own personal
favourites – the listings below are just a few worth searching out.
**Babka Bakery Cafe** 358 Brunswick St, Fitzroy ☏9416 0091.
Part bakery, part café, *Babka* serves simple Middle Eastern,
Russian and Jewish food. The antithesis of *Caffe e Cucina* (see
below) in style, it's unpretentious, bright and breezy with fresh
white walls and large windows. The coffee will win over the
most discerning caffeine addict, while a bowl of borscht with
rye bread can do wonders for the soul.
**Caffe e Cucina** 581 Chapel St, South Yarra ☏9827 4139.
Became *the* benchmark for Melbourne's restaurant/café style
when it opened in 1988, and has spawned a score of imitators
with its wood panelling, cute little table lamps and a creative
menu written up on a central blackboard. Rampantly Italian,
dark and small enough to make a toilet cubicle look spacious,
it is definitely a place to be entered with the right mental attitude. The immaculately dressed, theatrically aloof waiters have

put many a customer off, but when you're served sublime *al dente* pasta, mouthwatering *bigne* and one of the best coffees in town who cares?

**Don Camillo's** 215 Victoria St, West Melbourne ☏9329 8883; tram #109 from Collins St. Classic, unspoiled 1950s Italian café with a terrazzo floor and long bar. The walls are covered with photographs of AFL and other sporting stars, many of whom form part of the *Don's* clientele. The café keeps shortened hours, closing at 5pm.

**The Galleon** 9 Carlisle St, St Kilda ☏9534 8934. One of St Kilda's long-standing favourites, *The Galleon* was around long before the area was transformed from a run-down and forgotten beach resort to the funky place it is today. Large and grungy with lots of formica-topped tables, it's busy and noisy, the menu rarely changes, the coffee's good and the fried breakfasts are great.

## Bakers Café

**Map 5, G3.** 384 Brunswick St, Fitzroy ☏9419 7437.
Mon–Sat 7am–11pm, Sun 8am–11pm. Cheap.
The strip's longest-running restaurant is not as trendy as places like *Mario's* (see p.127), but the food (pasta, eggs, focaccia) is always tasty and filling.

## Bistro Inferno

**Map 5, G4.** 302 Brunswick St, Fitzroy ☏9416 0953.
Daily 6am–10.30pm. Moderate.
Relaxed setting with snazzy, civilized food like delicious vegetable pakoras and risotto cooked with a fair amount of chilli, but not so they're overly hot. Highly recommended.

## Black Cat

**Map 5, H4.** 252 Johnston St, Fitzroy ☏9419 2206.

CARLTON AND FITZROY

Daily 9am–1am. Cheap to inexpensive.
Fitzroy original and prototype of the groovy Brunswick Street café: *de rigueur* 1950s flair (laminex tables, vinyl chairs), jazz music and a useful noticeboard.

## Brunswick Street Noodle Bar
**Map 5, G4.** 328 Brunswick St, Fitzroy ✆9419 4296.
Mon & Tues 5–11pm, Wed–Sun noon–3pm & 5–11pm. Cheap.
Budget-friendly, exquisitely prepared dishes such as *Hokkien* mee in a restaurant with an upmarket feel.

## Café Provincial
**Map 5, G4.** Cnr Brunswick & Johnston streets, Fitzroy ✆9417 2228.
Daily noon–late. Inexpensive.
One of Melbourne's best grazing joints, this lovely café is set within the *Provincial Hotel*. Well-presented food, with a French-Italian pedigree (try the pesto and goat's cheese pizza), plus good blackboard specials and reasonably priced wines by the glass.

## Carmen Bar
**Map 5, G4.** 74 Johnston St, Fitzroy ✆9417 4794.
Mon–Sat 6pm–late. Cheap to inexpensive.
Atmosphere, authenticity, good food and a predominantly Spanish-speaking crowd makes this the best-value tapas bar in Fitzroy.

## Fitz
**Map 5, G4.** 347 Brunswick St, Fitzroy ✆9417 5794.
Daily 7am–late. Cheap.
*Fitz* has a deserved reputation for fuelling locals with one of the best and biggest breakfasts in town. The decor is simple, the Asian and European cuisine feel-good and down-to-earth, while the large outdoor area is ideal for catching the sun.

## Growlers

**Map 4, K1.** 153 Gertrude St, Fitzroy ℂ9416 4116.
Daily 6–11pm. Inexpensive.
Cluttered with bohemian tat, *Growlers* does big servings of traditional fare (steak, lamb shanks, mashed potatoes), and has free bread and olives plonked on each table. In winter, the open fires make this spot an ideal proposition.

## Guernica

**Map 5, G4.** 257 Brunswick St, Fitzroy ℂ9416 0969.
Mon–Fri & Sun noon–3pm & 6–10.30pm, Sat 6–10.30pm. Moderate to expensive.
This swish, stylish and invitingly intimate place offers highly original Australian food, yummy desserts and a few drops by the glass. Try the coconut fried garfish with Vietnamese noodles and see why *Guernica* has won all those awards. Heaven sent.

## Jimmy Watson's

**Map 5, D4.** 333 Lygon St, Carlton ℂ9347 3985.
Mon–Sat noon–11.30pm. Moderate to expensive.
Atmospheric restaurant which attracts locals, academics, students and anyone who loves a tipple. Simple bistro food downstairs (moderate) and formal dining upstairs (expensive), plus excellent Australian vintage wines from the cellar.

## La Porchetta

**Map 5, E1.** 392 Rathdowne St, Carlton ℂ9347 8906.
Daily 9am–midnight. Cheap.
Super-cheap prices for quality pizza, salad and pasta. Cacophony reigns come dinner time, when the takeaway crowds are piled five deep at the counter waiting for their order.

## Mario's

**Map 5, G4.** 303 Brunswick St, Fitzroy ℂ9417 3343.
Daily 7am–late. Cheap to inexpensive.

**CARLTON AND FITZROY**

Anyone who wants to get a true feel of Brunswick Street should home in on this European-style café, where you can eat brekkie (until midnight), lunch and dinner or just have a coffee or a drink. Although the staff are dauntingly smart, *Mario's* is by no means expensive or dressy. While waiting for a seat (it gets very busy at weekends), you can browse at the bookstores down the road.

### Piraeus Blues

**Map 5, G4.** 310 Brunswick St, Fitzroy ℂ9417 0222.
Mon, Tues, Sat & Sun 6pm–1am, Wed–Fri noon–2.30pm & 6pm–1am. Inexpensive.
Has gained a solid reputation for serving flavoursome, home-spun cooking like spicy sausages and spinach and fetta pie. A must for lovers of Greek food.

### Poppy's

**Map 5, D5.** 230 Lygon St, Carlton ℂ9663 3366.
Mon–Wed, Sat & Sun 5–10.30pm, Thurs & Fri noon–3pm & 5–10.30pm. Cheap to inexpensive.
Popular Thai restaurant serving well-prepared spring rolls and satay, and basic mains of curry and stir-fried dishes.

### Retro Cafe

**Map 5, G3.** 413 Brunswick St, Fitzroy ℂ9419 9103.
Daily 8am–11.30pm. Inexpensive.
Inviting and casual eaterie with a plethora of 1970s kitsch. Whether your preferences are for savoury pancakes, good coffee and cheap muffins, or pasta, syrupy-sweet desserts, even kangaroo, you'll be guaranteed to leave pleasantly stuffed. The window seats are a great place to people-watch.

### Rhumbarella's

**Map 5, G4.** 342 Brunswick St, Fitzroy ℂ9417 5652.
Daily 7am–1am. Cheap to inexpensive.

The neon sign in the window is one of the street's landmarks, and the inside of this stylish café is just as vibrantly coloured. *Rhumbarella's* hums to the sound of jazz and conversation. Breakfast until midday – eggs Benedict is a favourite – then anything from focaccia to steak.

## Sala Thai
**Map 5, G4.** 266 Brunswick St, Fitzroy ℭ9417 4929.
Daily 6pm–late. Cheap to inexpensive.
Dark interior with plenty of cushions scattered around the place, *Sala Thai* enjoys a deserved reputation for fine Thai food and cheery service.

## Shakahari
**Map 5, D4.** 201–203 Faraday St, Carlton ℭ9347 3848.
Mon–Sat noon–10.30pm, Fri & Sat noon–11.30pm. Inexpensive.
Excellent, well-priced and superbly presented favourites such as satays, curries and laksas. Great value.

## Tiamo
**Map 5, D4.** 303 Lygon St, Carlton ℭ9347 5759.
Mon–Sat 7.30am–11pm, Sun 10.30am–10.30pm. Cheap to inexpensive.
Fabulous family-run Carlton establishment with cheaper eating downstairs and a newer, posher dining room upstairs (inexpensive). The food, including Italian favourites such as lasagne and carbonara, isn't flash but is cheap and hearty. A decor of timber tables and walls adorned with 1950s posters, plus the strip's best coffee and tiramisu, makes this little gem a favourite with students and locals alike. *Tiamo 2*, next door (cheap to inexpensive), is more upmarket, but still excellent value.

## Toofey's
**Map 5, D4.** 162 Elgin St, Carlton ℭ9347 9838.
Tues–Sat noon–10pm. Moderate to expensive.

**CARLTON AND FITZROY**

A drawcard for local fishophiles, *Toofey's* extremely fresh seafood dishes are prepared in an adventurous Mediterranean or Middle Eastern style. There's steak and exquisite desserts too, and wines by the glass. Book ahead.

## Trotters

**Map 5, D4.** 400 Lygon St, Carlton ©9347 5657.
Mon–Fri 7.30am–10pm, Sat 8am–10pm, Sun 9.30am–10pm. Cheap to inexpensive.

A popular meeting place for breakfast, *Trotters* is a cosy place where you can plough through big servings of bacon and eggs, home-made cakes and good coffee.

## University Café

**Map 5, D5.** 255 Lygon St, Carlton ©9347 2142.
Mon–Fri 7am–11pm, Sat & Sun 7am–12.30am. Cheap to inexpensive.

The outdoor tables are possibly the best spot on the street for reading the newspapers, drinking lattes and eyeballing the locals. Food from the bar-cum-café is unpretentious but filling.

## The Vegie Bar

**Map 5, G3.** 378 Brunswick St, Fitzroy ©9417 6935.
Daily 8am–10pm. Cheap.

Cavernous in appearance, *The Vegie Bar* is popular and hip rather than hippie. Simple, fresh food such as tofu burgers and salads cooked to order with a range of healthy nibbles.

# RICHMOND AND HAWTHORN

## Burmese House

**Map 3, F4.** 303 Bridge Rd, Richmond ©9421 2861.
Mon, Tues & Sun 5.30–10pm, Wed–Sat 11.30am–10pm. Cheap.

Super curries, dumplings, salads and the national dish – *moh hin gha* soup – at dirt-cheap prices.

## Penang Coffee House
359 Burwood Rd, Hawthorn ✆9819 2092.
Tues–Fri & Sun 11.30am–9.30pm. Cheap to inexpensive.
Some of Melbourne's best hawker food in a suburban hideaway – try the curry laksa, *mee goreng* or sublime, chilli-infused *kway teow*, all served with "sky juice" (water) or Chinese tea.

## Richmond Hill Café and Larder
**Map 3, F4.** 48–50 Bridge Rd, Richmond ✆9421 2808.
Mon–Sat 8.30am–11pm, Sun 9am–3pm. Moderate to expensive.
Exquisite though pricey food from Stephanie Alexander, celebrated local chef and food writer. As well as a casual dining area, there's a grocery, cheese shop, and a bar which is perfect for a coffee whilst poring over the morning papers.

To reach Richmond and Hawthorn, take tram #75 or the Belgrave line from Flinders Street Station to Hawthorn.

## Tho Tho
**Map 3, F3.** 66 Victoria St, Richmond ✆9428 5833.
Daily 11am–midnight. Cheap to inexpensive.
This enormous, brasserie-style restaurant is much flasher than its neighbours. The Vietnamese food (yummy rice-paper rolls to crispy quail), though, is incredibly cheap, and the place is usually packed and very noisy.

## Thy Thy 1
**Map 3, F3.** 142 Victoria St, Richmond ✆9429 1104.
Daily 8am–10pm. Cheap.
Climb the stairs to one of the most popular Vietnamese restau-

RICHMOND AND HAWTHORN

rants in Melbourne. The food, which includes crispy spring rolls, noodles and chicken dishes, is basic but great.

### Tofu Shop
**Map 3, F4.** 78 Bridge Rd, Richmond ✆9429 6204.
Mon–Fri noon–9pm, Sat 10am–5pm. Cheap to inexpensive.
Treat your body to salads, bean curd and veggie dishes, or splurge on spring rolls, pasta and hummus dips with pitta bread.

### Vao Doi
**Map 3, F3.** 120 Victoria St, Richmond ✆9428 3264.
Daily 10am–11pm. Cheap.
Another much-frequented Vietnamese place. Reliable, with good soups and fish dishes, plus set lunch menus for the uninitiated.

### Vlado's
**Map 3, F4.** 61 Bridge Rd, Richmond ✆9428 5833.
Mon–Fri noon–3pm & 6–10.30pm, Sat 6–10.30pm. Moderate to expensive.
Sausages, hamburger, liver, steak, you name it – if it has four legs it'll probably be somewhere on the menu. Apart from the rivers of crimson, the only splash of colour comes courtesy of a hastily patched together salad. Mmmmm.

# SOUTH MELBOURNE

### est est est
**Map 3, D5.** 440 Clarendon St, South Melbourne ✆9682 5688.
Mon–Sat 6–11pm. Expensive.
Smart, almost invisible decor (white walls and red upholstered chairs), bevies of tailored waiting staff, and a handsome menu showcasing delectable French-inspired goodies and a dazzling array of wines. Come dressed to impress and don't forget to up the limit on your credit card.

## Isthmus of Kra

**Map 3, D5.** 50 Park St, South Melbourne ℗9690 3688.
Mon–Fri noon–11pm, Sat & Sun 6pm–11pm. Moderate.
Cornucopia of Asian flavours and very friendly service. In
summer, the best spot is the courtyard when the sun sets and
where you can take in the smells from the kitchen.

**To reach South Melbourne, take tram #1 or #96.**

## Kobe

**Map 3, D5.** 179 Clarendon St, South Melbourne ℗9690 2692.
Daily noon–3pm & 6.30–11pm. Inexpensive to moderate.
The area's first Japanese restaurant still packs them in with its
modest prices, kimono-clad waitresses and good fare.

## O'Connell's

**Map 3, D5.** Cnr Montague & Coventry streets, South Melbourne
℗9699 9600.
Tues–Sat noon–11pm. Expensive.
Street-corner pub with bar, bistro and superb grub from a
large, open-kitchen restaurant. Meat and vegetarian meals, all
tasty.

## Spirit of India

**Map 3, D5.** 401 Clarendon St, South Melbourne ℗9682 6696.
Daily 5.30–11pm. Inexpensive.
One of the city's few decent Indian restaurants, with crisp pap-
padums, huge samosas and finely flavoured dhals and curries.

# SOUTH YARRA, PRAHRAN AND TOORAK

## Caffe Grossi

**Map 6, C4.** 199 Toorak Rd, South Yarra ℗9827 6076.

Mon–Fri noon–3pm & 6pm–late, Sat 6pm–late. Moderate to expensive.

Fabulous Italian nosh and a breathtaking array of wines, served beneath an enormous print of Caravaggio's *St John the Baptist*. Lunch (around $20 for two courses, a glass of wine and coffee) is one of the best deals in town.

## Candy Bar
**Map 6, C8.** 162 Greville St, Prahran ℗9529 6566.
Daily noon–late. Inexpensive.
Funky joint popular for eating, drinking and bopping into the early hours. Sample a range of food from noodles and curries to polenta whilst sitting on comfy sofas under a giant mirror ball.

## Chinta Ria Jazz
**Map 6, C7.** 176 Commercial Rd, Prahran ℗9510 6520.
Daily noon–10.30pm. Cheap to moderate.
Consistently good hawker fare – the fat Hokkein noodles, roti bread and curry laksa, in particular, are to die for.

## Continental Café
**Map 6, C8.** 132–134 Greville St, Prahran ℗9510 2788.
Mon–Fri 7am–late, Sat & Sun 8am–late. Inexpensive to moderate.
Hugely popular restaurant and upstairs nightclub-cum-live music venue (see p.160), with waistcoated waiters and a smart, arty clientele. Breakfast all day, good pasta dishes, and a wide range of wines and liqueurs.

## D.O.M.O.
**Map 6, A2.** 175 Domain Rd, South Yarra ℗9866 3566.
Mon–Fri noon–10pm, Sat 8am–midnight, Sun 8am–3pm. Moderate.
Super-chic hangout favoured by South Yarra's Gucci-clad crowd. The unstuffy service and contemporary brasserie tucker

**134**

– coffee, snacks, larger meals such as duck and veal – are of a
uniformly high standard.

## Feedwell Cafe

**Map 6, B8.** 95–97 Greville St, Prahran ©9510 3128.
Mon–Thurs 9am–5pm, Fri 9am–10pm, Sat & Sun 11am–6pm.
Cheap.
One of Melbourne's vegan veterans, with cheap, healthy pies,
excellent sandwiches made from home-made bread, and plenty
of tasty drink. Pity about the tatty decor.

## France-Soir

**Map 6, A4.** 11 Toorak Rd, South Yarra ©9866 8569.
Daily noon–midnight. Moderate.
The food's modest but the wine list, sporting exceptional bottles
of French plonk, must rank as one of Melbourne's finest. Tables
are often filled with smug marrieds and overseas rich folk.

## Globe

**Map 6, C8.** 218 Chapel St, Prahran ©9510 8693.
Mon–Thurs 9am–10pm, Fri 8.30am–10pm, Sat 9.30am–10pm, Sun
10am–10pm. Cheap to inexpensive.
Fabulous breads and vegetarian food, a good wine list and
prompt, attentive service. Excellent value.

## Greville Bar Dining Room

**Map 6, B8.** 143 Greville St, Prahran ©9529 4800.
Daily noon–11pm. Moderate.
Dim and sexy downstairs with a sophisticated Japanese-style
menu, plus an upstairs "dining club" specializing in contemporary Australian cuisine.

## Jacques Reymond

**Map 6, F9.** 79 Williams Rd, Windsor ©9525 2178.
Tues–Fri noon–11pm, Sat 7–11pm. Expensive to very expensive.

SOUTH YARRA, PRAHRAN AND TOORAK

Jacques Reymond's shrine to fine food brings together eclectic ingredients from Europe, Australia, Asia and the Pacific to startling effect, but you'll need an eyeglass to pore over the very detailed menu. If you want to cut corners, lunch in the appealing courtyard pans out to a more moderate $30 a head. To get here, take tram #64 from Swanston Street.

## Lynch's

**Map 6, A2.** 133 Domain Rd, South Yarra ℗9866 2425.
Mon–Sat noon–11pm. Expensive.
Popular dining place for Croesus-like locals, who come for the first-class service, the private rooms, the old-fashioned food, the racy nudes hanging on the walls and the child-free environment.

## Pomme

**Map 6, B4.** 37 Toorak Rd, South Yarra ℗9820 9606.
Tues–Fri noon–11pm, Sat 6.30–11pm. Expensive.
Britpack chef Jeremy Strode's culinary sensation pays inordinate attention to detail, whether in the stark and minimalist decor or the theatrical, French-style food. You pay for the quality, although lunches are much more affordable.

# ST KILDA

## Bala's

**Map 7, E8.** 1c Shakespeare Grove ℗9534 6116.
Daily noon–10.30pm. Cheap.
Hugely popular restaurant that's perfect for a quick fuel stop or takeaway. Although the seating on large wooden tables is cramped, the food is fast and affordable, and includes Malaysian noodles, Thai curries, Indian samosas and delicious lassis.

## Big Mouth

**Map 7, F8.** 201 Barkly St ℗9534 4611.

Mon–Fri 5pm–1am, Sat 11am–late, Sun 10.30am–late. Cheap to moderate.

Relaxed and unpretentious, this large, triangular restaurant and bar has mix'n'match decor and food and great views of the street. The downstairs café (daily 9am–1am; cheap) is livelier and serves a variety of café-style fare to a hip local crowd.

### Café Barcelona

**Map 7, C6.** 25 Fitzroy St ℘9525 4244.
Mon–Thurs 4pm–1am, Fri–Sun noon–1am. Inexpensive to moderate.

A decent selection of tapas and mains, while the high ceiling and wood-panelled walls make for a warm atmosphere.

### Cafe Di Stasio

**Map 7, C5.** 31 Fitzroy St ℘9525 3999.
Daily noon–3pm & 6–11pm. Expensive.

Small and understated, *Cafe Di Stasio* was once the Melbourne dining equivalent of a young John McEnroe, where unpredictable outbursts from the waiting staff were the norm rather than the exception. It's mellowed with age, although the food – a masterful blend of traditional and modern Italian cooking – has remained constant.

### Chinta Blues

**Map 7, C6.** 6 Acland St ℘9534 9233.
Mon–Sat noon–2.30pm & 6–10.30pm, Sun noon–10pm. Inexpensive to moderate.

Asian restaurant with a blues music theme. Fortunately the authentic and reasonably priced dishes more than make up for the daft concept.

### Cicciolina

**Map 7, E8.** 130 Acland St ℘9525 3333.
Daily 11.30am–11pm. Moderate.

Tightly packed tables crammed into a small and always crowded space could easily be a downer, but it seems to work here. The atmosphere is social and the Italian food of a high standard. Doesn't take bookings, so be prepared to wait.

### Circa, The Prince

**Map 7, C5.** The Prince St Kilda, 2 Acland St ℰ9534 5033.
Tues–Thurs & Sat 6–11.30pm, Fri & Sun noon–3pm & 6–11.30pm.
Expensive to very expensive.
Part of the multimillion-dollar redevelopment that has transformed one of St Kilda's grungiest pubs into an Art Deco treasure. Touted as Melbourne's best new restaurant, it has a magnificently theatrical fit-out and boasts the talents of chef Michael Lambie, former protégé of the UK's Marco Pierre White. Book well in advance.

### The Dog's Bar

**Map 7, E7.** 54 Acland St ℰ9525 3599.
Mon–Fri 10am–1am, Sat & Sun 9am–1am. Inexpensive.
One of the first café-bars in St Kilda, and as popular as ever, even if its distressed paint finish and fake cracks are beginning to look more alarmingly genuine with every year. Italian-style food, simple and reasonably priced, and a good range of wines.

### Donovans

**Map 7, D8.** 40 Jacka Blvd ℰ9534 8221.
Daily noon–late. Moderate to expensive.
Originally a 1920s bathing pavilion, now a relaxed beach-house restaurant, complete with sofas, fireplace and ocean-front views. The homely atmosphere and mainly seafood menu create an interesting dining experience, and it's one of the best places for lounging around the fireplace during winter.

### 189 Espresso Bar

**Map 7, F8.** 189 Acland St ℰ9534 8884.

Mon 8.30am–6pm, Tues–Sun 8.30am–11pm. Cheap to inexpensive.
Stainless-steel tables, timber floors, huge *pides*, pizza, cakes and
and expertly made coffees. Outside tables make this a good
place for crowd surveillance.

## Il Fornaio

**Map 7, C6.** 2 Acland St ✆9534 2922.

Daily 7am–7pm. Cheap to inexpensive.

Hip bakery serving excellent breads, pastries and coffee.
Popular at breakfast time, with seating both inside and out.

## Luxe

**Map 7, F6.** 15 Inkerman St ✆9534 0255.

Mon–Thurs 5pm–midnight, Fri–Sun noon–3pm & 5pm–midnight.
Expensive.

Intimidatingly trendy, *Luxe* has a large concrete-filled space and
timber floors, but the industrial touch doesn't stop it from being
a welcoming place to eat. The atmosphere is loud, busy and
informal; the food European-bistro in style. Long lines usually
stretch outside for evening sittings, but it's worth the wait.

## Madame Joe Joe

**Map 7, C6.** 9 Fitzroy St ✆9534 0000.

Daily noon–11pm. Expensive.

One of Fitzroy Street's more established restaurant-brasseries,
*Madame Joe Joe* combines exciting contemporary cuisine with
classic stained glass, wooden floors, starched linen and a mar-
ble-topped bar.

## Melbourne Wine Room

**Map 7, E5.** The George Hotel, 25 Fitzroy St ✆9525 5599.

Daily noon–11pm. Inexpensive to expensive.

Excellent regional wine list and an innovative menu from
either the bar (inexpensive) or formal dining area (expensive).
Top service, top setting, top place.

ST KILDA

### Scheherezade

**Map 7, E8.** 99 Acland St ℅9534 2722.

Daily 9am–midnight. Inexpensive.

Hangout for elderly Eastern European émigrés, *Scheherezade*
was opened by a Jewish couple in the 1950s and has grown in
popularity to become an Acland Street institution. Famous for
its chicken broth (some swear it has medicinal properties) and
inexpensive mains, it's a great escape from modern-day cuisine.

### The Stokehouse

**Map 7, D8.** 30 Jacka Blvd ℅9525 5555.

Daily noon–3pm & 6–10.30pm. Inexpensive to expensive.

Boasting a spectacular beachfront location and views, this converted teahouse is one of most popular eating spots in
Melbourne. Both the café-bar downstairs (Mon–Fri 11am–late,
Sat & Sun 10am–late; inexpensive) serving brasserie-style
surf'n'turf (fish'n'chips, burgers, pizza slices, nibbles) and the
stylish restaurant upstairs (expensive) are always busy – the former sometimes annoyingly so. Although the restaurant menu
has a leaning towards seafood, there's always a wide variety of
inventive dishes available.

### Veludo

**Map 7, E8.** 175 Acland St ℅9534 4456.

Tues–Fri 7–11pm, Sat 10am–4pm & 7–11pm, Sun 10am–4pm.

Cheap to expensive.

Upstairs restaurant that mixes dark stained floorboards, red-
brick walls and 1950s decor with interesting and stylishly presented European dishes. The groovy downstairs bar area also
has simple but good food, like pies, mash and salads.

### Victory

**Map 7, E4.** 60 Fitzroy St ℅9534 3727.

Daily 7am–late. Cheap to inexpensive.

Located in the former St Kilda train station, *Victory* has large cooked breakfasts plus muffins, focaccias and bruschettas. Tables inside and out are mostly haunted by well-heeled locals and backpackers from the nearby hostels.

## Wall

**Map 3, F7.** 280 Carlisle St ✆9593 8280.
Mon–Fri 7.30am–6pm, Sat & Sun 8.30am–6pm. Cheap.
Restored kosher butcher's shop that's now one of the coolest cafés in the city, offering simple but delicious food (mostly toasted *pides*) and good coffee. Inside is a series of small alcoves and a larger space dominated by a wooden communal table perfect for round-table chit-chat. Check out the takeaway servery window and milk crates for seating outside.

## Wild Rice Wholefoods Cafe

**Map 7, F8.** 211 Barkly St ✆9534 2849.
Mon–Fri noon–10pm, Sat & Sun 11.30am–11pm. Cheap to inexpensive.
Small macrobiotic vegetarian café serving wholesome snacks and meals, including vegan dishes. The real treat is the court-yard garden hidden out the back – a pleasant escape from see-and-be-seen Acland Street. Also does takeaways.

# WILLIAMSTOWN

## Hobson's Choice Foods

**Map 3, A6.** 213 The Strand ✆9397 1891.
Daily 7.30am–11pm. Cheap.
Expansive menu has everything from eggs, home-made shep-herd's pie and laksa to croissants and pastries.

## Siam Orchid Restaurant

**Map 3, A6.** 147 The Strand ✆9397 5303.
Daily except Mon 5–11pm. Cheap to inexpensive.

WILLIAMSTOWN

Busy, comfortable place with friendly service and good, cheap Thai food.

### Sirens

**Map 3, A7.** Beach Dressing Pavilion, The Esplanade ℂ9397 7811. Daily 10am–10pm. Inexpensive to moderate.

Located in a former bathing pavilion, *Sirens* dishes up above-average seafood in its formal restaurant (moderate), while the cheaper bistro (inexpensive) serves a good spread of light meals. Great for grabbing a pot of beer and plate of chips, then heading to the deck for the fantastic beach views.

# Pubs, bars and clubs

Melbourne's love affair with drinking is reflected in its plethora of excellent **pubs and bars** – from places so obscure and cutting-edge you'll only know they exist by word of mouth to large establishments catering to broader and louder tastes. The push to revive Melbourne's once staid CBD has seen many older watering holes transformed into lively, youth-oriented venues, while cheap bar licences have meant that new spots are popping up each week. In addition, the relaxing of Melbourne's once draconian **licensing laws** has produced enlightened opening hours, meaning that it's now possible to drink from noon until dawn, while the advent of gaming machines in city pubs has boosted revenues, allowing owners to offer better food, a classier selection of grog and plenty of live entertainment. The only downside is that at some venues,

A number of Melbourne's drinking spots are key venues in the city's live music scene – see "Live music" (p.157) for further details.

**dress and style codes** are often rigidly enforced, and drinks can be expensive; some places will also have a cover charge if there's live entertainment or a DJ.

Melbourne has a thriving **club culture**, and all but the most resolute party animals will find plenty to keep them entertained until well into the small hours. Clubs focus on a myriad of dance styles, particularly house, techno and beats, while indie and retro heads are also well looked after. The hot spots are **Chapel Street** in South Yarra and the **CBD**, but clubs take root anywhere they can, from big commercial nights in the suburbs to obscure experimental sessions in inner-city nooks and crannies. Overseas DJs visit frequently, while local talent keeps Melbourne's club scene thriving and fairly progressive.

The bigger the night, the more you can expect **to pay**, although the cover charge rarely tops $10 unless there's an international guest. Most clubs offer discounted or even free entry to punters with a pass available free from record shops such as Gaslight Music (see p.203), some bars and fashion outlets. These places are also the source of Melbourne's essential clubbing guides: *Beat* and *Inpress* magazines.

# CITY CENTRE

## BARS AND CLUBS

### 44
**Map 4, I2.** 44 Lonsdale St ℄9654 9144.
Mon–Wed 4pm–3am, Thurs–Sat 4pm–7am.
Larger than it looks, *44* has pool tables, pinball machines, a dance floor, rear garden and a techno-happy atmosphere on weekends, when DJs play their beats. There's also a good range of beers on tap, including Guinness. Enter via the alleyway

the upside is that taxis are always waiting to whisk you away.
Entry $6–10.

## Meyers Place

**Map 4, I3.** 20 Meyers Place, off Bourke St ℅9650 8609.
Tues–Sat 4pm–4am.
Designed by rising Melbourne architectural firm Six Degrees,
this swish, dimly lit hole in the wall has proved a massive hit
with Melbourne's trendy office workers. The grooviest place to
fall down in town on a Friday night, bar none.

## Misty

**Map 4, H5.** 3–5 Hosier Lane, off Flinders St ℅9663 9202.
Mon & Sun 5–11pm, Tues–Sat 5pm–1am.
On Melbourne's coolometer, *Misty* can't be beat, although the
choice of tipples is limited. Most nights it's filled with hairdressers, students and assorted poseurs; just pull up a stool, pretend you're an architect, and you'll fit right in.

## Rue Bebelons

**Map 4, F3.** 267 Little Lonsdale St ℅9663 1700.
Tues–Fri noon–3am, Sat 11am–3am.
Small, smoky, European-style bar, with friendly service and a
simple but reasonably priced selection of beers; wine is also
available by the glass or bottle. Attracts a younger set, and is
an ideal place for a late-night drink or a quiet beer during
the day.

## Scubar

**Map 4, E3.** 389 Lonsdale St ℅9670 2400.
Mon–Wed 4pm–midnight, Thurs, Fri & Sun 4pm–3am, Sat
6pm–3am.
Sexy, 1970s-style underground hangout, populated in equal
parts by seedy-looking "intellectuals" and monied professionals, with live bands Thursday to Saturday ($3 entry) plus DJs

CITY CENTRE: BARS AND CLUBS

each night playing slinky contemporary grooves. Monday is backpacker night, with cheap beer and meals.

## Spleen

**Map 4, I3.** 41 Bourke St ℂ9650 2400.

Mon–Fri 5pm–3am, Sat & Sun 6pm–3am.

Long, narrow warren aimed squarely at precocious party animals, *Spleen* fills up rapidly on weekends with those warming up for a big night or having a drink after the movies. Sunday nights feature acid-jazz bands. Decent and inexpensive meals available.

## Troika

**Map 4, H2.** 106 Little Lonsdale St ℂ9663 0221.

Tues–Sat noon–12.30am, Sun 4–11pm.

Relaxed, casual atmosphere. Mixes an inner-city crowd with suburban trendies and creatives, while the selection of local and imported beers will satisfy the most discerning punter.

## Up Top Cocktail Lounge

**Map 4, H3.** Level 1, 163 Russell St ℂ9663 8990.

Wed, Thurs & Sun 4pm–3am, Fri & Sat 4pm–5am.

Slinky, stylish American-style joint with DJs Wednesday to Sunday (plus live jazz on Sundays). The decor is tacky but endearing, and there's a wide range of drinks, although little of it is non-alcoholic if you want a break. Enter via Bullens Lane.

## Velour Bar

**Map 4, I4.** 121 Flinders Lane ℂ9663 5589.

Mon–Wed noon–midnight, Thurs noon–2am, Fri & Sat noon–5am.

Incorporates a kitchen, dance floor and bar into a split-level design scattered with tables, bar stools, couches and mirror balls. Large and popular (especially on Saturday when it attracts a dancing crowd), with a comprehensive range of bottled beers and spirits.

### Charles Dickens Tavern

**Map 4, F4.** 290 Collins St ✆9654 1821.

Daily 11am–1.30am.

Comfy place for homesick Brits, with bitter and Guinness on tap, pint glasses, and live soccer and rugby on a big-screen TV.

### Stork Hotel

**Map 4, E1.** 504 Elizabeth St ✆9663 6237.

Mon–Sat 10am–midnight, Sun noon–midnight.

This phlegmatic watering hole, located in a historic hotel from the goldrush era, features lovely Art Deco fittings, emphysemic regulars and superb artwork on the walls from some of Australia's finest cartoonists, including Melbourne-based Michael Leunig.

### Young & Jackson's

**Map 4, G5.** Cnr Swanston & Flinders streets ✆9650 3884.

Mon–Thurs 9am–10pm, Fri 9am–1am, Sat 9am–midnight, Sun 9am–8pm.

Victoria's oldest and most famous boozer (see p.36) is as good a place as anywhere to start drinking your way around town. In winter, a boisterous footy crowd usually descends after matches.

# FITZROY

### Bar Open

**Map 5, G4.** 317 Brunswick St ✆9415 9601.

Daily noon–2am.

Funky little bar attracting an arty crowd, popular at weekends, when free live jazz spills out into the rear courtyard. Get in early to secure a window seat.

## The Binary Bar
**Map 5, G5.** 243 Brunswick St ℂ9419 7374.
Daily 3pm–1am.
Spacious bar with a great front window for some solid people-watching. Free Internet access with helpful and friendly service and a wide range of reasonably priced cocktails. DJs spin ambient techno Thursday to Saturday, and it's a popular hangout for travellers and locals alike.

## The Night Cat
**Map 5, H4.** 141 Johnston St ℂ9417 0090.
Thurs–Sun 8pm–1am.
Beautiful and spacious, *The Night Cat* has two bars and is particularly fun on weekends, when jazz bands belt out dance-floor classics and twisters strut their stuff. There's a minimal cover charge on weekends, but it's a great spot if you're techno-fatigued and like dressing up and dancing shamelessly.

**PUBS**

## The Builders Arms
**Map 5, F7.** 211 Gertrude St ℂ9419 0818.
Mon–Thurs & Sun 5pm–1am, Fri & Sat 12.30pm–1am.
Groovy without being exclusive, *The Builders Arms* has guest DJs on weekends, when it's easily identifiable by the punters queuing to get in. Meals and snacks are available, and the atmosphere is laid-back and unpretentious. The "No Pokies" sign above the door has become a Melbourne landmark.

## The Napier Hotel

**Map 5, H6.** 210 Napier St ℓ9419 4240.

Mon–Wed 3–11pm, Thurs 3pm–midnight, Fri 3pm–1am, Sat 1pm–1am, Sun 1–11pm.

Small and eclectic pub with friendly service and seven beers on tap. The beer garden and outside tables are ideal for summer, and the cosy lounge with pool table is perfect for a wintry day. There's also down-to-earth grub at reasonable prices.

## Punters Club Hotel

**Map 5, G4.** 376 Brunswick St ℓ9417 3006.

Mon, Tues & Sun noon–2am, Wed–Sat noon–3am.

Legendary knees-up drinking hole boasting a rough-and-ready band scene each night and obscenely cheap pool tables. Hunker down at the bar for a session and enjoy the passing parade of soused locals. Peerless entertainment.

## The Rainbow Hotel

**Map 5, G5.** 27 St David St ℓ9419 4193.

Daily 3pm–1am.

Cosy little boozer featuring free live music (jazz, blues, funk or country) nightly and on weekend afternoons. Although crowded on weekends, the front bar is comfortable and relaxing, and the bands aren't so loud as to spoil conversation.

## The Rose Hotel

**Map 5, H3.** 406 Napier St ℓ9417 3626.

Mon–Wed 10am–11.30pm, Thurs–Sat 10am–1am, Sun noon–11pm.

Good example of what inner-city pubs were like before pokies and architects axed much of their character. Although busy on weekends and evenings, it's retained the feel of a family-run pub, with a basic range of alcohol. You can also chew the fat with the locals over hearty meals like T-bone steak.

FITZROY: PUBS

# SOUTH YARRA AND PRAHRAN

## BARS AND CLUBS

### Blue Bar

**Map 6, C7.** 330 Chapel St, Prahran ℗9529 6499.

Mon–Wed & Sun 11am–1am, Thurs–Sat 11am–3am.

Intimate, Japanese-influenced bar that spills out onto the street at weekends, with groovers checking each other out while sipping mineral water. Good range of local and imported beers, as well as an extensive – if not particularly cheap – menu. There's no sign, so look for the blue neon bar above the door.

### Candy Bar

**Map 6, C8.** 162 Greville St, Prahran ℗9529 6566.

Daily noon–3am.

Twenty-something, party-going crowd, and a good place to head for if you feel like some solid drinking and dancing. Dress up, however, or you may have trouble getting past the fashion police at the door.

### Chasers

**Map 6, C7.** 386 Chapel St, South Yarra ℗9827 6615.

Fri–Sun 10pm–5am.

Veteran of the Melbourne club scene, *Chasers* was extensively renovated in 1998. Its regular nights focus on accessible house, retro and electronic beats, presented in the spacious main room and two snug lounges. Entry around $7.

### Globe Back Bar

**Map 6, C8.** 218 Chapel St, Prahran ℗9510 8693.

Mon–Fri 8.30am–midnight, Sat & Sun 10am–10.30pm.

Drop-dead sexy bar frequented by equally gorgeous people. Small but comfortable, it provides a mellow start to an evening

# Cigar and supper clubs

Melbourne's smart society is currently flourishing, as witnessed by the city's increasing number of **cigar and supper clubs**. Popular with older punters, these nightspots are guilt-free havens for cigar smokers, whose dark and leathery confines offer plenty of cheap food and live or recorded music. All are open late, and usually charge no admission.

**Victorian Cigar Room**, Ground Floor, Como Centre, 299 Toorak Rd, South Yarra (⌀9827 3131). Comfortable leather armchairs, cognac, single-malt whiskeys and an array of Latin-American cigars. You'll need to dress up to get through the door, and also to conceal your scepticism about its location in the bland Como Centre complex.

**Fidel's Cigar Room**, Lower Ground Floor, Crown Casino, 8 Whiteman St, Southbank, City (⌀9292 6885). A must for aficionados of fine liquor and cigars, which range in price from $9 to over $100. The interior is filled with antiques, leather armchairs, humidors, rare books and stylish modern furnishings. Although expensive, drinks are generous, and cover everything from armagnacs to aged whiskeys.

**Melbourne Supper Club**, Level 1, 161 Spring St, City (⌀9654 6300). This convivial upstairs lounge room opposite Parliament House exudes an air of decadence and attracts a lively mix of hospitality types and late-night roisterers. As well as an excellent drinks list, the club offers cigars, inexpensive food, and deep leather sofas and chairs in which to enjoy them.

**Tony Starr's Kitten Club**, 267 Little Collins St, City (⌀9650 2448). Sleek and stylish interior tricked out with slightly Oriental furnishings, conducive to lolling on comfy sofas and ottomans while cradling a cocktail (reputedly Melbourne's best) and nibbling on Asian-inspired food from the grill. There's also live music every Tuesday, Thursday and Saturday night.

CIGAR AND SUPPER CLUBS

with a few drinks and perhaps something to eat. Enter via Anchor Place.

## Revolver

**Map 6, C8.** 229 Chapel St, Prahran ☏9521 5985.
Daily noon–3am.

A recent addition to the Prahran scene, *Revolver* has recently established itself as a popular venue with Melbourne's drinking and dancing crowd. Electronic beat DJs and artists create a cool vibe every night, and bands play most weekends (a modest cover charge applies), and it's the perfect place on a Saturday afternoon, when DJs spin throbbing reggae and dub sounds. You can grab a snack in the Thai restaurant, lounge around with a drink in the spacious, comfortable main area, or boogie in the back room. Entry is free early in the week; prices vary later in the week according to guests.

**PUBS**

## Bridie O'Reilly's

**Map 6, D6.** 462 Chapel St, South Yarra ☏9827 7788.
Mon–Thurs 11am–1am, Fri & Sat 11am–3am.

Irish-themed pub incongruously housed in an old church and saved from terminal tackiness by the pleasant front patio. Has meals and plenty of memorabilia from the Emerald Isle. Can get raucous on weekends, but it's fun if you're desperate for a Guinness or British beer.

# ST KILDA

**BARS AND CLUBS**

## Doulton Bar

**Map 7, F6.** 202 Barkly St ☏9534 2200.

Mon–Wed & Sun 10am–11.30pm, Thurs–Sat 10am–1.30am.

Part of the *Village Belle Hotel* on the corner, but don't bother with the front bar as it's little more than a betting shop. Enter the old-fashioned *Doulton Bar* via a discreet door between the bottle shop and main bar and you'll find a relaxing oasis from the St Kilda crowds, with a one-way window overlooking the street.

## The George Public Bar

**Map 7, E5.** 127 Fitzroy St ℂ9534 8822.
Mon–Thurs & Sun noon–1am, Fri & Sat noon–3am.

Very cool underground bar with an upbeat design. Favoured by locals, it has a large range of beers on tap, plus a pool table and free live music on Saturday afternoons. The service is friendly and the kitchen is open until 11pm each night, serving a wide range of snacks and good-value meals. Table seats outside.

## The Mansion

**Map 7, E1.** 83 Queens Rd ℂ9521 1711.
Fri & Sat 11pm–7am.

Club set in a converted Victorian mansion with an ambience of slightly dilapidated elegance. House is the main groove, although techno gets a look in too. In summer the rooftop is open for cooling off and stargazing. Entry is around $8.

## Mink Bar

**Map 7, C5.** The Prince St Kilda, 2b Acland St ℂ9537 1322.
Daily 6pm–2am.

Carved out of the remade part of *The Prince St Kilda*, this sub-terranean space has back-lit refrigerated shelves stacked high with an astonishing array of Russian, Polish, Swedish, Finnish, Lithuanian and – gulp – Japanese vodka. There are also private booths for intimate tête-à-têtes and a portrait of Karl Marx hanging from the wall. If you're hungry, try the antipasto platters, or head straight for the caviar and Cuban cigars. A great place for convivial quaffing and mellowing.

ST KILDA: BARS AND CLUBS

### Sunset Strip

**Map 7, E5.** 16 Grey St ℅9534 9205.

Daily noon–5am.

Cross between a strip joint and a cabaret lounge on a cruise ship. With a deafening sound system, cheap drinks and a late close, it's a popular place with backpackers from the nearby hostels.

### Veludo

**Map 7, E8.** 175 Acland St ℅9534 4456.

Mon–Thurs & Sun noon–1am, Fri & Sat noon–2am.

Magnet for St Kilda fashion plates, *Veludo* sports a bar downstairs with interesting and cheap food, and a smart restaurant upstairs (see p.140) overlooking Acland Street. Spacious and stylish, it really gathers steam on the weekends.

---

**PUBS**

### The Esplanade Hotel

**Map 7, C6.** 11 Upper Esplanade ℅9534 0211.

Daily noon–1am.

Famous for its beachside views, this hotel is the epicentre of St Kilda's drinking scene and shouldn't be missed. Bands play every night and there are inexpensive meals from *The Espy Kitchen* at the rear, plus pool tables and pinball machines.

### The Prince St Kilda

**Map 7, C5.** 29 Fitzroy St ℅9536 1177.

Daily noon–3am.

Defiantly local and no-frills, the downstairs public bar at *The Prince* has an air of stubborn resistance in the face of St Kilda's freewheeling gentrification. Frequented in equal parts by colourful local identities and desperadoes, this hotel is not for the faint-hearted.

# Live music

**M**elbourne has arguably the best **live rock music** scene in Australia – on any given night you'll find scores of bands playing at venues around the city, covering everything from grunge rock and techno to blues and jazz. Unlike Sydney, where developers and the introduction of "pokies" has largely decimated the city's best rock pubs, Melbourne's music scene has remained healthy and remarkably resilient. The city's rock and pop heritage is a rich one. During the 1970s and 1980s, acts like the Skyhooks, Daddy Cool, the Sports, The Birthday Party, and Hunters and Collectors performed their first gigs in pubs across the city, while the Melbourne-based indie label Mushroom Records (see box on p.162) was responsible for launching the vocal talents of singers like Kylie Minogue and Peter Andre onto an unsuspecting world.

**Listings** of bands and venues can be found in the free *Beat* and *Inpress*, or the "EG" insert in the Friday edition of *The Age*, or tune into one of Melbourne's community radio stations, such as 3RRR (102.7 FM) or 3PBS (106.7 FM). For larger events like the annual Big Day Out (a one-day outdoor concert featuring myriad national and overseas acts), you may need to book in advance through Ticketmaster (℡13/6100), or at music stores like Gaslight

Music (see p.203). At pubs and smaller venues you can pay at the door; entry to gigs ranges from about $3 to $25 depending on the calibre of the band.

Melbourne is also blessed with a fine **classical music** scene. The Melbourne Symphony Orchestra gives regular performances at the Melbourne Concert Hall in the Victorian Arts Centre and Melbourne Town Hall. Opera Australia has productions during the season (March–May & Nov–Dec) at the State Theatre in the Arts Centre and the newly renovated Opera Centre at 35 City Road, Southbank, while chamber music can be heard at the Melbourne Concert Hall and Melbourne Town Hall. Expect to pay $30–70 for classical music performances, $50–120 for opera; tickets from Ticketmaster on ✆13/6100.

# INDIE AND MAINSTREAM ROCK

## CITY CENTRE

### The Hi Fi Bar and Ballroom
**Map 4, G4.** 125 Swanston Street ✆9654 7617.
Reasonably spacious underground space with two bars on different levels where you can view acts in relative comfort and avoid the overheated mosh-pit below. A mainstay venue for high-profile local and international indie-rock bands.

## CARLTON AND FITZROY

### The Arthouse
**Map 5, A7.** Cnr Elizabeth & Queensberry streets, Carlton ✆9347 3917.
Something of a dive, with punk and metal bands most nights of the week aimed squarely at those who like their music at ear-

bleeding volumes. Despite its hardcore credentials, occasional poetry readings and film screenings are also held here.

## The Empress Hotel

**Map 3, E1.** 714 Nicholson St, North Fitzroy ℗9489 8605.
A mecca for Melbourne's quirkier bands, with a friendly and low-key atmosphere, cheap meals and the occasional screenings of cult films. To reach North Fitzroy, take tram #11.

## Evelyn Hotel

**Map 5, G3.** 351 Brunswick St, Fitzroy ℗9419 5500.
Recently transformed from a gloomy hotel into a stygian post-modern cave, this stalwart of the Fitzroy scene is a good introduction to Melbourne's alt-rock bands, which play here nightly.

## The Punters Club

**Map 5, G3.** 376 Brunswick St, Fitzroy ℗9417 3006.
A boisterous pub renowned for showing its patrons a good time, *The Punters Club* presents up-and-coming international acts, as well as those better known on the Melbourne scene. The low, nicotine-stained ceilings, sticky carpet and steady stream of guitar-oriented alt-rock bands remain a constant, as do the feral and grunge clientele, who have more bark than bite. Reasonable cover charges ($5 most bands) and drinks.

## Rochester Castle Hotel

**Map 5, H4.** 202 Johnston St, Fitzroy ℗9416 3133.
Casual atmosphere with top-notch bands playing each night. Entry is usually free, or not more than $5.

## The Royal Derby Hotel

**Map 5, G2.** 446 Brunswick St, Fitzroy ℗9417 2321.
Bare-boards pub with a party vibe that gets down to live music ranging from banging guitar bands to stomping outfits each weekend. Just don't mention that Elvis is dead.

INDIE AND MAINSTREAM ROCK: CARLTON AND FITZROY

### The Club

**Map 5, I7.** 132 Smith St, Collingwood ℡9417 4039.

Small and claustrophobic, featuring mainly unknown acts performing on weekends only until late into the night. There's also an upstairs bar, where you can drink until 7am and play pool. Minimal cover charge ($3–5).

### The Corner Hotel

**Map 3, F4.** 57 Swan St, Richmond ℡9427 7300.

Dark, grungy, but reasonably spacious hotel with two bars showcasing bands of varying quality most nights. Ageing rocker Mick Jagger performed here when on tour with The Rolling Stones a few years ago.

### The Tote

**Map 5, I5.** 71 Johnston St, Collingwood ℡9419 5320.

Classic Melbourne rock'n'roll venue, with sharp-tongued staff, stained carpet and plastic beer glasses. Home to Melbourne's punk and hardcore scene, with nightly bands that will blow your socks off. If you've ever owned a Ramones record, this is the place for you.

........................................................................

To reach Collingwood, take tram #86 or the
Hurstbridge line from Flinders Street Station. For
Richmond, take tram #75 or the Belgrave line from
Flinders Street Station.

........................................................................

**PRAHRAN**

### The Continental

**Map 6, C8.** 134 Greville St, Prahran ℡9510 2788.

This elegant venue attracts mainly solo performers, or two- or three-piece acts, and an older clientele. It's slightly more expensive than other venues ($8–15 show only, $45 dinner and show), although the quality of the acts and the civilized atmosphere make it eminently worthwhile. Advance bookings advisable.

## Revolver

**Map 6, C8.** 229 Chapel St, Prahran ☏9521 5985.

Catering mainly to a techno crowd, *Revolver* has bands at weekends, and also doubles as a nightclub (see p.154). Always something going on and plenty of room to dance.

## ST KILDA

## The Esplanade Hotel

**Map 7, C6.** 11 Upper Esplanade, St Kilda ☏9534 0211.

Long-established fixture in Melbourne's pub-rock and drinking scene (see p.156), attracting both established and fledgling acts. Bands nightly, either free in the front bar, or with a nominal cover charge in the Gershwin Room at the rear. No frills, but hugely enjoyable.

## The Greyhound Hotel

**Map 3, E5.** 1 Brighton Rd, St Kilda ☏9534 4189.

A bit seedy, but still a good place to see established local artists as well as younger bands strutting their stuff. Bands nightly, with an emphasis on stripped-down rock'n'roll. There's usually a small cover charge ($3–5).

## The Palace

**Map 7, D7.** Lower Esplanade, St Kilda ☏9534 7558.

One of Melbourne's larger indie venues, *The Palace* also doubles as a nightclub and place for dance parties. Can get suffocating when packed, but it's still one of the few places where

INDIE AND MAINSTREAM ROCK: ST KILDA

# Mushroom Records

Until its sale in 1998, **Mushroom Records** was the largest independent record label in Australia, handling over four hundred local artists, with over eight thousand releases and sales of more than eight million. The label was founded in 1972 by Michael Gudinski, an ambitious 19-year-old who quickly rose to become the most successful entrepreneur in the Australian music industry. His encouragement of domestic talent spawned a whole swag of memorable pop songs, including Split Enz's "I Got You" (their album *True Colours* was the label's first international hit), Skyhooks' "Living in the '70s", Paul Kelly's "Before Too Long" and, er, Kylie Minogue's "'I Should Be So Lucky". Gudinski's patronage of Australian music gave exposure to Melbourne-based acts the Sports, Black Sorrows and Hunters and Collectors, while expatriates like Nick Cave and the megaselling Kylie Minogue and Peter Andre also graced the Mushroom roster, delivering several no.1 UK hits and contributing substantial revenue to the label's coffers.

Twenty-six years of Mushroom Records ended in 1998, when Gudinski flogged his remaining stake to News Limited for $40 million. As a last hurrah, Gudinski staged a mammoth "Concert of the Century" at the MCG, where groups ground their way through past Mushroom songs to over 70,000 dewy-eyed fans.

mid-range local and international acts play to large audiences without resorting to stadiums such as Melbourne Park or the MCG.

## The Prince St Kilda

**Map 7, C5.** 29 Fitzroy St, St Kilda ℂ9536 1166.
This landmark venue has been a breeding ground for local bands, as well as hosting visiting acts from overseas. Although

revamped, it's lost little of its character and continues to show-case Melbourne's best bands each weekend (and occasionally in the week). It also attracts an incredibly diverse range of punters, from gays and skinheads to young city professionals.

# BLUES AND FOLK

### Café Bohemio
**Map 5, I4.** 354 Smith St, Collingwood ©9417 7626.
Charmingly laid-back, the licensed *Café Bohemio* has free bands most nights. Latin-American influences abound, although the music varies from jazz and blues to Brazilian folk. The food is also very good.

### The Dan O'Connell Hotel
**Map 5, F2.** 225 Canning St, Carlton ©9347 1502.
Comfortable, friendly hotel with a large back room where there's often an expatriate Irish crowd in full swing. Bands most nights of the week, usually Irish folk or excellent acoustic blues, either free or with only a minimal door charge.

# JAZZ

### Bar Deco
**Map 4, H4.** Hyatt Hotel, 123 Collins St, City ©9657 1234.
Located just off the hotel's lobby, *Bar Deco* has an exclusive lounge-like ambience, where you can settle back with a marti-ni and a good cigar and watch live jazz from Wednesday to Saturday (10.30pm–1am; free).

### Bennett's Lane Jazz Club
**Map 4, H2.** 25 Bennett's Lane, off Little Lonsdale St, City ©9663 2856.

Cramped and smoky, with archetypal 1950s-style decor, *Bennett's Lane* is Melbourne's leading venue for live jazz, with high-quality local and touring acts most nights of the week. Entry is around $8.

## The Night Cat
**Map 5, G4.** 141 Johnston St, Fitzroy ☎9417 0090.
Stylish, roomy venue with bands most nights playing a variety of jazz from good-time swing to slinky lounge music. Weekends are busy, when a cover charge applies ($5 after 9.30pm), and it's worth getting in early to grab a table. Not for purists, but invariably lots of fun.

# Gay Melbourne

**A**ttitudes to homosexuals and transgendered people in Australia are among the most relaxed in the world. There are pockets of gay and lesbian life all over inner-city Melbourne, especially along **Commercial Road**, which bisects the suburbs of Prahran and South Yarra and houses popular nightclubs, bookstores, boutiques, cafés and gymnasiums. Saturday morning at **Prahran Market** (see p.202) is the time to people-watch, while **Brunswick Street** in Fitzroy and nearby **Smith Street** in Collingwood also offer a large and eclectic range of gay-oriented eateries, retail outlets and nightspots. The final must-go area is **St Kilda**, especially Acland and Fitzroy streets, which have one of the highest concentrations of lesbian and gay residents in Australia. There's an official **gay beach** at Port Melbourne, near the sand dunes (known as "Screech Beach"), while the beaches at Elwood, St Kilda and the stretch between Middle Park and Port Melbourne are also popular.

Festivals to watch out for are the **Midsumma Festival** (mid-Jan to early Feb; ✆9525 4746) and the **Melbourne**

---

Melbourne's best gay bookshop, Hares & Hyenas (✆9824 0110), is at 135 Commercial Road (there's a second branch in Smith Street, Collingwood)

---

**Queer Film and Video Festival** (mid-March; ✆9510 5576). Two free local **gay and lesbian newspapers** – *Brother Sister* and *MSO* – and the inexpensive monthly magazine *Lesbiana* are available at gay and lesbian book-shops, where you will also find free interstate newspapers and guides to sights and activities. Other good sources of **information** are the Alternative Life Style Organisation (ALSO), 35 Cato Street, Prahran (Mon–Fri 9am–5pm; ✆9510 5569), the Gay and Lesbian Switchboard (Mon, Tues & Thurs–Sun 6–10pm, Wed 2–10pm; ✆9510 5488 or freecall ✆1800/631 493), the 24-hour Gay and Lesbian Entertainment Info Line (✆0055/12504), or tune into the radio station Joy Melbourne 90.7 FM. For **accommodation**, ring Gay Share (✆9650 0200), which arranges house-shares.

Entry to pubs and clubs in the following listings is free most nights of the week, although a door charge (no more than $5) occasionally applies at the weekend.

## PUBS, BARS AND CLUBS

### Barracuda
**Map 5, H7.** 64 Smith St, Collingwood ✆9419 2869.
Mon–Sat 5pm–late.
Located in a converted theatre, and popular with both gays and lesbians, *Barracuda* boasts three separate bars: the Front Bar (pool tables, games, videos, snacks, drinks and coffee); the Panama Lounge cocktail bar; and the Zinc dance bar (Fri & Sat 10pm–late).

### The Glasshouse Hotel
**Map 4, M1.** 51 Gipps St, Collingwood ✆9419 4748.
Fri & Sat 11am–3am, Sun 11am–1am.
Relaxed and friendly hotel popular with Melbourne's pool-

playing lesbians and their admirers. Good, inexpensive meals available nightly, and bands often play on Sunday evenings.

## The Laird
**Map 4, N1.** 149 Gipps St, Abbotsford ©9417 2832.
Mon–Thurs 5pm–1am, Fri & Sat 5pm–3am, Sun 5pm–midnight.
Melbourne's sole men-only pub attracts a mainly leather crowd. The atmosphere is relaxed and welcoming, and accommodation for gays and lesbians is also provided by the hotel and its affiliate, the *Norwood Guesthouse*, just across the street. To get there, take the Epping line to Collingwood Station.

## Peel Dance Bar
**Map 4, M1.** Cnr Peel & Wellington streets, Collingwood ©9419 4762.
Wed–Sun 10pm–dawn.
Dance floor, music videos and shows. A longstanding favourite with a mainly male crowd.

> **To reach Collingwood, take tram #86, or the
> Hurstbridge line from Flinders Street Station.**

## 3 Faces
**Map 6, C7.** 143 Commercial Rd, South Yarra ©9826 0933.
Thurs–Sun 9pm–5am; $5–10.
Melbourne's largest and most popular gay-and-lesbian club. Regular drag shows complement the high jinks on the dance floor, or take a breather at the cocktail bar, pool tables or pinball machines.

# CAFÉS

## Blue Elephant
**Map 6, C7.** 194 Commercial Rd, Prahran ©9510 3654.
Daily 7am–late.

CAFÉS

One of the sceniest gay cafés in Melbourne – with a menu that has nothing over $10 and service that isn't top-heavy with attitude. While the body beautiful is still on display, the last couple of years have seen a more mixed crowd enjoying the café's cheap eats and party atmosphere.

## 189 Espresso Bar

**Map 7, F8.** 189 Acland St, St Kilda ℗9534 8884.
Mon 8.30am–6pm, Tues–Sun 8.30am–11pm.
Popular coffee bar and eaterie attracting a mainly young, gay clientele, although straights won't feel out of place. The coffee's great and the food selection's limited but tasty, with none of the regular menu items over $10. If the music gets too loud, cross the street to *Big Mouth* (see p.136).

## Jackie O

**Map 7, F8.** 204 Barkly St, St Kilda ℗9537 0377.
Daily 7.30am–late.
St Kilda's first recognized gay café, *Jackie O* has quickly risen to become the most popular place to be gay (and be seen) in Melbourne. The food is standard, but portions are large and incredibly cheap, while the view along Acland Street is well worth the price of a drink from the bar.

# Theatre, comedy and cinema

**M**elbourne's standing as the centre of Australian **theatre** has been recognized since 1871, when visiting English novelist Anthony Trollope remarked on the city's excellent venues and variety of performances. Nowadays, you can see a host of quality productions most nights of the week, from big musicals to experimental drama. And, judging by box-office returns, they're generally well supported. **Tickets** can be booked through Ticketmaster (✆13/6100) and Ticketek Victoria (✆13/2849), while Half-Tix (Mon & Sat 10am–2pm, Tues–Thurs 11am–6pm, Fri 11am–6.30pm; ✆9650 9420), in the middle of Bourke Street Mall, has discounted tickets (cash only) on the day of performance. A highlight of the city's theatrical year is the Melbourne Festival (see p.180), which runs for a couple of weeks in late October.

Melbourne is also the heart of Australian **comedy**, with regular performances by home-grown and overseas comedians in pubs and clubs. Don't miss the Melbourne International Comedy Festival (see p.178) in late April, when more than a thousand comics converge on the city.

There are plenty of mainstream **cinemas** in Melbourne, mostly in and around Bourke Street, plus a growing number of plush arthouses. Discounts are usually available on Monday and Tuesday, when the price of a ticket drops from $11.50 to $7.50. The centrepiece of Melbourne movie life is the annual International Film Festival (see p.179), which runs for two weeks during late July in venues like the Village Centre and the Forum, showcasing hundreds of local and international releases.

For theatre, comedy and cinema **listings**, check *The Age* (especially Friday's comprehensive arts and entertainment guide, "EG") and "Hit", the Thursday supplement of the *Herald Sun*. Another good source is *Melbourne Events*, a free monthly calendar to citywide events, available from the Victorian Visitor Information Centre (see p.25), leading newsagents and information booths.

# THEATRE

### Athenaeum Theatre
**Map 4, G4.** 188 Collins St, City ℗9650 1500.
Built in 1842, the Athenaeum Theatre stages everything from Shakespearean drama to comedy and fringe performances.

### CUB Malthouse
**Map 4, G9.** 113 Sturt St, South Melbourne ℗9685 5111.
Former brewery now transformed into state-of-the-art performance-and-gallery complex. Contains the small 200-seater Beckett Theatre, the larger Merlyn Theatre and the newish Tower Room. The resident company – the Playbox Theatre Centre – produce contemporary Australian plays. To get there, take tram #1 from Swanston Street or St Kilda Road.

THEATRE

## Her Majesty's Theatre

**Map 4, H2.** 219 Exhibition St, City ☏9663 3211.
Fabulously ornate theatre built in 1886 – now features popular retro throwbacks like *Chicago* and *Grease*.

## La Mama

**Map 5, D4.** 205 Faraday St, Carlton ☏9347 6948.
A Carlton institution for over thirty years, *La Mama* hosts low-budget, innovative works by local playwrights. Ticket prices are probably the cheapest in town.

## Playhouse Theatre

**Map 4, H6.** Victorian Arts Centre, 100 St Kilda Rd, City ☏9281 8000.
Wide-ranging choice of programmes, usually performed by the renowned and very popular Melbourne Theatre Company, who are currently resident here until their new 500-seater home in Southbank is completed in 2000.

## Princess Theatre

**Map 4, I2.** 163 Spring St, City ☏9299 9800.
Established at the height of the goldrush, this small, exquisitely restored theatre is one of the city's best-loved venues, and stages musicals and mainstream theatrical productions.

## Regent Theatre

**Map 4, G4.** 191 Collins St, City ☏9299 9500.
Opened in 1929, this mammoth, lavishly restored theatre presents razzle-dazzle West End/Broadway productions like *Sunset Boulevard* and *Showboat*.

## Theatreworks

**Map 7, D6.** 14 Acland St, St Kilda ☏9534 4879.
Cutting-edge Australian plays in a reasonably large, wooden-floored space that was formerly a church hall.

THEATRE

# COMEDY

## The Comedy Club
**Map 5, D4.** 380 Lygon St, Carlton ℂ9348 1622.
Slick, cabaret-style space with two rooms featuring mainstream domestic and international acts.

## The Esplanade Hotel
**Map 7, C6.** 11 Upper Esplanade, St Kilda ℂ9534 0211.
*The Esplanade Hotel* has a long and legendary comedy tradition, with gigs twice a week – Tuesday nights for more established

## Laughing matter

Melbourne has long been regarded as the home of Australian **comedy**. During the 1970s, a comedy cabaret scene developed around small theatre-restaurants like *The Flying Trapeze* and *The Comedy Café,* later evolving into a healthy stand-up circuit in the 1980s at venues such as *The Last Laugh* and the *Prince Patrick Hotel*. Founded in 1987, the **Melbourne International Comedy Festival** (see p.178) has grown to become (along with Toronto and Edinburgh) one of the world's top three comedy festivals, during which around a thousand national and international comics descend on the city. Some of Melbourne's comedy stalwarts include Greg Fleet, a wonderfully surreal stand-up comic who gained enormous exposure in the long-running TV show *Neighbours*; Anthony Morgan, whose tear-streaming comic timing and deadpan delivery have made him one of Australia's most adored performers; and fully fledged "national treasure" Rod Quantock, who dreams of moving the Phillip Island penguin parade to the City Square, and recently sought to host the Second Coming in Melbourne for the year 2000.

acts, and Sunday afternoons for newer performers. It's a relaxed introduction to the world of stand-up comedy in Melbourne, and when the jokes wear thin you can order a cheap meal from the *Espy Kitchen* or catch one of the bands playing in the front bar.

### Prince Patrick Hotel

**Map 4, N2.** 135 Victoria Parade, Collingwood ℂ9419 4917.
Leading venue for some of Australia's hottest performers since the mid-1980s, despite only hosting comedy acts one or two nights a week. Many of Melbourne's most famous acts, such as Anthony Morgan, Greg Fleet and Judith Lucy, have cut their comedy teeth at "the Pat", which continues to showcase some of the most inventive and bizarre comedy draws in town.

### Star & Garter Hotel

**Map 3, C5.** 70 Nelson Rd, South Melbourne ℂ9690 5062.
Regular and reliable Thursday-night comedy gigs. Was previously the home base for expat UK comics like Jimeoin and Bob Franklin before they got established in Australia.

# CINEMA

### Astor Theatre

**Map 3, F6.** Cnr Chapel St and Dandenong Rd, St Kilda ℂ9510 1414.
Built in 1936, the Astor's fabulous Art Deco ambience and popular front steps have made it a favoured meeting place for film buffs or anyone who appreciates architectural glamour. It now shows a mix of classics, recent releases and cheesy double bills.

## Cinema Como

**Map 6, D4.** Cnr Toorak Rd and Chapel St, South Yarra ℘9827 7533.
Boutique, three-cinema complex stuck in the giant Como
Complex. Screens international and new releases.

## Cinema Nova

**Map 5, D4.** Lygon Court Plaza, 380 Lygon St, Carlton ℘9347 5331.
Labyrinthine theatre noted for its lurid crimson-and-purple
decor. Arthouse and European films a speciality.

## Cinemedia at Treasury Theatre

**Map 4, J3.** 1 MacArthur Place, East Melbourne ℘9651 1515.
The recently upgraded Cinemedia is dedicated to promoting
cinema culture through independent films and festivals, ranging
from screenings of domestic and international films to anima-
tion and documentaries. Check their Web site
(*www.cinemedia.net/venues/*) for upcoming events.

## George Cinema

**Map 7, E5.** 133–137 Fitzroy St, St Kilda ℘9534 6922.
New independent releases, mostly from the USA, and has
excellent choc-top ice creams. *Café Diva*, on the same floor,
overlooking Fitzroy Street, is ideal for supper or an after-movie
coffee.

## IMAX Theatre

**Map 5, E6.** Rathdowne St, Carlton ℘9663 5454.
Recently opened as part of the new Museum of Victoria complex (see p.69), IMAX has kitsch interiors and awesome technology, including a gigantic screen and film reels so big they
require a fork-lift to move them. Shows both 2-D and 3-D
films, usually lasting between 45min to 1hr, mostly documentaries on inaccessible places or anything involving a tyran-
nosaurus rex. The complex also includes two candy bars, a
licensed bar and restaurant.

CINEMA

## Kino

**Map 4, I4.** 45 Collins St, City ℂ9650 2100.

Sophisticated and civilized complex beneath the Collins Place atrium showing new – predominantly arthouse – releases.

## Lumiere

**Map 4, H2.** 108 Lonsdale St, City ℂ9639 1055.

A beacon for moviegoers seeking quality avant-garde movies, classic re-releases and alternative films from around the world.

## Moonlight Cinema

**Map 4, L9.** Royal Botanic Gardens

Outdoor screenings (Dec–March) of arthouse, cult and classic movies on the central lawn of the Royal Botanic Gardens (see p.64), weather permitting (8.45pm; $11.50; call in advance on ℂ1900/933 899 for movie programmes). Tickets can be bought at Gate D, Birdwood Avenue, or through Ticketmaster (ℂ13/6100).

## Village

**Map 6, D5.** Jam Factory, 500 Chapel St, South Yarra ℂ9827 2424.

Sprawling multiplex containing two movie houses: an eleven-screen cine-city showing a steady stream of money-spinning blockbusters, and (opposite on the same level) the opulent Cinema Europa (ℂ9827 2440), which has three small arthouse cinemas in which Australian short films precede the main event. Big, roomy seats at both cinemas, although the food and drink from the "Lollywood" candy bars is hideously expensive.

**CINEMA**

# Festivals

M elbourne has an abundance of **festivals**, which bring together an array of Australian and international talent to collaborate on events featuring everything from music, comedy and film to flowers, food and wine. The following are the major festivals only; for one-offs or smaller goings-on, pick up a copy of *Melbourne Events* – available from hotels, newsagents or the Victorian Visitor Information Centre (see p.251) – which lists monthly happenings throughout the city. For most festivals, **tickets** can be obtained through the booking offices of Ticketmaster (℡13/6100), Ticketek Victoria (℡13/2849) and Half-Tix (℡9650 9420), or at the venue concerned.

## JANUARY

### Chinese New Year Festival
**January 30–February 1.** Melbourne's Chinatown hosts a packed arts and cultural programme, featuring music, dance, food, and an appearance by Dai Loong, the world's longest ceremonial dragon (℡0419/350 477).

# FEBRUARY

### St Kilda Festival
**Early February.** Ear-blistering events on St Kilda's foreshore, the Esplanade and Acland Street, with live bands, exhibitions, food stalls and street performers (℘9209 6327).

# MARCH

### Antipodes Festival
**March 1–April 12.** Greek film, arts and crafts, sport and commerce featured in venues throughout the city (℘9662 2722).

### Melbourne Moomba Festival
**March 9–19.** One of Australia's largest outdoor festivals, focusing on the Yarra, the adjacent Alexandra Gardens and city centre, with a mixture of cultural and sporting events like water-skiing, dragon-boat racing and night parades (℘9699 4022).

### St Kilda Film Festival
**March 27–31.** St Kilda's National Theatre stages this small but good survey of contemporary Australian short films and videos, with a spotlight on emerging film-makers (℘9209 6217).

### Melbourne Food and Wine Festival
**March–April.** Australia's premier food-and-wine event, at various venues in Melbourne and regional Victoria, showcasing specially prepared dishes by some of the city's finest chefs and excellent wines from around the state. Events include the "World's Longest Lunch" and guided tours of Melbourne's best-known eating streets (℘9628 5008).

# APRIL

### Melbourne International Flower and Garden Show

**April 5–9.** Held in Carlton Gardens, this is Australia's largest and most prestigious horticultural event, with hundreds of floral and landscape displays against the backdrop of the Royal Exhibition Building and the new Museum of Victoria (☏9569 4400).

### Melbourne International Comedy Festival

**Late April.** Leading laughathon that attracts more than a thousand home-grown and overseas comics. Based in the Melbourne Town Hall, but with programmes in over fifty other city venues, spanning stand-up comedy, plays, film, TV and street theatre (☏9417 7711).

# MAY

### Next Wave Festival

**May 15–31.** Cutting-edge multimedia, visual arts and writing, created and performed by emerging Australian artists, mainly in inner-city pubs and other locations in Fitzroy (☏9417 7544).

# JULY

### Maverick Arts

**Mid-July.** One of Melbourne's more alternative festivals, held at a variety of smaller venues throughout the city, Maverick Arts assembles a variety of cutting-edge performance and visual artists, singers, comedians and writers for a week of arty frolics that usually begin and end in a pub. Book through Ticketmaster (☏13/6100).

## Melbourne International Film Festival

**Late July.** Hugely popular fortnight with a big focus on Australian films, and a new multimedia component highlighting the latest in film technology. Hundreds of films from a variety of countries are shown, while a who's who of local and overseas film-makers attend to talk about their work. Venues city-wide (✆9417 2011).

# AUGUST

## Melbourne Writers' Festival

**August 21–30.** Hundreds of Australian and overseas writers converge on Melbourne, where they get completely plastered, forget their hotel keys, wangle deals with publishers and, when sober, give talks and lectures to fawning members of the book-loving public. Activities centre on the CUB Malthouse in South Melbourne, except for the keynote address – setting the tone for the festival (and always good for a writerly stoush) – which takes place at the Melbourne Town Hall (✆9685 5111).

# SEPTEMBER

## Royal Melbourne Show

**September 17–27.** Eleven-day agricultural bonanza at the Royal Melbourne Showgrounds, preceded by a parade of animals and farm machinery down Swanston Street. Rides, baked potatoes and candyfloss compete with contests featuring everything from Jersey-Holstein cows to wood-choppers ($14; ✆9281 7444).

## Asian Food Festival

**Late September.** Various venues around town celebrate and promote Melbourne's Asian culture and cuisine. The month-long event also includes food tours, cooking classes, banquets and more ($9690 4053).

## Melbourne Fringe Festival

**Late September.** Kicks off the day after the AFL Grand Final with the outrageous Brunswick Street parade and all-day party, and ends in a raucous gathering of feral types in an inner-city venue. Other debauched events typically include street raves, saucy plays and watching people having their bodies pierced. Tickets available from the Fringe Caravan ($9654 5645) parked outside the Melbourne Town Hall.

# OCTOBER

## Melbourne Oktoberfest

**October 23–25.** Three-day beer- and foodfest at the Royal Melbourne Showgrounds, where revellers can scull a range of local and imported beers, then tuck into pork shanks and schnitzels for extra staying power. If you're still standing, you can watch folk bands or large men bundled into lederhosen dancing up a storm ($10; $9281 7444).

## Lygon Street Festa

**October 24–25.** Founded in 1978, Australia's oldest street festival was masterminded by the traders and restaurateurs of Carlton's cappuccino belt. Crowd favourites include the waiters' race, the pizza-throwing competition, bocce, fencing and ballroom dancing, Italian-style ($1900/931 575).

## Melbourne Festival

**Late October.** One of Australia's pre-eminent annual arts events, the festival has a cast of thousands drawn from the fields of music, opera, dance and theatre. Ticketed and free performances are held both indoors and on Melbourne's streets ($13/6166).

# Sport and outdoor activities

T he acknowledged **sporting capital** of Australia, Melbourne is home to a string of major events including the AFL Grand Final, the Australian Grand Prix, the Australian Tennis Open and the Melbourne Cup. Its leading position has recently been enhanced by the development of major sporting facilities such as the Colonial Stadium and the Multi-Purpose Venue, both due for completion in 2000 (see p.62), while the famous Melbourne Cricket Ground (MCG) continues to draw mammoth crowds. Visitors can watch a range of spectator sports, including Aussie Rules, basketball, cricket, rugby union and soccer. In addition to its regular calendar of sporting events, Melbourne offers a number of **recreational sports**, with cycling, rollerblading, swimming, surfing and sailing all widely enjoyed.

# AUSTRALIAN FOOTBALL LEAGUE (AFL)

The **Australian Football League** ("Aussie Rules", or simply "the footy") is a Melbourne institution. Originally contested by the city's suburban teams, the AFL has now grown into a national league, with teams from Melbourne, Adelaide, Perth, Sydney and Brisbane playing games each weekend from March to September, culminating in the AFL Grand Final at the MCG on the last Saturday in September. Melbourne has ten of the sixteen AFL teams – Carlton, Essendon, North Melbourne and Hawthorn are some of the most successful – and consequently hosts the majority of games.

The most accessible stadiums are the MCG (tram #75 along Wellington Parade, or the Epping line train from Flinders Street Station to Jolimont Station) and the Optus Oval in Carlton (tram #19 from Elizabeth Street), although the Colonial Stadium (see p.62), due to open at the start of the AFL season in 2000, will be even more central. Tickets cost around $12 per person, or $30 for a family of four, and can be bought from the grounds or through Ticketmaster (℃13/6100). Ticket availability is generally good, and they can usually be bought on the day.

# BASKETBALL

There are over 600,000 registered **basketball** players in Australia, and games involving Melbourne's two teams – the Melbourne Tigers and the newly formed Victorian Titans – enjoy considerable support. The city's main basketball

# The rules of Rules

To those unfamiliar with the game, **Australian Football** may seem bizarre, but once you've experienced it live and understand a few basic rules, you'll be richly rewarded. The game was originally conceived as a winter fitness routine for Melbourne's cricketers, which is why it's played on a cricket oval. At each end of the oval are two upright posts, with another two (shorter) posts on either side of these. Each team is made up of eighteen players, plus four reserves or interchange players, who run around in incredibly tight shorts attempting to kick the football – in size and shape somewhere between a rugby ball and an American football – between the posts. A goal (worth six points) is when the ball is kicked through the two inner posts; a "behind" (worth one point) is when the ball passes between the two outer.

The game has four quarters of twenty minutes each. There are no offside rules, and players can run with the ball, although they must bounce it every 15m. A tackle can only be made below the shoulders and above the hips, but there's plenty of scope in the rules for a legal "bump" with the hip or shoulder which, when done correctly, produces an intensely violent level of body contact. If a player catches a ball which has travelled over 10m before it bounces, he's awarded a free kick. This produces the game's trademark signature: a player leaping for a mark or "speccie", often high enough to rest his knees or feet on an opponent's shoulders. An incredible seven umpires (don't call them "refs") officiate – two goal umpires, two boundary umpires and three main umpires on the field. Umpires are traditionally booed whenever they run onto the ground and throughout the game, but the animosity from the one-eyed, scarf-waving fans is mostly good-natured.

venue is Melbourne Park ($\textcircled{c}$9286 1234), Australia's largest indoor entertainment arena, in Yarra Park near the MCG. This is where the Tigers and Titans play, and it's easily accessible by tram #75 along Wellington Parade (which runs along the southeastern corner of Fitzroy Gardens), or the Epping line train from Flinders Street Station to Jolimont Station. Tickets cost $15–20 and can be obtained through Ticketek Victoria ($\textcircled{c}$13/2849).

# CRICKET

When the footy season is over, the **cricket** begins. The MCG hosts all the major games, such as the Boxing Day test match and four-day Sheffield Shield matches involving the Victorian state team, plus limited-overs day-and-night matches involving state and national teams (usually held between December and February), which regularly attract huge crowds. There are also eighteen club and district teams such as Carlton and St Kilda, which compete in the Light Ice Cup one- and two-day cricket competition between October and April at various suburban grounds (contact the Victorian Cricket Association on $\textcircled{c}$9653 1100 for fixtures and locations).

# CYCLING

Melbourne has an extensive network of quality **cycling tracks**. Popular routes include the Yarra riverside track from Southgate to Eltham (see p.89) and the bayside trail from Port Melbourne to Brighton. Bicycle Victoria, at 19 O'Connell Street in North Melbourne (Mon–Fri 9am–5pm; $\textcircled{c}$9328 3000), organize rides from 10km to 100km ($18–60) and hand out *Great Cycling Victoria*, a free brochure on bike rides in Victoria and interstate. Another free publication is *Fun on Trails*, a fold-out map available from the Victorian Visitor Information Centre (see p.25); cycle enthusiasts can also purchase a copy of the booklet *Discovering Victoria's Bike Paths* from bookshops and newsagents. For details of bike rental, see p.211.

# GOLF

There are no fewer than eighty **golf courses** around the city, four of them ranked in the world's top one hundred courses. Although some are members-only, there are also dozens of public courses. Typical green fees are around $15–20 for an eighteen-hole round, but check in advance. One of the best and most accessible courses is the Albert Park Public Golf Course on Queens Road (daily 6.30am–sunset; $18.50; ©9510 5588; tram #72 from St Kilda Road), which has sixty tee-off bays, four target greens and an eighteen-hole course. Albert Park also has an excellent driving range at Aughtie Drive, Albert Park ($6 for fifty balls; ©9696 4653). Other good courses include the nine-hole Royal Park Public Golf Course, Popular Road, Parkville (©9387 3585) and the eighteen-hole Sandringham Golf Links, Cheltenham Road, Cheltenham (©9598 3590). Most have pro shops where you can rent clubs and buggies, or book lessons.

# GYMS AND FITNESS CENTRES

Melbourne has plenty of **gyms and fitness centres**. Gym fees are around $10 per session for aerobics, weights or circuits. The Melbourne City Baths, at 420 Swanston Street (Mon–Fri 6am–10pm, Sat & Sun 8am–6pm; ©9663 3977), have excellent facilities, including a large gym, massage room, pools, floor and water aerobics classes, and saunas and spas. Other good centres include the Melbourne Fitness Club, Level 1, 385 Bourke Street (Mon–Fri

6am–8.30pm, Sat 9am–3pm; ✆9642 0288) and the St Kilda Sports and Fitness Centre, 97 Alma Road, St Kilda (Mon–Thurs 6am–10pm, Fri 6am–8pm, Sat & Sun 9am–6pm; ✆9510 9409).

# HORSE AND GREYHOUND RACING

**Horse racing** is a popular spectator sport, especially during the Spring Racing Carnival from October to November. The centrepiece is the 3.2-kilometre **Melbourne Cup**, arguably the top event in the country's entire sporting calendar, which is run on the first Tuesday in November ("Cup Day", a Victorian public holiday) at the Flemington Racecourse at Epsom Road, Flemington (✆9371 7171; tram #57 from Elizabeth Street). Known throughout the country as "the race that stops a nation", the Melbourne Cup attracts over 100,000 visitors, who come to admire the horseflesh, or use the occasion to strut their fashion stuff at the numerous corporate marquees. Melbourne's other metropolitan racecourses are the Caulfield Racecourse, Station Street, Caulfield (✆9572 7200), the Sandown Racecourse, Princess Highway, Springvale (✆9518 1350), and the Moonee Valley Racing Club, McPherson Street, Moonee Ponds (✆9373 2222), which also has night racing on weekdays.

If you fancy a flutter on the dogs, there's **greyhound racing** at the Sandown Greyhound Racing Club on Lightwood Road, Springvale (✆9546 9511; $5) – take the Dandenong line from Spencer Street Station, to Sandown Station. For information on race meets at other

---

When betting at the tote at trackside, "call out" your picks to the operator at the counter (who then gives you a ticket), rather than filling out a betting slip.

---

city locations or throughout the state, contact the Melbourne Greyhound Racing Association (℡9428 2145).

# MOTOR SPORTS

The **Australian Grand Prix**, the opening race of the Formula One World Championship season, is held over four days each year in March at Albert Park (tram #96 from Bourke Street or #12 from Collins Street). Tickets can be bought through Ticketmaster (℡13/6100), or via the Grand Prix hotline (℡13/1641). For general admission, expect to pay around $37–70 (depending on the day) for a one-day ticket, $120 for a four-day ticket, or between $299 and $475 for a grandstand seat.

Melbourne's other major motor-sports event, the **Qantas Australian Motorcycle Grand Prix**, is held at the Phillip Island Racing Circuit over three days in early October.

# ROLLERBLADING

**Rollerblading** is all the rage in summer, especially along St Kilda's bayside bike tracks. Skates and equipment can be hired from Bob's Boards and Blades, 17 Fitzroy Street, St Kilda (Mon–Fri 11am–6pm, Sat & Sun 10am–7pm; ℡9537 2118), and Apache Junction Skate Hire, 16 Marine Parade, St Kilda (daily 10am–5pm; ℡9534 4006). Around $7 will get you a pair of skates for an hour; $20 for a day.

# RUGBY

**Rugby union** has experienced slow growth in Melbourne, which now has twenty club sides, eight of them in the first division, including reigning and past champions Melbourne Rugby Club and Harlequins. Although the game in Melbourne lags behind Sydney and Brisbane in terms of popularity, the MCG holds the Australian attendance record (90,119) for a match, when the New Zealand All Blacks played the Australian Wallabies in a 1997 Bledisloe Cup test.

Like union, **rugby league** traditionally received little support in Melbourne, at least until the creation in 1998 of a new city team, the Melbourne Storm. Formed the previous year as part of the National Rugby League's push to nationalize the code, the Storm enjoyed remarkable success, beating more highly fancied Sydney- and Brisbane-based clubs to reach the finals. In doing so, they captured Melbourne's imagination, drawing healthy crowds to their home ground at Olympic Park.

Both union and league are played from April to September. Matches involving the Melbourne Storm are held at Olympic Park; the MCG is reserved for international games.

# SOCCER

**Soccer** is well supported in Melbourne, especially by the city's Italian and Croatian communities. There are currently four clubs in the city – South Melbourne, Carlton, Melbourne Knights and the Gippsland Falcons – which compete in the Ericsson Cup national league (call the Victorian Soccer Federation on ☏9682 9666 for details). The season runs from October to May; venues include the Bob James Stadium in South Melbourne (tram #12 from Collins Street to the end of the line) and the Optus Oval on Royal Parade, Carlton (tram #19 from Elizabeth Street). Admission is around $10–15.

# SWIMMING AND WATERSPORTS

The coastline of Port Phillip Bay offers ample opportunities for **watersports** enthusiasts. **Swimming** is popular over the hot summer months, when Melburnians pack the metropolitan beaches at Port Melbourne, Middle Park, St Kilda and Elwood, and the beaches further afield at Brighton, Sandringham and Mentone (all accessible by public transport). There's also a nude beach south of Melbourne at Half Moon Bay, Beach Road in Black Rock. Pools include the cavernous Melbourne Sports and Aquatic Centre on Aughtie Drive, Albert Park (Mon–Fri 5.30am–8pm, Sat & Sun 7am–8pm; $4; ©9926 1555; tram #96 from Bourke Street), the Fitzroy Pool, corner of Alexander Parade and Young Street, Fitzroy (Mon–Fri 6am–8pm, Sat & Sun 8am–6pm; $3; ©9417 6493; tram #11 from Collins Street) and the Prahran Aquatic Centre, 41 Essex Street, Prahran (Mon–Fri 6am–7.30pm, Sat & Sun 8am–6pm; $2.80; ©9522 3248; tram #6 from Swanston Street).

---

**If you're going to marinate in the sun, wear a hat and apply lots of sunscreen – Australia's ultraviolet levels and skin cancer rates are amongst the highest in the world.**

---

There are a number of **sailing** schools dotted around the bayside suburbs. The Jolly Roger School of Sailing (©9690 5862) on Aquatic Drive, Albert Park, holds sailing lessons ($40hr) on the Albert Park Lake; while Yachtpro at the Royal Melbourne Yacht Squadron, Pier Road, St Kilda (©9525 5221), has basic courses in sailing and navigation ($195 for 8hr tuition). One of Melbourne's more scenic sailing spots is on the Yarra at Boathouse Road, Kew, where Studley Park Boathouse (©9853 1972) rents out boats for $10 per half hour, $18 per hour. **Sailboarding** is also popular: Repeat Performance Sailboards, at 87 Ormond Road in Elwood (©9525 6475), rent sailboards and offer individual windsurfing lessons ($39hr, or $28 per person for groups of three or more).

SWIMMING AND WATERSPORTS

For **surfing**, you'll have to journey further afield. Some of Victoria's more popular surfing spots include Phillip Island, Mornington Peninsula, Torquay and nearby Bell's Beach, which hosts the international Rip Curl Pro and Quit Women's Classic each Easter for professional surfers. For daily surf reports, call the Triple J Surfline (©1900/922 996) or ©1900/983 268 (Mornington Peninsula only), or log on to the Surf Shop Victoria Web site (*www.surfshop.com.au*), which has comprehensive information on Victoria's beaches, surf events and where to buy equipment.

# TENNIS

The highlight of Melbourne's **tennis** season is the annual Ford Australian Open, one of the world's four grand slam tennis events, which takes place over two weeks from January to February at the National Tennis Centre in Melbourne Park, next to the MCG. Tickets range from $20 to $90 (bookings ©9286 1234; a Ticketmaster office operates in the foyer Mon–Fri 9am–5pm; tram #75 along Wellington Parade, or the Epping line train from Flinders Street Station to Jolimont Station). If you want a hit, the Tennis Centre has 21 outdoor and five indoor public courts (Mon–Fri 7am–11pm, Sat & Sun 9am–6pm; bookings ©9286 1244). Rates are around $14 per hour during the day, $22 per hour in the evening. Other public courts include the Collingwood Indoor Tennis Centre at 100 Wellington Street, Collingwood (©9419 8911), and the Albert Reserve Tennis Centre, on the corner of St Kilda Road and Hanna Street, South Melbourne (©9510 3311).

# Shopping

**M**elbourne's eclectic **shopping** scene accurately reflects the preoccupations of its lifestyle-conscious citizens, from the chic boutiques of Collins Street and South Yarra to the ethnic foodstalls of the Queen Victoria Market. Although the recent closure of the Terence Conran-inspired Georges department store may have deprived the city centre of some of its glamour, it has done little to dampen the spirits of most Melbourne shopaholics.

**Shopping hours** are generally Monday to Wednesday 9am–5.30pm, with late-night shopping until 7pm or 9pm on Thursday and Friday evenings; many places are also open on weekends from around noon to 5pm. Shops in some suburban areas such as Carlton, Fitzroy, South Yarra and St Kilda open seven days a week and keep varying hours, as noted in the following listings. Shopping hours are also extended by up to two hours during daylight-saving months (Nov–March).

Bargain hunters should make a beeline for the suburb of Richmond (especially Bridge Road and Church Street; trams #48 or #75 from Flinders Street), a clearance centre for some of Australia's most popular designers, or look out for stocktake sales during January and July. Otherwise, copies of *The Bargain Shopper's Guide to Melbourne* and *Pam's Guide to Discount Melbourne* are available from newsagents and bookshops.

# BOOKS AND MAPS

## CITY CENTRE

### Foreign Language Bookshop
**Map 4, G4.** 259 Collins St ℰ9654 2883.
Mon–Thurs 9am–5.30pm, Fri 9am–7.30pm, Sat 10am–5pm.
One of Australia's largest selections of travel guides and maps, plus foreign-language novels, magazines, dictionaries, videos and over seventy language-learning kits.

### Haunted Bookshop
**Map 4, F4.** 15 McKillop St, off Bourke St ℰ9670 2585.
Mon–Fri 10am–6pm, Sat noon–5pm, Sun 1–5pm.
Decked out with dim lighting, red velour curtains and a resident black cat, this is Australia's only paranormal and mystical bookshop – titles range from lycanthropy and vampirism to spellcraft and demonology. The shop also holds regular tarot readings and seances, and organizes tours (Wed 6.30–9pm; $25) of some of Melbourne's spookier haunts.

### Mapland
**Map 4, E4.** 372 Little Bourke St ℰ9670 4383.
Mon–Thurs 9am–5.30pm, Fri 9am–6pm, Sat 9am–4pm.
Travel guide and map specialist, plus globes, compasses and moneybelts.

### Page One
**Map 4, G4.** 179 Collins St ©9654 3886.

Mon–Sat 10am–9pm, Sun 11am–5pm.

Melbourne's preferred destination for those who like architecture, graphic design, photography and fine art. Marvel at its sloping bookshelves and sharp corners.

### CARLTON AND FITZROY

### Polyester Books
**Map 5, G4.** 330 Brunswick St, Fitzroy ©9419 5223.

Mon–Wed 10am–9pm, Thurs–Sat 10am–11pm, Sun noon–9pm.

Controversial store that's been denounced for its racy and offbeat titles. Among the popular culture, drug titles, adult comics and magazines are works by literary outlaws William Burroughs, Lenny Bruce, Jean Genet, the Marquis de Sade and Adolf Hitler.

### Readings
**Map 5, D4.** 309 Lygon St, Carlton ©9347 6633.

Mon–Sat 9am–11pm, Sun 10am–11pm.

Shelves of food, wine, history, children's and literary titles dominate this Carlton institution, while there's enough cultural theory detritus to stone a dozen academics, and a music section bulging with jazz, classical and world music CDs. Other branches in South Yarra, Hawthorn and Malvern.

### SOUTH YARRA AND PRAHRAN

### Borders
**Map 6, D5.** The Jam Factory, 500 Chapel St, South Yarra ©9824 2299.

Daily 9am–midnight.

Melbourne's first mega-bookstore crams over 200,000 books, CDs, videos, magazines and newspapers onto its shelves. Also has loads of discounts, a licensed café, children's playing area and regular in-store events like live music and author signings.

## Kill City

**Map 6, C8.** 126 Greville St, Prahran ©9510 6661.
Mon–Wed & Fri 10.30am–6pm, Thurs & Sat 10.30am–5pm, Sun 11.30am–5pm.
The store for all those with a fixation on hard-boiled characters. Titles by Elmore Leonard, James Ellroy, Carl Hiasen, Robert Cray and Patricia Highsmith, plus cards, posters and excellent "Kill City" T-shirts.

**ST KILDA**

## Cosmos

**Map 7, E8.** 112 Acland St, St Kilda ©9525 3852.
Daily 10am–10pm.
Everything from the latest bodice ripper to the most obscure items of esoterica, plus a comprehensive music catalogue.

## Metropolis

**Map 7, E8.** 160 Acland St, St Kilda ©9525 4866.
Daily 10am–10pm.
Art and architectural titles jostle with travel, film and fashion selections; there's also a shelf filled with hard-to-find local and international magazines.

# CLOTHES, SHOES AND JEWELLERY

**CITY CENTRE**

## Calibre

**Map 4, G4.** 3/182 Little Collins St ©9654 8826.

Mon–Thurs 9.30am–6pm, Fri 9.30am–9pm, Sat 9.30am–5pm, Sun noon–5pm.

Small shop in the groovy "menswear alley" of Little Collins Street, with a great range of tailored pants, shirts and jackets for the calorie-challenged male, and an impressive selection of imports, ranging from Helmut Lang and Vivienne Westwood to Patrick Cox. Has another store in South Yarra.

## Cose Ipanema
**Map 4, H4.** 113 Collins St ℗9650 3457.
Mon–Thurs 9.30am–6pm, Fri 9.30am–8pm, Sat 9.30am–4.30pm.

Fashion frontliner harbouring super-chic labels like Issey Miyake, Yohji Yamamoto and Dolce & Gabbana, plus exquisite jewellery from ex-Melburnian Sarah Harmarnee. Their sales often provoke a buying frenzy as normally expensive labels are snaffled up.

## Genki
**Map 4, G5.** Shop 5, Cathedral Arcade, 37 Swanston St ℗9650 6366.
Mon–Thurs 11am–7pm, Fri 11am–8pm, Sat 11am–6pm.

Japanese for "happy, healthy and feeling fine", Genki is a store for quirky Melburnians, with sequinned purses, pocket Polaroid cameras, Japanese pretzels dipped in chocolate, and other assorted knick-knacks and food items from around the world.

## Kozminsky's
**Map 4, F4.** 421 Bourke St ℗9670 1277.
Mon–Fri 10am–5.30pm, Sat 10am–3pm.

Esteemed antique and twentieth-century jewellery firm housed in an elegant former stock and station agent's premises. Upstairs a newly refurbished art gallery boasts works by Brett Whitely and Arthur Streeton, among others.

CLOTHES, SHOES AND JEWELLERY: CITY CENTRE

## Le Louvre

**Map 4, I4.** 74 Collins St ✆9650 1300.

Mon–Fri 9am–5.30pm.

Melbourne's A-list come here for eat-your-heart-out Gallianos, Givenchys and Richard Tylers, all hidden away behind closet doors. If the atmosphere doesn't intimidate you, the prices will.

## Makers Mark

**Map 4, I4.** 101 Collins St ✆9654 8488.

Mon–Thurs 9.30am–5pm, Fri 9.30am–7pm, Sat 10am–3pm.

Showcases the crop of the country's top designers, with monthly exhibitions featuring everything from opera rings to handcrafted pens.

## Mortisha's

**Map 4, F4.** Shop 8–10 Royal Arcade, off Bourke St ✆9654 1586.

Mon–Thurs 10am–5.30pm, Fri 10am–8.30pm, Sat 10am–5pm, Sun noon–4pm.

Superbly sewn velvet gowns, brocade coats and velour capes, plus accessories like glow-in-the-dark bats or handmade coffin handbags. Popular with Siouxsie Sioux wannabes and prospective brides, who queue up for wedding gowns from $300.

## Nike Superstore

**Map 4, G3.** Cnr Bourke & Swanston streets ✆8660 3333.

Mon–Wed & Sat 10am–6pm, Thurs 10am–7pm, Fri 10am–9pm, Sun 11am–6pm.

Nike's first superstore in the Southern Hemisphere – and only the second of its kind in the world – is a two-storey affair of immense video screens, footwear, apparel, accessories and equipment.

## Scanlan & Theodore

**Map 4, G4.** 279 Little Collins St ✆9650 6195.

Mon–Thurs 10am–6pm, Fri 10am–9pm, Sat 10am–5pm, Sun noon–5pm.

Women's clothing from Melbourne duo Fiona Scanlan and Gary Theodore, who specialize in contemporary classics in simple shades cut from couture-grade fabrics.

## Zambesi
**Map 4, H4.** 161 Collins St ☏9654 4299.
Mon–Thurs 10am–6pm, Fri 10am–8pm, Sat 10am–5pm.
Prestigious and stylish store showcasing the new millennium Gothic designs of New Zealand label Zambesi, with a solid range of imports – Dirk Bikkemberg, Helmut Lang and Costume National – on board.

**FITZROY**

## Dangerfield
**Map 5, G4.** 289 Brunswick St ☏9416 2032.
Mon–Thurs & Sat 10am–6pm, Fri 10am–9pm, Sun noon–6pm.
Reasonably priced club- and streetwear with just a touch of glamour. In front are crotch-clutching cords, US workwear and jewellery for guys and girls, while out back trained staff will staple rings to noses and navels at the drop of a Kangol cap.

## It Inc
**Map 5, G6.** 188 Brunswick St ☏9415 1339.
Mon–Wed & Sat 10am–6pm, Thurs 10am–7pm, Fri 10am–8pm, Sun 11am–6pm.
Eye-catching contemporary jewellery, designer clothing, period furniture and homewares spread over two floors of an enormous warehouse. Has another store in Greville Street, Prahran.

**SOUTH YARRA**

## Christopher Graf
**Map 6, D5.** 509 Chapel St ☏9826 4711.

CLOTHES, SHOES AND JEWELLERY: FITZROY, SOUTH YARRA

Mon–Sat 10am–6pm, Sun 12.30–5.30pm.

Innovative mix of "modern retro" clothing for women. Worth a visit just for the interior – a palette of hot pink, lime green and sharp turquoise colours given further oomph by the paintings of Melbourne artist Ian Russell.

## Collette Dinnigan

**Map 6, D5.** 553 Chapel St *©*9827 2111.

Mon–Thurs & Sat 10am–6pm, Fri 10am–7.30pm, Sun 1–5pm.

Intricate, opulent and expensive fare from the New Zealand-born, Sydney-based, Paris-feted designer extraordinaire.

## Country Road

**Map 6, D4.** Cnr Chapel St & Toorak Rd *©*9824 0133.

Mon–Thurs 9.30am–6pm, Fri 9am–9pm, Sat 9am–5pm, Sun noon–5pm.

Flagship store offering a small but considered selection of homewares, plus good basic clothing, shoes and accessories for men and women. Fashion foodies can inspect their purchases over coffee in the café upstairs.

## Dinosaur Designs

**Map 6, D5.** 562 Chapel St *©*9827 2600.

Mon–Sat 10am–6pm, Sun noon–5pm.

Chunky Flintstone-like resin and sterling silver jewellery, crockery and cult-in-the-making glassware. Affordable.

## Marcs

**Map 6, D6.** 459 Chapel St *©*9827 5290.

Mon–Thurs 10am–6pm, Fri 10am–9pm, Sat 9.30am–5.30pm, Sun noon–5pm.

Huge range of men's and women's wear, including T-shirts, button-downs, jeans, suits, knits and shoes. Does a good line in the maverick Italian fashion house Diesel.

CLOTHES, SHOES AND JEWELLERY: SOUTH YARRA

## Mooks

**Map 6, D6.** 491 Chapel St ✆9827 9966.
Mon–Thurs 9.30am–6pm, Fri 9.30am–9pm, Sat 9.30am–5.30pm,
Sun noon–5pm.
Covetable casual wear and accessories, including beanies, back-packs, quirky T-shirts and, topping the I-want-list, military drill cargo pants.

## Succhi

**Map 6, D6.** 500 Chapel St ✆9827 9137.
Mon–Thurs 10am–6pm, Fri 10am–9pm, Sat 10am–5pm, Sun noon–5pm.
Cave-like shoe shop good for imitation snakeskin shoes, high-heeled sneaker boots or, for those with sparrow-like ankles, fab sandals in metallic colours.

# CRAFTS AND SOUVENIRS

## Monds Gifts and Souvenirs

**Map 4, G4.** 133 Swanston St, City ✆9650 1739.
Mon–Thurs 9am–6pm, Fri 9am–9pm, Sat 9am–5.30pm, Sun 11am–5pm.
A riot of fair-dinkum Aussie souvenirs and tacky collectables. Come for the wood-and-plastic plaques with "Greetings from Melbourne", souvenir blowflies, non-PC Aboriginal dolls, or a bottle opener fashioned from a kangaroo's front leg.

# DEPARTMENT STORES

## Daimaru

**Map 4, F2.** Melbourne Central, 30 Lonsdale St, City ✆9922 1100.
Mon–Thurs & Sat 10am–6pm, Fri 10am–9pm, Sun 11am–6pm.
Japanese department store selling everything from men's and

women's wear to ceramics and Badtz-maru cartoon characters. Also has an excellent food hall where you can stop for a coffee and a snack; alternatively, you can browse the Cooksworld grocery, which does a good line in local and Asian tucker.

### David Jones
**Map 4, F4.** Bourke St Mall, City ☎9643 2222.
Mon–Thurs 9.30am–6pm, Fri 9.30am–9pm, Sat 9am–6pm, Sun 10am–6pm.
Upmarket retailer with stores either side of Bourke Street Mall. Renowned for its domestic and international designer range, beauty section and food hall.

### Myer
**Map 4, F4.** Bourke St Mall, City ☎9661 1111.
Mon–Wed, Sat & Sun 10am–6pm, Thurs 10am–7pm, Fri 10am–9pm.
Six floors spread across almost two blocks with perfumes, lipsticks, jewellery, homewares, electrical goods, local and imported fashion, books, records, and a giant sporting emporium.

# MARKETS

### Camberwell Market
Station St Carpark, Camberwell ☎9509 0535.
Sun 6am–12.30pm.
A Melbourne institution for over twenty years, this early-morning market is set in a car park that metamorphoses into a sea of trestle tables and racks buried under secondhand clothing, furniture, watches, records, cards, stuffed toys, curios – you name it. To get there, take tram #75 from Flinders Street.

### Chapel St Bazaar
**Map 6, C8.** 217 Chapel St, Prahran ☎9529 1727.

Daily 10am–6pm.

An Aladdin's Cave with over sixty dealers' stalls displaying everything from Coca-Cola memorabilia to Royal Doulton china. Eclectic, to say the least.

### St Kilda Arts and Craft Market
**Map 7, C7.** The Esplanade, St Kilda ℂ9386 1368.
Sun 10am–5pm.
Arts and crafts market that's been a major draw for locals and tourists for years, though you'll have to do a little rummaging before you find a bargain. Paintings, jewellery, leatherwork and didgeridoos are just some of the goods on offer.

### Queen Victoria Market
**Map 4, D1.** Cnr Victoria and Elizabeth streets, City ℂ9320 5822.
April–Oct Tues & Thurs 6am–2pm, Fri 6am–6pm, Sat 6am–3pm, Sun 9am–4pm; Nov–March same hours plus Wed 6.30–10.30pm.
Fantastically sensory experience combining the heady aromas of fresh produce with the musty whiff of secondhand clothing and century-old fittings.

# FOOD AND DRINK

### Becco
**Map 4, I3.** 11–25 Crossley St, off Bourke St, City ℂ9663 3000.
Daily 9am–10pm.
Food shop tagged on to the popular restaurant of the same name. Stocks chic food such as pinot sourdough bread, plus fresh fruit and veg, fish, meats and cheeses.

### King and Godfrey
**Map 5, D4.** 293 Lygon St, Carlton ℂ9347 1619.
Mon–Sat 9am–9pm.

FOOD AND DRINK

Established in 1870, this Carlton landmark boasts a great deli with Italian pasta, cheeses, breads, small meats, sweets, biscuits and crackers, plus a superb stock of wine, beer and spirits.

### Prahran Market

**Map 6, C7.** Commercial Rd, Prahran ©9522 3301.
Tues, Thurs & Sat dawn–5pm, Fri dawn–6pm.
Excellent, upmarket food emporium selling fish, meat, fruit, vegetables and delicatessen for the gourmand.

### Richmond Hill Café and Larder

**Map 3, F4.** 48 Bridge Rd, Richmond ©9421 2808.
Mon–Fri 10am–5pm, Sat 8am–5pm, Sun 9am–5pm.
Owned by well-known Australian chef and food writer Stephanie Alexander, with a good though pricey selection of groceries including bread, preserves, savouries, sweets and magnificent cheeses.

## RECORDS AND CDS

### Au Go Go

**Map 4, F3.** 349 Little Bourke St, City ©9670 0677.
Mon–Wed 9.30am–6pm, Thurs 9.30am–7pm, Fri 9.30am–9pm, Sat 9.30am–5.30pm.
Small but stacked with alternative CDs, vinyl collectables and imported fanzines like *Gearhead*. Upstairs houses secondhand records, T-shirts and posters.

### Basement Discs

**Map 4, F4.** 24 Block Place, off Little Collins St, City ©9654 1110.
Mon–Wed 10am–6pm, Thurs 10am–7pm, Fri 10am–9pm, Sat 9am–6pm, Sun 11am–6pm.
Discreet underground space with an exhilarating range of jazz

and blues displayed amidst inviting sofas, flower displays and excellent listening stations stocked with lollies.

## Discurio
**Map 4, F5.** 105 Elizabeth St, City ©9600 1488.
Mon–Thurs 9am–6pm, Fri 10am–11pm, Sat 9am–11pm, Sun 11am–6pm.
Broad range of jazz, R&B, soul, country, classical, world music and movie soundtracks in a sleek environment. You can also grab the latest issue of *Jazz Times* to go with your Coltrane.

## Gaslight Music
**Map 4, I3.** 85 Bourke St, City ©9650 9009.
Mon–Wed 10am–8pm, Thurs 10am–9pm, Fri 10am–11pm.
Renowned for its huge music collection, Gaslight gained infamy for its annual "Nude Day" celebrations (now sadly scrapped), when music buffs disrobed and browsed the racks in the buff.

## Missing Link
**Map 4, G5.** 262 Flinders Lane, City ©9654 5507.
Mon–Thurs 9.30am–6pm, Fri 9.30am–8pm, Sat 9.30am–5.30pm, Sun noon–5pm.
Punk, hardcore and indie music, plus a magazine section where you can case local fanzines and imported copies of *Punk Planet*.

## Rhythm and Soul Records
**Map 6, C8.** 128 Greville St, Prahran ©9510 8244.
Mon–Thurs 10.30am–7pm, Fri 10.30am–9pm, Sat 10.30am–6pm, Sun noon–5pm.
Aimed at boys and girls who love their beats phat and furious, this store is also where Melbourne and Australia's foremost DJs come to shop. Hours are flaky at best, so ring in advance.

RECORDS AND CDS

# Kids' Melbourne

**M**elbourne has a wide range of **activities for children**, from splashing about at the Melbourne Sports and Aquatic Centre, feeding the animals at the Collingwood Children's Farm, or checking out the exhibits at the Scienceworks and Toy museums. Other childproof diversions include amusement parlours, indoor play centres and recreational areas such St Kilda beach and foreshore, while most major parks have playgrounds.

## Creche facilities

**East Melbourne Child Care Co-operative**, Cnr Grey & Simpson streets, East Melbourne ℃9419 4301. Children up to 5 years. Book early as there may be a waiting list. Mon–Fri 7.30am–6pm; $36 full day, $18 half day.
**Kids on Collins**, Level 3, 600 Collins St ℃9629 4099. Children up to 6 years. Mon–Fri 7am–7.30pm; $65 full day, $40 half day or $10 per hour (minimum 2hr).
**Young Melbourne Child Care**, 77 Parks St, South Melbourne ℃9686 6366. Children 3 months to 5 years. Mon–Fri 7am–7pm; $47–55 full day, $30–44 half day (cost varies according to child's age).

Children are generally welcome in Melbourne's **cafés and restaurants**, especially the city's ethnic varieties. Most also provide child-sized portions and free "baby chinos", a local interpretation of a child's cappuccino – milk froth sprinkled with chocolate.

**Action plans** can be plotted by scouring *The Age*'s Friday entertainment supplement, "EG", which lists a range of family activities, and the "Applause" section in *The Sunday Age*. Another good resource is *Melbourne Events*, a free monthly calendar available from the Victorian Visitor Information Centre (see p.25), hotels and newsagents.

## INDOOR

### Australian Toy Museum

**Map 5, I6.** 174–180 Smith St, Collingwood ℭ9419 4138. Tram #86. Daily 10am–5pm; $6, under-16s $4, under-18 months free.

Historic building housing both frilly and functional toys from the 1880s to the present, including a permanent display of dolls and dolls' houses. There's also a garden with a miniature steam train and the *Magic Pudding Café*, with gourmet delights for children.

### Bernard's Magic Shop

**Map 4, F3.** 211 Elizabeth St, City ℭ9670 9270. Mon–Fri 9.30am–5.30pm, Sat 10am–3pm.

Chock-a-block with puzzles and games, plus silly glasses, exploding dog turds, jumbo tongues and plenty of copies of that perennial children's favourite, *Teach Yourself Rope Magic*.

### Classic Cinema

**Map 3, F7.** 9 Gordon St, Elsternwick ℭ9523 9739. Sandringham line from Flinders St Station to Elsternwick Station. Sat & Sun, daily during school holidays; $7.

INDOOR

The oldest continually running cinema in Melbourne and the perfect place for junior film buffs. Weekend "Kids Pics" sessions screen a mix of new releases and old favourites; new releases are also shown each day of the school holidays.

## Fun Factory

**Map 6, D4.** 257 Toorak Rd, South Yarra ©9826 8276.
Daily 10am–1am; free.

One of the largest indoor amusement centres in Melbourne, Fun Factory has Daytona racing machines, pinball, shooting and skill test games, plus pool tables, a rollerblade rink and dodgem cars.

## IMAX Theatre

**Map 5, E6.** Rathdowne St, Carlton ©9663 5454.
Films screened every hour Mon–Thurs & Sun 10am–10pm, Fri & Sat 10am–11pm; $13.95, under-15s $9.95 (extra $1 for 3-D films).

Adjoining the new Museum of Victoria (see p.69), IMAX has big comfy seats in which to enjoy 2-D and 3-D films (lasting 45–60min) on a giant eight-storey-high screen. The complex also has two candy bars, a licensed bar and restaurant.

## Melbourne Sports and Aquatic Centre

**Map 3, D5.** Aughtie Drive, Albert Park ©9926 1555. Tram #96.
Mon–Fri 6am–10pm, Sat & Sun 7am–8pm; $4, under-14s $3.

Part sporting facility, part fun park, the centre has a wave and toddlers' pool, water slide, pool garden and a diving complex. Childcare is available (Mon–Fri 9am–noon; ©9926 1533; $3/90min), and the centre also runs an excellent day-long school-holiday programme, "Planet Sport", for 5- to 12-year-olds ($25/day), and a Saturday-morning kids' session (9–10am; $8) with games, sports and arts and crafts activities.

## Pipsqueak

**Map 6, G9.** 811 High St, Armadale ℗9500 9181. Tram #6 or the Frankston line from Flinders St Station.

Mon–Thurs 9.30am–5.30pm, Fri 9.30am–6pm, Sat 9.30am–3pm.

This shop's wardrobe resembles a Lilliputian collection fresh from the catwalks of Paris and Milan, with the extravagant partywear upstairs being the ultimate turn-on for little lords and ladyships.

## Red Bear's Playhouse

**Map 4, D9.** 134 York St, South Melbourne ℗9645 0788. Tram #1 or #12.

Mon–Thurs 9.30am–6.30pm, Fri 9.30am–8pm, Sat & Sun 8.30am–8pm; $5.

Australia's largest indoor play centre has piles of plastic tubing shaped into tunnels, ladders and miniature junkyards, which are suitable for all ages. Parents can avail themselves of cappuccinos, telly and free newspapers and magazines.

## Scienceworks

**Map 3, A5.** 2 Booker St, Spotswood ℗9392 4800. Williamstown and Werribee lines from Flinders St Station to Spotswood Station.

Daily 10am–4.30pm; $8, under-15s $4, under-4s free.

Learn about science and technology through a series of interactive exhibitions on sport, insects and, erm, contraception. There's also a digital planetarium and plenty of hands-on activities, as well as school-holiday programmes on the human mind and body, and touring exhibitions (see also p.87).

**OUTDOOR**

## Collingwood Children's Farm

**Map 3, G3.** St Heliers St, Abbotsford ℗9205 5469. Epping line from Flinders St Station to Victoria Park Station.

Daily 9am–5pm; $4, under-14s $2.

OUTDOOR

Feed animals like "Lazy Charlie", a Wessex saddleback, other porkers and piglets, or goats (daily 9–10am). Kids can also help with farm chores, have a go at milking a cow or do a farm tour and learn about plants and animals. Family days (first day of the month) include horse treks, and have a yummy farm lunch thrown in as well.

## Luna Park
**Map 7, D8.** 18 Lower Esplanade, St Kilda ℗9525 5033.
Fri 7–11pm, Sat 2–6pm & 7–11pm, Sun 2–6pm; free.
Old-fashioned roller-coaster, ferris wheel and ghost-train rides, plus newer harum-scarum attractions like the "Gravitron", which will have you and your child hanging on for dear life.

## Melbourne Zoo
**Map 3, D2.** Elliot Ave, Parkville ℗9285 9300. Tram #55, #56 or #68.
Daily 9am–5pm; $14, under-15s $7, under-4s free.
Apart from watching monkeys scratching their privates, children can line up for daily meet-the-keeper sessions (wombats 11.15am, seals 2pm, pelicans 2.30pm, penguins 3.30pm; free) or go on twilight tours (Fri–Sun in Feb and the first weekend in March; free) for better views of the nocturnal animals. Other highlights include National Zoo Month (Oct) and the Freddo Frog Festival (Nov), as well as various school-holiday children's activities (see also p.71).

## Polly Woodside Maritime Museum
**Map 4, C7.** Lorimer St East, Southbank ℗9699 9760.
Daily 10am–4pm; $7, under-16s $4, under-5s free.
Clamber over the tall ship *Polly Woodside* (see p.61), wander through nautical displays and relics, then venture to the playground with its wooden pirate ship. From the museum, cruises go to Port Melbourne and Williamstown, and there's a water taxi to Southbank.

OUTDOOR

## Royal Botanic Gardens

**Map 4, L9.** Birdswood Ave, South Yarra.

Daily: April–Oct 7.30am–5.30pm; Nov–March 7.30am–8.30pm; free.

Young ones can feed the swans or wander along winding leafy paths. School-holiday programmes are especially fun, as they allow children to dig for worms, hunt for slugs and spiders, or do a spot of face painting (under-15s $10, accompanying adults free).

## Victoria's Open Range Zoo

**Map 2, F4.** K. Rd, Werribee ℗9731 9600. Werribee line from Flinders St Station to Werribee Station.

Daily 10am–5pm; $14, under-14s $7, under-3s free.

Great place for watching a bunch of African wildlife (rhinos, hippos, zebras and giraffes) cavorting in their natural environment. Highlights include a bus safari (first at 10.30am, last at 3.40pm), the thirty-minute Volcanic Plains Walking Trail, and the Savannah Discovery Centre (see also p.92).

# Directory

**Airlines** Air France ✆9920 3868; Air New Zealand ✆13/2476; Alitalia ✆9600 0511; American Airlines ✆1300/650 747; Ansett Australia ✆13/1300; British Airways ✆9603 1133; Canadian Airlines ✆1300/655 767; Cathay Pacific ✆13/1747; Garuda ✆1300/365 330; Japan Airlines ✆9654 2733; KLM ✆9654 5222; Lauda Air ✆1800/642 438; Malaysia Airlines ✆13/2627; Qantas (domestic) ✆13/1313, (international) ✆13/1211; Singapore Airlines ✆13/1011; Thai Airways ✆9650 5066; United Airlines ✆13/1777.

**Airport enquiries** ✆9297 1600.

**Airport tax** The international departure tax from Melbourne's Tullamarine Airport of $27 is included in your airline ticket.

**American Express** 233–239 Collins St (Mon–Fri 8.30am–5.30pm, Sat 9am–noon; ✆9633 6333).

**Banks and exchange** Standard banking hours are generally Monday to Friday 9.30am to 4pm (Fri until 5pm), although some branches of the Bank of Melbourne, including the one at 142 Elizabeth St, are open on Saturday (9am–noon). Most banks have 24-hour automatic teller machines (ATMs), which accept a variety of cash, credit and debit cards. There are several foreign exchange desks at the airport. In town, try Thomas Cook, 257 Collins St (Mon–Fri 8.45am–5.15pm, Sat 9am–5pm); other branches are at 330 Collins St and 261 Bourke St.

**Bicycles** Bikes and cycling equipment can be rented from Bicycle Victoria, 19 O'Connell St, North Melbourne (☎9328 3000); Borsari Cycles, 193 Lygon St, Carlton (☎9347 4100); Fitzroy Cycles, 224 Swanston St (☎9639 3511); Freedom Machine, 401 Chapel St, South Yarra (☎9827 5014); Hire a Bicycle, beneath Princes Bridge (☎9758 7811); St Kilda Cycles, 11 Carlisle St, St Kilda (☎9534 3074).

**Car rental** The main rental companies are Avis ☎9663 6366; Budget ☎13/2727 or ☎9203 4844; Delta ☎13/1390 or ☎9662 2366; Hertz ☎13/3039; and Thrifty ☎9663 5200. Used-car companies with cheaper rates include Backpacker Car Rentals ☎9329 4411; Rent-A-Bomb ☎9428 0088; and Ugly Duckling ☎9525 4010. Campervans are available from Brits:Australia ☎9483 1888 and Maui Campervans ☎9484 7740.

**Disabled travellers** The Travellers Aid Society of Victoria, 2nd Floor, 169 Swanston St (Mon–Fri 9am–5pm, Sat & Sun 11am–4pm; ☎9654 2600), provides information and assistance for the disabled. It has another branch at Spencer Street Station (Mon–Fri 7.30am–7.30pm, Sat & Sun 7.30–11.30am; ☎9670 2873). Other resources include the Disability Resource Centre, 306 Johnston St, Abbotsford (☎9419 5535); Disability Information Victoria (☎1300/650 865; *www.disabilityinfo.org.au*); Para Quad Association, 208 Wellington St, Collingwood (☎9415 1200); and Travellers Aid Disability Access Service (TADAS) (phone only: ☎9654 7690). Assistance at metropolitan, suburban, country and interstate stations can be obtained by calling the

Met Information Centre (℃13/1638). The Melbourne City Council produces a free mobility map of the CBD showing accessible routes and toilets in the city centre, available from the front desk of the Melbourne Town Hall. For wheelchair-accessible taxis, call Central Booking Service (℃1300/364 050).

**Electricity** 240 volts, AC 50 cycles, with three-pronged plugs the norm. Most hotels have provision for AC 110 volts. British and North American devices will require a transformer and adapter, available at most leading hotels or hardware and electrical stores.

**Email and Internet access** There are plenty of cybercafés throughout Melbourne. Most charge around $10 per hour online and there's usually an extra charge for printing out emails (around 25c for a laser printout). Melbourne's best cybercafés include *Myer Internet Café*, on Level 4 of the Myer department store, Bourke Street Mall (Mon–Wed & Sat 10am–6pm, Thurs & Fri 10am–7pm); *Café Wired*, 363 Clarendon St, South Melbourne (Mon–Fri 9am–9pm, Sat noon–6pm), and *Surf-Net City Café*, 140 St Kilda Road, St Kilda (Mon–Fri 9.30am–9pm, Sat noon–6pm).

**Embassies** Austria, 107 Wellington St, Windsor (℃9533 6900); Canada, 1st Floor, 123 Camberwell Rd, Hawthorn East (℃9811 9999); China, 77 Irving Rd, Toorak (℃9804 3683); France, 492 St Kilda Rd (℃9820 0921); Germany, 480 Punt Rd, South Yarra (℃9828 6888); Greece, 34 Queens Rd (℃9866 4524); Hungary, 115 Collins St (℃9650 8636); Indonesia, 72 Queens Rd (℃9525 2755); Italy, 509 St Kilda Rd (℃9867 5744); Japan, 360 Elizabeth St (℃9639 3244); Malaysia, 492 St Kilda Rd (℃9867 5339); Norway, Suite 2, 416 High St, Kew (℃9853 3122); Spain, 540 Elizabeth St (℃9347 1966); Sweden, 61 Riggall St, Broadmeadows (℃9301 1888); Switzerland, 420 St Kilda

Rd (✆9867 2266); Thailand, 277 Flinders Lane (✆9650 1714); UK, 17th Floor, 90 Collins St (✆9650 4155); USA, 553 St Kilda Rd (✆9526 5900).

**Emergencies** Ring ✆000 for fire, police or ambulance.

**Hospitals and clinics** Major hospitals include the Alfred Hospital, Commercial Rd, Prahran (✆9276 2000), Royal Children's Hospital, Flemington Rd, Parkville (✆9345 5522), Royal Melbourne Hospital, Grattan St, Parkville (✆9342 7000), and St Vincent's Hospital, Victoria Parade, Fitzroy (✆9807 2211). Useful clinics include the Travellers Medical and Vaccination Centre (TMVC), 2nd Floor, 393 Little Bourke St (✆9602 5788), or the free Melbourne Sexual Health Centre, 580 Swanston St, Carlton (✆9347 0244 or ✆1800/032 017).

**Immigration office** Visas can be extended at the Department of Immigration and Multicultural Affairs at 2 Lonsdale St (Mon, Tues, Thurs & Fri 9am–4pm, Wed 9am–3am; ✆13/1881). You'll need to fill in Form 601; make sure you apply at least a month before your visa expires, as the process can take some time.

**Laundries** Most hostels and hotels have their own laundry. Commercial laundries include City Edge Laundrette, 39 Errol St, North Melbourne (daily 6am–11pm); The Soap Opera Laundry & Cafe, 128 Bridport St, Albert Park (Mon–Fri 7.30am–9.30pm, Sat & Sun 8am–9pm), and Blessington Street Launderette, 22 Blessington St, St Kilda (daily 7.30am–9pm).

**Left luggage** There are lockers at Flinders Street Station (daily 9.30am–4.30pm; $2.10), Spencer Street Station (daily 6am–10pm; $2) and Travellers Aid, 169 Swanston St (Mon–Fri 9am–5pm; $1–1.50); another branch of Travellers Aid is at Spencer Street Station. There are also lockers at the airport in the international terminal (24hr; $4–8).

**Lost property** Trains: Bayside Trains ℂ9610 5854, Flinders Street Station ℂ9610 7512, Hillside Trains ℂ9610 7512. Trams: Swanston Trams ℂ9610 3383, Yarra Trams ℂ9610 3382. For buses and taxis, call the respective companies in the White or Yellow Pages.

**Newspapers and magazines** Melbourne's two daily newspapers are *The Age* (its Sunday edition is called *The Sunday Age*) and the tabloid *Herald Sun*. Two national newspapers are also available – the Rupert Murdoch-owned *Australian* (Mon–Sat) and the *Australian Financial Review* (Mon–Sat). Magazines to look out for include *Melbourne Events*, a free monthly listings publication; *The Big Issue*, which supports Melbourne's homeless; and *Beat* and *Inpress*, two free and informative indie music magazines. Domestic and international publications can also be perused at the State Library (see p.42) or bought from major newsagents such as McGills, 187 Elizabeth St.

**Parking** Parking is often hard to find in the city centre, even though there are over 10,000 metered spaces and 40,000 off-street car spaces. Meters are mostly coin-operated; for car-park spaces, expect to pay around $5 an hour, or $10–15 daily.

**Pharmacies** Robert Jenyns Pharmacy, 517 St Kilda Rd, City (Mon–Fri 8.30am–9pm, Sat 10am–6pm, Sun 10am–3pm); Rodney P. Cohen Pharmacy, 173 Acland St, St Kilda (Mon–Fri 9am–7pm, Sat 9am–6pm, Sun 10am–6pm).

**Police** Call ℂ11 444, or ℂ000 for emergencies.

**Post offices** Melbourne's General Post Office (ℂ9203 3044), on the corner of Elizabeth and Bourke streets, is open Monday to Friday 8.15am to 5.30pm, and Saturday 10am to 1pm. Suburban post offices are generally open Monday to Friday 9am to 5pm. Stamps can also be purchased from Australia Post shops, newsagents, and some pharmacies and milk bars, as well as from the National Philatelic Centre, Ground Floor, 321 Exhibition St (©9204 7736). Stamps cost 45c for a letter within Australia; 75–85c for a letter to New Zealand and Southeast Asia; $1.05 to the USA and Canada; and $1.20 to the UK and Europe. Postcards within Australia and to New Zealand and Asia are 5c cheaper than standard letters; 95c to the USA and Canada; and $1 to the UK and Europe.

**Public holidays** New Year's Day; Australia Day (January 26); Labour Day (first or second Monday in March); Easter (Good Friday, Easter Saturday and Monday, usually late March or early April); Anzac Day (April 25); Queen's Birthday (second Monday in June); Melbourne Cup Day (first Tuesday in November); Christmas Day; Boxing Day.

**Public toilets** See p.32.

**Taxis** Major firms include Arrow Taxi Services (©13/2211); Black Cabs Combined (©13/2227); Embassy Taxis (©13/1755); and Silver Top Taxi Service (©13/1008).

**Telephones** Local calls from a payphone cost a minimum of 40c. Many phones also accept phonecards, which can be purchased from Telstra shops, post offices, duty-free stores and newsagents. Melbourne's General Post Office has several payphones plus a range of directories, including White and Yellow Pages. Overseas calls can be made by dialling 0011 (the overseas access code), followed by the country code, area code and required number. The cheapest time to make international calls is at off-peak periods (Mon–Fri 6pm–midnight, Sat & Sun). For more information, see the

DIRECTORY |

back of the White Pages L–Z. For emergencies phone
Ⓒ000; for operator services, call Ⓒ1223 (local, country and
interstate numbers), Ⓒ1225 (international numbers;
reverse-charge calls) or Ⓒ12550 from a private or public
payphone (both domestic and international). If you want to
know how much an interstate or international call will cost,
ring Ⓒ12552. The prefixes Ⓒ13 or 1300 indicate a toll-free
number. The area code for domestic calls to Melbourne
from outside the city is Ⓒ03. If ringing from overseas, dial
the international access code followed by 61 3, then the
number.

**Television and radio** The government-funded Australian
Broadcasting Corporation (ABC), the national broadcaster,
provides Channel 2. Another government-sponsored station
is the excellent multicultural Special Broadcasting Service
(SBS) on Channel 28. Australia's major commercial stations
are Channel 7, Channel 9 and Channel 10. The ABC provides a range of national radio channels (both AM and FM),
including Radio National (frequency 621), 3LO (774) and
Triple J (107.5), an alternative station geared for younger
listeners. Melbourne also has a host of commercial radio
stations, and more community stations per head than any
other city in the world – try 3RRR (102.7) and 3PBS
(106.7), both of which showcase new independent music.

**Ticket agencies** Tickets for festivals, concerts, sporting
events, and film and theatre performances can be obtained
through Ticketmaster (Ⓒ13/6100), Ticketek Victoria
(Ⓒ13/2849) and Half-Tix (Ⓒ9650 9420).

**Time** Melbourne follows Australian Eastern Standard
Time (AEST), half an hour ahead of South Australia and
the Northern Territory, two hours ahead of Western
Australia, ten hours ahead of Greenwich Mean Time
(GMT) and fifteen hours ahead of US Eastern Standard

Time. Clocks are put forward one hour in November and back again in March for daylight savings.

**Travel agents** Backpackers Travel Centre, Shop 19, Centreway Arcade, 258 Flinders Lane (℃9654 8477); Flight Centre, 19 Bourke St (℃9650 2899); STA Travel, 208 Swanston Street (℃9639 0599, telephone bookings ℃1300/360 960); Student Uni Travel, Shop 4, 440 Elizabeth St (℃9662 4666); YHA Travel, 205 King St (℃9670 9611).

# BEYOND THE CITY

# Mornington Peninsula and Phillip Island

J ust south of Melbourne, the **Mornington Peninsula** is a favourite seaside holiday destination boasting elegant beachfront towns like Sorrento and Portsea, prolific bush and native wildlife in the Mornington Peninsula National Park, excellent surfing and swimming spots, lookouts, walking trails and wineries. Southeast of here is scenic **Phillip Island**, whose main tourist drawcard is the Penguin Parade, where hordes of penguins wade ashore each evening at sunset.

## MORNINGTON PENINSULA

Map 2, F5–G5.

Curving around Port Phillip Bay from Frankston to Point Nepean, the **Mornington Peninsula** has traditionally been popular with Victoria's less affluent holidaymakers, whose caravans and tents dot the peninsula's tea tree-studded foreshore, although the towns of Sorrento and Portsea at the tip of the peninsula remain the preserve of Melbourne's wealthy, many of whom decamp here for extended periods during the summer months. Water-based activities like surfing and swimming with dolphins are the main attractions, along with some excellent wineries, walking trails, sweeping views and historical sites.

Regular **bus services** to all major towns on the Mornington Peninsula operate from Frankston, which is on the Frankston line from Flinders Street Station. In Frankston, Peninsula Bus Lines (©9786 7088) and Portsea Passenger Services (©5986 5666) operate services from departure bays immediately outside Frankston Station. Visitors can also purchase a package-deal "Round the Bay in a Day" ticket ($36) from main train stations, allowing you to circle Port Phillip Bay on a combination of train, bus and ferry; contact V/Line Holidays for details (©9619 8080). If you're travelling **by car**, take the Nepean Highway from Melbourne and then the Mornington turn-off.

## Frankston to Cape Shanck

The peninsula starts at **Frankston**, 40km south of Melbourne, beyond which the peninsula's western coast is a succession of beaches, all crowded and traffic-snarled in summer. Twelve kilometres further on, the old fishing port of **Mornington** has few attractions, although the lookout at the Matthew Flinders obelisk at Schnapper Point has great views. Beyond here, the coast road leads to **Dromana**, where seaside development begins in earnest. Inland from Dromana, the granite outcrop of **Arthur's Seat** rises to a height of 305m, providing breathtaking views of Port Phillip Bay. A chair lift makes the trip to the top, leaving from the picnic area on Arthur's Seat Road, just off the Mornington Peninsula Freeway (Sept–June daily 11am–5pm; July & Aug Sat & Sun 11am–5pm, weather permitting; $7.50 return)

Interspersed among the peninsula's bushland and orchards are over twenty **wineries**, which produce superb, if pricey, pinot noir and shiraz. The most notable wine-growing area is **Red Hill**, southeast of Arthur's Seat. Overlooking the calm waters of Western Port Bay, Red Hill Estate (daily 11am–5pm; ℗5989 2838) has tastings, sales and light lunches, with restaurant dining on Friday and Saturday evenings.

Further south, on the ocean side of the peninsula, **Cape Shanck** is the site of an 1859 lighthouse from where a timber staircase and boardwalk lead from the dramatic basalt cliffs down to the sea along a narrow neck of land, providing magnificent coastal views.

## Sorrento

Near the tip of the peninsula, **Sorrento** is the area's oldest and most affluent town (and recent attempts by wealthier residents to fence off sections of the beach for their private use have not made the hoi polloi feel any more welcome). The smell of money is everywhere – in the wide, tree-lined residential streets, the spectacular cliff-top properties hidden behind high fences, and in the town centre's abundant antique shops, galleries, cafés and restaurants.

......................................................................................

**Swimming with dolphins has become one of the area's prime attractions. One of the longest-serving operators, Moonraker, departs twice daily from the Sorrento pier (Sept–May 9am & 1pm; ℗5984 4211; $50 for swimmers, $25 for observers).**

......................................................................................

SORRENTO

The **Collins Settlement Historic Site** (open access 24hr), 3km southeast in Sullivan Bay, is where in 1803 Captain David Collins attempted the first permanent European settlement of the Melbourne area, only to abandon the site less than a year later because of its chronic lack of water. The tourist office (daily 10am–4pm; ℂ5984 5678) at 2 St Aubins Way has information about the failed settlement, and on the life of the local Aborigines who lived in the area previously.

From Sorrento, **ferries** run across the mouth of the bay to Queenscliff on the Bellarine Peninsula (see p.251), departing every two hours from 8am to 6pm, returning from Queenscliff every two hours from 7am to 5pm. There are additional later services (no set times) on Friday and Sunday during peak periods. It's $34/14 each way for cars/motorbikes, plus $3 per passenger; pedestrians pay $7. Bookings are not necessary unless your vehicle is longer than 5.5m (ℂ5984 1602).

## Portsea and the Mornington Peninsula National Park

A few kilometres further on, **Portsea** is quieter than Sorrento, with the houses of its wealthy inhabitants contentedly secluded in the coastal scrub. In summer, Front Beach and Shelley Beach are crowded with beautiful people, while on the other shore Portsea Ocean Beach attracts surfers and hang-gliders. There are several stunning **walking trails** nearby – one leads to Cheviot Hill, from where you can see Cheviot Beach, the spot where Australian Prime Minister Harold Holt disappeared, presumed drowned, in 1967.

Beyond Portsea at the tip of the peninsula, **Point Nepean** is where the **Mornington Peninsula National Park** begins, extending along 40km of the peninsula's ocean-facing coastline. The park is covered with original bushland, and is home to kangaroos, bandicoots and echidnas, as well as many species of forest and ocean birds. At the point of the peninsula, historic **Fort Nepean** has tunnels, fortifications, glorious views of the Port Phillip Heads and walking tracks leading off into secluded bushland.

# PHILLIP ISLAND

**Map 2, G5.**

Just under two hours' drive from Melbourne, and connected to the mainland by bridge, **Phillip Island** is one of Victoria's most popular destinations, largely on account of the Penguin Parade, although the island also has large colonies of seals and koalas, fine coastal scenery and good swimming beaches.

Massive investment has boosted the Phillip Island's infrastructure in recent years, but getting around still poses problems. From Spencer Street Station, there is a daily V/Line **bus** to Cowes (Mon–Fri 3.50pm, Sat 9.36am & 5.30pm, Sun 9.05am & 5.05pm; travelling time 3hr 20min; $13.80 one way), the main settlement on the island, but little public transport once you get there. If you're short of time, a bus **tour** from Melbourne is a good way to see the penguins, and most also take in other island attractions as well. Details of operators are available from the Victorian Visitor Information Centre (see p.25). Access **by car** is via the South Gippsland and Bass highways.

## Penguin Parade

Daily at sunset; $9.50; for credit-card bookings, call the Phillip Island Nature Park ©5956 8300. Information, maps and tickets for the Penguin Parade are available from the tourist office in Newhaven, the first town on the island as you cross over the bridge from the mainland (daily 9am–5pm; ©5956 7447).

The enormously popular **Penguin Parade** takes place at Summerland Beach, near the western end of the island. Each evening at sunset, several thousand cute Little Penguins (sometimes known as "Fairy Penguins") emerge from the surf and waddle to their nesting areas on the foreshore. It's an impressive spectacle, although the penguins are almost outnumbered by the hordes of tourists who look down from concrete stands onto the floodlit beach. The parade takes about fifty minutes, after which you can move onto the extensive boardwalks over the burrows and continue watching the penguins' antics for several more hours. The crowds are smaller in winter, but rug up, as winds blowing in from Bass Strait can make the experience unbearably chilly.

Just above Summerland Beach, the excellent **Penguin Parade Visitor Centre** (daily 10am–7.30pm) offers presentations on penguins and other local fauna, plus meals and souvenirs.

## Around the island

A few kilometres beyond the Penguin Parade, at the western end of the island, the **Seal Rocks Sea Life Centre** (daily 10am–dusk; $15) at Point Grant boasts cafés, souvenir shops, interactive displays on local marine life and glass-walled viewing areas from which to observe the resident seals. Below here, the **Nobbies** are two huge rock stacks with stunning views across to Cape Shanck on the Mornington Peninsula, while **Seal Rocks** are known for their thriving colony of Australian fur seals.

Other highlights of the island include the **Koala Conservation Centre** on the Phillip Island Tourist Road between Newhaven and Cowes (daily 10am–5.30pm; $5), where elevated walkways allow visitors to observe these tree-top dwellers at close range, and **Cowes** itself, which has a wide sheltered beach and a lively Sunday market.

# The Dandenong Ranges

The peaceful and inviting hills of the **Dandenong Ranges,** 30km east of Melbourne, have been a popular weekend retreat for city dwellers for over a century. Modest in height (their most elevated point, Mt Dandenong, is only 633m), they are famous for their undulating woodland scenery, interesting fauna and excellent walking possibilities. There are also a few worthwhile tourists attractions: the historic **Puffing Billy** steam train; the lovely gardens and sculptures of the **William Ricketts Sanctuary** and the towering mountain ash trees and varied wildlife of the **Dandenong Ranges National Park**.

Parts of the Dandenongs are easily accessible by **public transport**. Trains run from Flinders Street Station to Upper Ferntree Gully and Belgrave, from where buses go to many other destinations in the ranges, including the villages of Olinda, Emerald, Gembrook, Sassafras, Kallista, Monbulk and Menzies Creek – for more details, contact the Met Information Centre (℧13/1638). If you're travelling **by car**, a good route to take is the Burwood Highway to Upper Ferntree Gully, from where you're ideally placed to explore the area – the drive from Upper Ferntree Gully via the Mount Dandenong Tourist Road to the quaint villages of Sassafras and Olinda and the Mount Dandenong Observatory is particularly good.

The best place for **tourist information** is the tourist office at 1211 Burwood Highway in Ferntree Gully (9am–5pm; ℅9758 7522), which has walking guides and maps, and can help with a range of accommodation. If you're travelling by train, get off at the Upper Ferntree Gulley Station; the office is a five-minute signposted walk from there. In the city, the Victorian Visitor Information Centre (see p.25) has the *Yarra Valley, Dandenongs and the Ranges* brochure, which has listings of events, attractions and accommodation, plus a map and instructions on how to get to the Dandenong Ranges from Melbourne.

# PUFFING BILLY

**Map 2, G4.** Old Monbulk Road. Daily, usually at 10.30am, 12.30pm & 2.30pm; $14.50 return. For inquiries, bookings, and timetable and fare information, call ℅9754 6800.

Perhaps the most enjoyable and comfortable introduction to the Dandenongs is by the **Puffing Billy**, a narrow-gauge steam railway which has run more or less continuously since entering service in the early 1900s. It starts a short signposted walk from Belgrave Station then winds the 24km to Gembrook, with other stops at Menzies Creek, Emerald and Lakeside. If you want to break up the two-hour round trip, Emerald Lake Park (adjacent to Emerald Station) has paddle boats, bush walks, a water slide and swimming pool, kiosk and tearoom, as well as free picnic and barbecue facilities, although it's a rather shabby and clamorous place, especially on the weekends, when it's full of children preternaturally interested in running away from their parents.

To get to Puffing Billy, take a **train** to Belgrave, 40km east of Melbourne, from Flinders Street Station. Trains run daily (Mon–Fri 5.20am–12.05am & Sat 6.09am–12.05am on the Belgrave line, Sun 7.34am–11.30pm on the Lilydale line; change at Lilydale); the journey takes just under an hour.

# DANDENONG RANGES NATIONAL PARK

**Map 2, G3–G4.**
Stretching north of the railway line between Upper Ferntree Gulley and Gembrook, the mountain ash forests of the **Dandenong Ranges National Park** are well worth a visit, as are the tourist-friendly villages and townships of Olinda, Sassasfras, Kallista, Monbulk and Menzies Creek in the same area.

The park is divided into three areas, of which **Sherbrooke Forest** (a 15min signposted walk from Belgrave Station) and **Ferntree Gulley National Park** (a 5min walk from Upper Ferntree Gulley Station) are the most accessible. **Sherbrooke Falls** is a popular destination within the Sherbrooke Forest section – an easy 2.5-kilometre return walk signposted from Sherbrooke Picnic Ground, off Sherbrooke Road (reached from the Mt Dandenong Tourist Road). It's also one of the few places in Victoria where you might get to see the beautiful but elusive lyrebird – named for the lyre-shaped tails of the male – in the wild; you can try your luck by taking the magnificent seven-kilometre **Eastern Sherbrooke Lyrebird circuit walk** (information and maps available from the Dandenong tourist office in Ferntree Gully, as well as from Parks Victoria).

## North to the William Ricketts Sanctuary

The **Alfred Nicholas Memorial Garden** (daily 10am–5pm; $4) in nearby Sherbrooke has bush walks and a stunning mix of indigenous and exotic plants. Heading north, the village of Olinda is home to the **National Rhododendron Gardens** (daily 10am–5pm; $6.50), featuring thousands of rhododendrons, camellias and azaleas, and the **R.J. Hamer Forest Arboretum** (open access 24hr; free), a vast expanse of woodlands with over 150 species of native and exotic trees. Just off the Mount Dandenong Tourist Road towards the top end of the park is the **William Ricketts Sanctuary** (daily 10am–5pm; $5). Ricketts, a sculptor, worked here for many years until his death in 1993 at the age of 94; set within the sanctuary are some of the kiln-fired clay figures he created out of the experience of living among Aboriginal people in central Australia.

# The Yarra Valley

**H**alf an hour's drive northeast of the city, the **Yarra Valley** is home to more than thirty of Victoria's best wineries. Visitors with parched palates flock to the region throughout the year, but if you can drag yourself away from the cellar door, there are also plenty of non-alcoholic attractions, from scenic Kinglake National Park, north of the valley, to Healesville Sanctuary, an outstanding wildlife park, to the south. In and around you'll find a healthy selection of walking and cycling tracks in the magnificent Yarra Ranges National Park, hot-air ballooning in pretty Yarra Glen, Aboriginal history at the Galeena Beek Living Cultural Centre, and quality local produce from a variety of food and retail outlets.

The southwestern gateway to the Yarra Valley is the Melbourne outer suburb of **Lilydale** on the Maroondah Highway, and a one-hour train journey from Flinders Street Station on the Lilydale line. From Lilydale, bus #685 travels to the valley's two main townships: **Yarra Glen** (to the north) and **Healesville** (to the northeast). If you're coming by car, take the Eastern Freeway from Fitzroy to Springvale Road and turn right; the Maroondah Highway to Lilydale is about 3km south down Springvale Road.

Before you go, get a copy of *The Yarra Valley Tourist Route Map & Locality Guide* from the Victorian Visitor

Information Centre in the Melbourne Town Hall. In addition to a comprehensive map of the valley, it lists wineries, recreational activities, tours, festivals, attractions and places to eat. The *Yarra Valley Accommodation Guide* is also handy if you intend staying here.

# LILYDALE AND BEYOND

**Map 2, G3.** Lilydale line from Flinders St Station.

Drab and uninspiring, **Lilydale** is around an hour's drive east of Melbourne. The only attraction of note is the **Museum of Lillydale** at 33 Castella Street (Wed–Sun 11am–4pm; ℂ9739 7230; $3), which has everything you might wish to know about famous Australian soprano Dame Nellie Melba, who, when she wasn't touring, spent much of her time in the small township of **Coldstream**, just north of Lilydale. Her former home, Coombe Cottage, is set behind a vast hedge at the junction of Melba and Maroondah highways, and is now privately owned.

Heading north along the Melba Highway, you'll come to the **Yarra Valley Dairy** on McMeikans Road in Yering (Mon–Thurs & Sun 10.30am–5pm, Fri & Sat 10.30am–10pm; ℂ9739 0023). If you take your cheese seriously, this is the place for you, with everything from washed rind to Persian fetta and goat's cheeses. Beyond here, the township of **Yarra Glen** lies in the centre of the valley. In Bell Street, the main drag, you'll find the National Trust-

---

**Sunrise balloon flights, followed by a champagne breakfast at a local winery, are a popular way of seeing the valley. Contact Go Wild Ballooning (ℂ9890 0339) or Global Ballooning (ℂ1800/627 661) for details. Packages cost around $200.**

---

# Yarra Valley wineries

The **Yarra Valley** – Melbourne's so-called "grape escape" – is a favourite day-trip from the city, especially for those wanting a tipple and a chance to meet local winemakers. The region's highest concentration of wineries is found in the triangle formed by Yarra Glen, Healesville and Dixon's Creek. Around Dixon's Creek you can hop from one vineyard to the next – **Fergusson's**, **De Bortoli**, **Allinda** and **Lovey's Estate**, among them. Between Healesville and Coldstream are a cluster of fine wineries on or near the Maroondah Highway. Closest to Healesville is the award-winning **Eyton On Yarra Winery** (daily 10am–5pm), a cool, architect-designed winery with a large and airy restaurant that relies almost entirely on superb local produce, while the nearby **Oakridge Estate** (daily 10am–5pm) is renowned for its wines and innovative food. On the highway, **Domaine Chandon** (daily 10.30am–4.30pm), owned by Möet et Chandon, has arguably Australia's best *méthode champenoise* sparkling wine, and a stunning main building that's every bit as good as the product. Other good places include **Yarra Burn Winery** at 60 Settlement Road in Yarra Junction (daily 10am–6pm) to the south of the valley; the **Kellybrook Winery** on Fulford Road in Wonga Park (Mon–Sat 9am–6pm, Sun 11am–6pm), the region's oldest licensed winery, at the valley's western end; and, just south of Yarra Glen, **Yering Station** (daily 10am–5pm), site of the valley's first planting in 1838, and one of its great vineyards.

One of the best times to visit the Yarra Valley is during the annual **Grape Grazing Festival** (first weekend in March). For winery tours of the region, contact Link Tours (©9699 8422), Victorian Winery Tours (©9621 2089) and Yarra Valley Winery Tours (©5962 3870).

classified **Yarra Glen Grand**, a beautifully restored nine-teenth-century hotel. On the first Sunday of the month from October to June, the **Yarra Glen Craft Market** (9am–2pm) is held at the Yarra Glen Racecourse, 200m east of Bell Street.

Just north of Yarra Glen on the Melba Highway, the National Trust's **Gulf Station** (Wed–Sun & public holidays 10am–4pm; $7) is a large pastoral property which was once home to the Bell family, Scottish immigrants who lived here from 1854. There are ten hand-built farm buildings from the 1850s, representing the best-preserved slab-and-shingle complex in Victoria, and a glorious kitchen garden, while the avenue of quince trees leading to the cottage explodes with colour when in bloom in September and October.

# KINGLAKE NATIONAL PARK AND AROUND

**Map 2, G2–G3.**

As the Melba Highway heads north past Dixon's Creek it leaves the valley and enters state forest. Around 15km north of Yarra Glen, turn west onto the Kinglake to Healesville road and you'll come to the huge **Kinglake National Park**, a huge tract of eucalyptus forest and native bush with walking trails, picnic and barbecue spots, and lookouts. The park is divided into three distinct areas: the eastern Mount Everard section; the western Mount Sugarloaf section, beyond the township of Kinglake; and the northern Wombelano section. There are several sign-posted walking tracks across the park, and two small waterfalls – Masons Falls in the Mount Sugarloaf section and Wombelano Falls to the north – noted for their views and platoons of native birds, while the Mount Everard section includes Jehosophat Gully, a small but beautiful picnicking area.

> **Information and maps are available from the tourist office in the Old Courthouse on Harker Street, Toolangi (daily 9am–5pm; ©5962 2600).**

Just east of here, the small timber town of **Toolangi** is where the Australian poet C.J. Dennis wrote "The Songs of a Sentimental Bloke" in 1915, a bawdy tale of larrikin Bill and his "ideal bit o'skirt", Doreen. In the same year, Dennis and his wife Biddy planted the pleasant **Singing Gardens of C.J. Dennis**, which have tearooms serving devonshire teas and lunches (Mon–Thurs, Sat & Sun 10am–5pm; closed August). **Toolangi Forest Discovery Centre**, on the town's Main Road (daily 10am–5pm), introduces visitors to the forest ecosystem, and has audiovisual displays and a Sculpture Trail – nine sculptures presented to the centre in 1996 after a UNESCO-sponsored event invited Asian-Pacific artists to represent their culture's relationship to the environment.

# HEALESVILLE

**Map 2, H3.**

Heading south back into the Yarra Valley, Myers Creek Road brings you to the small town of **Healesville**, nestling beneath the forested slopes of the Great Dividing Range. On Sundays and public holidays, the **Yarra Valley Tourist Railway** operates rides on old trolleys between Healesville and Yarra Glen (every 30min 11am–4.30pm; $5). The town's main attraction, **Healesville Sanctuary**, on Badger Creek Road (daily 9am–5pm; $14), is one of Australia's outstanding conservation parks, and shouldn't be missed. Established in 1934, this sanctuary has the largest collection of Australian wildlife in the world, as well as a long and proud tradition of caring for injured and orphaned animals

– some are returned to the wild, while those that are threatened or endangered join the park's education and breeding programmes. Visitors can experience close encounters with a number of native Australian fauna including platypuses, koalas, kangaroos and wombats, or go on meet-the-keeper sessions to learn more about the animals. There's also a licensed bistro, and picnic and barbecue facilities.

Opposite here, at 22–24 Glen Eadie Avenue, the excellent **Galeena Beek Living Cultural Centre** (daily 9am–5pm; $6) was built on the former site of the Coranderrk Aboriginal Mission. The mission was closed in 1924 to make way for a soldier settlement, with the majority of residents packed off to Lake Tyers in northeast Victoria. As well as a permanent exhibition on Aboriginal history and artefacts, the centre features dance performances, didgeridoo and boomerang lessons, and has guided walks exploring the secrets of bush medicine and bush tucker.

# YARRA RANGES NATIONAL PARK

**Map 2, H3.**

About 10km east of Healesville is another massive wilderness area, the **Yarra Ranges National Park**, which has spectacular mountain ash forests, fern gullies, picnic areas and marked walking trails. At the southern end of the park, **Mount Donna Buang** has prime walking tracks and Melbourne's most accessible tobogganing slope, and is easily reached by car by taking the Mount Donna Buang Road from **Warburton**, 20km southeast from Healesville. For almost a century, Warburton's cool climate and hill-station atmosphere has attracted droves of urban dwellers seeking respite from the city; to get here, take the Warburton Highway turn-off 3km south of Coldstream. There's no public transport.

# Macedon Ranges, Daylesford and Hepburn Springs

Sixty kilometres northwest of Melbourne, the **Macedon Ranges** feature pleasant townships like Macedon and Woodend, panoramic views and Hanging Rock, an austere lump of lava mythologized in book and film. Further west, **Daylesford** and **Hepburn Springs** are two of Victoria's most welcoming country towns, with hundreds of natural mineral springs dotting the surrounding hills – the reason why they are collectively known as the Spa Centre of Australia. Each weekend tourists flood the area to indulge in the languid comforts of the spas, but you'll also find fine food, scenic surroundings and assorted communities of hippies, artists and greenies.

From Melbourne, the Macedon Ranges, Daylesford and Hepburn can be reached by **train** to either Woodend or Ballarat from Spencer Street Station. From either of these destinations, you can take a connecting **bus** to Daylesford.

The combined train and bus fare is $12.20 one way, regardless of which route you take. There are three trains a day to Woodend between Monday and Friday, ten a day to Ballarat; services at the weekend are extremely patchy. Alternatively, you can **drive** by taking the Western Highway towards Ballarat and turning off just beyond Ballan, from where Daylesford is only 30km distant.

# WOODEND AND HANGING ROCK

**Map 2, F2.**

The bucolic township of **Woodend** has some characterful old pubs and a rather expensive antiques gallery. Six kilometres northeast from here, the eerie, boulder-strewn **Hanging Rock** provided the setting for Joan Lindsay's famous novel *Picnic at Hanging Rock* (filmed by director Peter Weir in 1975), concerning the mysterious disappearance of two schoolgirls and a teacher on Valentine's Day 1900. Entry to the parking area at the base of the rock costs $5 per car.

........................................................................................

**Hanging Rock is also the venue for two horse-racing meetings: one on New Year's Day, the other on Australia Day (January 26). Around February 20, it's the venue for the Harvest Picnic, a food-and-wine festival.**

........................................................................................

There are more than a dozen **wineries** around Woodend and Hanging Rock, including Hanging Rock Winery (☎5427 0652) and Mount Macedon Winery (☎5427 2735). For information and maps, the **Woodend Tourist Office** (daily 9am–5pm; ☎5427 2033) is on the High Street, on the left as you drive out of town towards Hanging Rock. In September, the majority of wineries band together for the Macedon Budburst, a celebration of local produce.

If you haven't got your own **transport**, you can reach Hanging Rock by getting off the train at Woodend and walking 500m down the road to the Woodend Tourist Office, where you can fill up on water and maps, then trek the beautiful 6km to Hanging Rock. Alternatively, the tourist office can arrange a taxi (approximately $8).

# MOUNT MACEDON

**Map 2, F2.**

Just east of Woodend lies **Mount Macedon**, an extinct thousand-metre volcano. In 1983 the Ash Wednesday bush-fires swept through the area, scorching land and destroying a number of houses. Since then, homes have been rebuilt and the flora has grown back, although some scars remain. In autumn, Mount Macedon is particularly beautiful as the deciduous trees form spectacular russet avenues.

On the summit of Mount Macedon, a huge **memorial cross** was erected by William Cameron in 1935 to com-memorate his son and others killed in World War I. On a clear day there are great views across to Port Phillip Bay in the southeast and Hanging Rock to the north. On the drive to the summit, you pass a parking area and walking trail to Camels Hump, a lava outcrop popular with rock-climbers.

# DAYLESFORD

**Map 2, E2.**

Forty-five kilometres west of Woodend, **Daylesford** sports well-preserved Victorian and Edwardian streets and boasts a large and vibrant gay, lesbian and alternative-lifestyle popu-lation. On Vincent Street, the main drag, you'll find several good cafés, and a **tourist office** (daily 9am–5pm; ℭ5348 1339) with information on accommodation, including a useful publication listing gay- and lesbian-run establishments. It also stocks pamphlets on local health practitioners, walking trails and mineral springs, and has a handy selection of maps. From here, **buses** travel around three times daily to neighbouring Hepburn Springs.

The **Daylesford Historical Museum** (Sat & Sun 1.30–4.30pm; $2.50), next door to the tourist office, traces the town's origins in the 1850s goldrush. The museum's ramshackle collection of goldmining ephemera is housed in a former School of Mines, while the adjoining yard has numerous items of farm equipment and a tiny post office – once claimed to be the smallest in Victoria.

Down the hill from the museum are the picturesque **Lake Daylesford** and the Edwardian-style **Central Springs Reserve**. At the lake's edge, a pleasant café rents out paddle boats ($10/30min), while the reserve has several walking trails and mineral springs. The sixteen-kilometre **Tipperary Walking Track** runs from Lake Daylesford to Hepburn Mineral Springs Reserve (see opposite), passing through undulating open-forest country and several old gold-diggings.

Wombat Hill rises above the town to the east. At the top, the **botanical gardens**, established in 1861, contain magnificent elms, conifers and oaks, and a lookout tower with views of the local countryside. Just below the gardens, the **Convent Gallery** is on the corner of Daly and Hill streets (daily 10am–6pm; $3). A former convent, religious retreat and gold commissioner's residence, it now has three levels of galleries selling arts, crafts and antiques, plus a café and gift shop at the front of the complex.

The old Daylesford **train station** is down the road from Wombat Hill, where the Midland Highway enters town. On Sundays, the Central Highlands Tourist Railway runs from here through the Wombat State Forest to the nearby towns of Musk and Bullarto, a return journey of just under an hour (10am–3pm; $7 return to Bullarto). Also on Sundays, the station car park is the site of a lively **arts and crafts market** (9am–3pm).

# HEPBURN SPRINGS

**Map 2, E2.**

Leaving Daylesford, Vincent Street heads on to **Hepburn Springs**, a few kilometres north. For more than a century, Australia's only mineral spa resort has been a major destination for affluent tourists, although in recent years it has attracted more alternative types and some of the worst unemployment rates in Victoria.

As you enter the town, you'll pass the National Trust-listed **Old Macaroni Factory** on the left. Built in 1859, it was the first pasta factory in Australia; visitors can call ahead to arrange a tour of the frescoed interior ($2; ©9457 7035). Further down the hill, on the corner of Tenth Street, **The Palais** is a lovingly restored 1920s theatre hosting everything from torch-song performances to gypsy swing bands, and has a good-value restaurant and bar.

At the bottom of Tenth Street, you'll pass through the Soldiers Memorial Park to the **Hepburn Mineral Springs Reserve**. There are four springs in the immediate area, and a visit to any of them with a few empty containers is a must. Old-fashioned hand pumps dispense the $H_2O$, with each spring having a distinctive, effervescent taste. Most have a more robust flavour than the bland, filtered variety you can buy in shops, and all are better tasting than the local tap water which, ironically, is quite undrinkable (the local council can't afford to upgrade the town's water-treatment facilities).

The renovated **Hepburn Spa Resort** (Mon–Fri 10am–8pm, Sat & Sun 9am–8pm; ©5348 2034) built in 1895, lies at the centre of the Hepburn Mineral Springs

Reserve. Public facilities include a relaxation pool, spa and heavy mineral salt pool (Mon–Fri $8, Sat & Sun $9); there are also packages available using its extensive private facilities, including an aerospa bath, massage and flotation tanks. Prices range from $38 for an aerospa bath and fifteen-minute massage, to $210 for a pedicure, aerospa, facial, flotation, massage and two-course lunch; book at least six weeks in advance.

# Ballarat

Just over 100km west of Melbourne, **Ballarat** holds a pivotal place in Australia's history. In the 1830s, white pastoralists fanning out from Port Phillip Bay were quick to appreciate the grazing potential of the lightly wooded hills and plains to the northwest. In August 1851, gold was discovered near Ballarat, which brought immense wealth to the town but also led to the country's only civil uprising – the bloody Eureka Rebellion (see p.247) – as put-upon prospectors revolted against the authorities. By the decade's end, Ballarat had grown into a prominent Australian city: gorgeous Victorian architecture lined its wide tree-lined avenues, and the city took on the airs and graces of a prosperous and conservative provincial centre.

With gold long gone – the last seam was exhausted in 1918 – tourism and information technology (IBM has its southeast Asian headquarters here) have now taken over as Ballarat's major sources of income, while a large student population from the University of Ballarat has challenged the town's more insular inclinations. However, reminders of its glory days can still be seen in elegant nineteenth-century buildings on and around **Lydiard Street**, while further south lies Ballarat's outstanding attraction, **Sovereign Hill**, a fabulous re-creation of the mining shafts, hotels and shops of the goldrush era. Beyond Ballarat, the tacky but endearing Kryal Castle warrants a visit, as does the Arch of Honour, a solemn memorial to those killed in war.

> **The Ballarat Tourist Office at 39 Sturt Street (daily 9am–5pm; ©5332 2694) is well stocked with maps, guides and tourist information; it also has a route map of the Eureka Trail (see p.246).**

**Trains** run daily from Spencer Street Station to Ballarat, while V/Line **buses** depart twice daily from Spencer Street

Station, arriving at Ballarat Station, centrally located in Lydiard Street. Both bus and train take ninety minutes each way and cost $27.60 return. If you're **driving**, take the Westgate Freeway out of Melbourne, then turn onto the Western Ring Road before taking the Western Highway to Ballarat; the trip takes just over an hour.

# LYDIARD STREET AND AROUND

The heart of Ballarat contains one of Australia's best-preserved nineteenth-century streetscapes: **Lydiard Street**. Running from the centre up past the train station, the street has several two-storey terraced shopfronts, with verandahs and decorative iron-lace work, mostly from the period 1862–89. Among the stately buildings, the former Mining Exchange (1888) has been recently renovated to its former splendour, and the architecture of Her Majesty's Theatre (1875) also proclaims Ballarat's goldrush-era heyday. Also on Lydiard Street are a collection of fine hotels that once watered thirsty diggers, and include *Craig's Royal Hotel* at no. 10 and the *George Hotel* at no. 27, which are still an integral part of Ballarat's architectural heritage. Sadly, during the 1970s, the council forced most of the old pubs to pull down their verandahs on the grounds that they were unsafe, so very few survive in their original form.

The highlight of the street, however, is the superb **Ballarat Fine Art Gallery** at 40 Lydiard Street North (daily 10.30am–5pm; $4). Established in 1884, this is Australia's largest and oldest regional gallery, home of the original Eureka flag (frayed but still impressive), a fine collection of colonial and Heidelberg School paintings by artists such as Tom Roberts and Arthur Streeton, contemporary art and works by members of the talented Lindsay family, who lived in nearby Creswick. One room of the gallery is given over to a reconstruction of the Lindsay household's sitting room.

A short distance west of Lydiard Street, **Lake Wendouree** was the site of the 1956 Olympics rowing events. The **Ballarat Botanical Gardens**, situated on the western boundary, features the striking Robert Clark Conservatory, which opened in 1995 and has dazzling variety of flowers and shrubbery. On Wednesday afternoon, Saturday, Sunday and public holidays, visitors can take a ride around the lake on a tram along Wendouree Parade ($3.50).

## THE EUREKA TRAIL AND CENTRE

Starting at the Post Office on the corner of Lydiard and Sturt streets, the 3.5-kilometre **Eureka Trail**, opened in 1996, follows the path the troops took during their march to the Eureka Stockade (see box). Starting on the site of the former government camp, the trail winds its way through the city along the Yarrowee River and through the city's older residential suburbs before arriving at the **Eureka Stockade Centre** in Eureka Street (daily 9am–5pm; $6). Opened in 1998, the centre was built close to where the stockade is thought to have stood, and features a number of dull figures of soldiers and diggers, as well as multimedia galleries highlighting the main events behind the rebellion. Above, the huge **Eureka Sail** guarantees that the building can be seen for kms; inside, a fragment of the original flag has pride of place in the centre's central Contemplation Space. If you don't want to walk to the centre, take a Davis Bus Lines bus from Curtis Street just east of Lydiard Street ($2.45).

## SOVEREIGN HILL

Daily 10am–5pm; $18.50; ℗5331 1944. 15min walk from Sturt Street, or take a Davis Bus Lines bus from Curtis Street ($2.45).

# The Eureka Rebellion

In 1854 miners at Ballarat were doing it hard: the goldfields administration was corrupt and overbearing, miners were forced to pay an excessive 30 shillings for a gold licence and, to add insult to injury, they didn't even have a franchise. In response, miners started burning their gold licences and, under the leadership of Peter Lalor, barricaded themselves in a flimsy stockade, above which fluttered a blue flag featuring the Southern Cross.

Just before dawn on the morning of December 3, almost three hundred troops summoned from Melbourne slipped out of the government camp and made their way through the sleeping city. Upon reaching the stockade, they loaded muskets, fixed bayonets and charged. In less than fifteen minutes, more than thirty miners lay dead and 114 had been taken prisoner. Six troopers died in the assault. Public opinion, however, sided firmly with the miners. Thirteen were charged with high treason but acquitted three months later, and within the year Peter Lalor was elected to the Victorian Parliament and the miners had earned the right to vote.

Ballarat's undoubted highlight, **Sovereign Hill**, is on Bradshaw Street just south of the city centre. This reconstruction of the goldmining township of Ballarat in the 1850s is complete with working mineshaft, actors dressed in period costume, horse-drawn carriages and a Chinese Temple, and is well worth the admission price. Activities such as wheelwright demonstrations, gold pourings and mine tours run throughout the day, while the evening sound-and-light show "Blood on the Southern Cross" (daily; $22.50; booking essential on ©5333 5777) lavishly recreates the Eureka Rebellion. On entry to Sovereign Hill, visitors are given a map and an itinerary of activities – it's

THE EUREKA REBELLION

worth spending a few minutes plotting your day before continuing. The site also has plenty of cafés, restaurants and picnic areas.

Directly opposite here, the interesting **Gold Museum** (daily 9.30am–5.20pm; free with Sovereign Hill entry) is crammed with coins, nuggets and temporary exhibitions.

# AROUND BALLARAT

An unmistakable sight on the Western Highway 8km east of Ballarat, **Kryal Castle**, on the slopes of Mount Warrenheip (daily 9.30am–5.30pm; $12.50), is an ersatz castle-cum-medieval theme park whose mishmash of exhibits include a gloriously tacky dungeon and torture chamber, where pretend whippings and hangings are conducted daily at 1.30pm.

Five kilometres west of Ballarat on the Western Highway, the Arch of Victory heralds the entry to the 23-kilometre **Avenue of Honour**, a beautiful if sobering stretch of road – flanking either side are over 3700 ash, elm, poplar, maple and plane trees dedicated to local soldiers who fought in World War I.

# Geelong and Bellarine Peninsula

**G**eelong, around 75km southwest of Melbourne, is Victoria's second-largest city and gateway to the Bellarine Peninsula. Don't come looking for extraordinary natural landscapes or brilliant sunsets, however, because its attractions are predominantly man-made. Long the centre of Australia's wool industry, Geelong's main draw is its magnificent National Wool Museum, but you'll also find a modicum of other sights like the town's excellent art gallery, botanic gardens and fine examples of colonial architecture. In addition, Deakin University and the Gordon Institute have attracted a younger population, and there's now a small arts community and healthy band scene which lend a patina of hipness to the city. Beyond Geelong, the **Bellarine Peninsula** offers the graceful beachfront town of Queenscliff, quaint fishing villages, some of Victoria's finest views, and activities such as surfing and swimming with dolphins.

The easiest way to get to Geelong is by **train** (hourly from Spencer Street Station; $8.60 one way), a sixty-minute journey. By **car**, it's an hour's drive southwest of

Melbourne on the Princes Freeway. From Geelong, a **bus service** departs from Brougham Street (next to the National Wool Museum) for Ocean Grove and Barwon Heads, Point Lonsdale via Queenscliff, and St Leonards via Portarlington.

# GEELONG

Map 2, E4.

Industrial **Geelong** is not a particularly attractive city – the fact that the **National Wool Museum** at 26 Moorabool Street (daily 10am–5pm; $7) is the main attraction will give you some idea of the place. Housed in an imposing blue-stone building, the museum proves that Australia really did ride on the sheep's back. Inside, displays concentrate on the social history of the Geelong and Australian wool industry, with reconstructions of typical shearers' quarters, turn-of-the-century looms (still in use), and sounds and images evocative of the past. Also here, a tourist office (daily 9am–5pm; ☏1800/620 888) provides lots of brochures and maps; for details of what's going on in the city, pick up a copy of the free magazine *Forte*, available from cafés, book-shops, galleries and cinemas.

Many of the town's best Victorian buildings are on **Little Malop Street**, three blocks south of the National Wool Museum in the city centre, including the elegant **Geelong Art Gallery** (Mon–Fri 10am–5pm, Sat & Sun 1–5pm; $3), which has an extensive selection of works by nineteenth-century Australian artists such as Tom Roberts and Frederick McCubbin, plus contemporary Australian paint-ings and sculpture. From Malop Street, Moorabool Street leads down to Corio Bay, where a number of bicycle and walking trails head off along its western shore. Overlooking the bay are the lovely **Geelong Botanic Gardens** (daily 7.30am–5pm; free), surrounded by lush parkland.

Twenty kilometres north of Geelong is the little-known **Serendip Sanctuary**, at 100 Windermere Road in Lara (daily 10am–4pm; $5; no public transport). A refuge for endangered Victorian birds, the sanctuary is renowned for its captive breeding programme of brolgas, magpie geese and Australian bustards. Kangaroos and other marsupials, including the rare pademelon wallaby, can also be viewed here in special enclosures.

# BELLARINE PENINSULA

Map 2, F4–F5.

Less exciting than the popular Mornington Peninsula which it faces across Port Phillip Bay, **Bellarine Peninsula** manages even so to summon up enough sights to make for a worthwhile visit. The most obvious attraction is the quiet seaside resort of **Queenscliff**, with its historic buildings, fishermen's cottages and Victorian hotels, while nearby is an evocative lighthouse and a collection of interesting small coastal communities.

For details of "Round the Bay in a Day" excursions, incorporating the Mornington and Bellarine peninsulas, see p.222.

## Queenscliff

From Geelong the Bellarine Highway runs 31km southeast to **Queenscliff** at the tip of the Bellarine Peninsula. From its humble beginnings as a sea pilot's station and fishing village, Queenscliff became a fashionable resort in the 1880s before falling out of favour, and has only recently begun to enjoy a revival in popularity. The town's position near the narrow entrance to Port Phillip Bay made it strategically

BELLARINE PENINSULA

important: **Fort Queenscliff** guards the entrance, facing the fort opposite at Point Nepean (see p.225). The fort was planned during the Crimean War in 1861 in response to the perceived threat of a Russian invasion. It is now the home of the Australian Army Command and Staff College, and can be visited on guided tours (Sat & Sun 1pm & 3pm; $4), when you can see tunnels built during the goldrush period and muzzle-loading cannons. Further north on Weerona Parade, the **Queenscliff Maritime Centre and Museum** (daily 1.30–4.30pm; $4) focuses on the many shipwrecks caused by "The Rip", a fierce current that passes through the mouth of Port Phillip Bay.

Queenscliff's range of **water activities** includes boat rides and swimming with dolphins off the bay; one reliable tour operator for the latter activity is Sea All Charters, which departs from the car ferry wharf (daily 1pm; $50 swimmers, $35 sightseers; bookings essential on ✆0411/873 777). Every Sunday, the **Bellarine Peninsula Railway** operates ninety-minute steam trips from the old Queenscliff Railway Station to Drysdale, 20km northwest (11am & 2.30pm; $12), while the **Queenscliff Sunday Market** is held on the last Sunday of each month from August to May on Symonds Street.

Regular ferries link Queenscliff and Sorrento on the Mornington Peninsula – see p.223 for details.

## Around Queenscliff

From Queenscliff it's about 5km to peaceful **Point Lonsdale** and its 120-metre-high lighthouse (tours Sun 9.30am–1pm; $5) overlooking The Rip. Built in 1902, it's visible for 30km out to sea and has sweeping views across to Point Nepean on the Mornington Peninsula. Beneath the lighthouse, on the edge of the bluff, "Buckley's Cave" is where the famous **William Buckley** reputedly made his home. A convict in the 1803 expedition by Captain David Collins, Buckley escaped and was adopted by local Aborigines, living with them for over thirty years. When the "wild white man" was seen again by settlers he could scarcely remember how to speak English; his survival against all odds has been immortalized in the phrase "Buckley's chance".

Fifteen kilometres west of Queenscliff, **Ocean Grove** and **Barwon Heads** face one another across the Barwon River – the former has one of Victoria's safest surf beaches and a pleasant summer climate cooled by breezes blowing in from Bass Strait, while the latter is a pretty town with a long sandy river foreshore, jetties, delightful rockpools and a popular beach. North of Queenscliff, **St Leonards** was founded in 1840 as a fishing base for Geelong, while at **Portarlington** there's the beautifully preserved, steam-powered **Portarlington Mill** at Turner Court (Wed, Sat & Sun noon–4pm; $2). Four storeys of solid stone, this National Trust property was built in 1857 and is well worth visiting if you're interested in seeing how bluestone was once put to industrial use. Portarlington also has a safe family beach and splendid views across the bay to the You Yangs Regional Park (see p.92), an eerie volcanic outcrop northeast of Geelong.

AROUND QUEENSCLIFF

# The Great Ocean Road

The **Great Ocean Road** stretches from Torquay, 20km south of Geelong, all the way along the rugged Victorian coast to Warrnambool, almost 300km to the west. When construction began in 1919, this scenic route was intended as a memorial to those who fell in World War I. As the Great Depression took hold it also became a source of much-needed work for thousands of unemployed ex-servicemen. After fourteen years of difficult and sometimes dangerous work, the Great Ocean Road was completed in 1932. Now regarded as one of the world's great coastal journeys, the road takes you within a day through some of Australia's most stunning scenery, dotted with picturesque coastal communities, and with plenty of opportunities for walking, surfing and whale-watching en route.

Although it makes for exhilarating driving, the Great Ocean Road is best enjoyed from the passenger seat. From Melbourne, a **bus** goes along the coast to Geelong and Apollo Bay, then on to Warrnambool (departures every Friday at 8.49am, arriving in Warrnambool at 5pm; $45.20 one way; for further details, contact V/Line on ©13/2232).

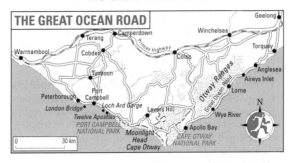

West Coast Railways (℡5221 8966) operate a **train service** between Melbourne and Warrnambool (Mon–Fri three departures daily; $34 one way), a journey of around three hours. In addition, a host of companies offer **tours** down the Great Ocean Road, either on its own or as part of a longer trip – contact the Victorian Visitor Information Centre (see p.25) for details.

# FROM TORQUAY TO AIREYS INLET

Gateway to the Great Ocean Road, **Torquay** is a nirvana for surf-seekers. Surfing is big business here (the town's annual turnover is more than $200 million), culminating each Easter in the Rip Curl Pro and Quit Women's Classic for professional boardriders. If you don't know a point break from a reef break, call into the **Surfworld Museum** (Mon–Fri 9am–5pm, Sat & Sun 10am–4pm; $6) at the rear of the Surfcoast Plaza on the Surfcoast Highway. The world's largest surfing museum, it has a wave-making tank, interactive displays like paddling machines, and a collection of antique surfboards and Hawaiian shirts. Also here, a small **tourist office** (same hours; ℡5261 4219) hands out tidal reports and maps of local breaks, as well as information on where to rent boards and wet suits. To check out the real thing, follow the signs to two of Victoria's best surf beaches: **Jan Juc** and **Bells Beach**. The former is also the starting point for the 25-kilometre Surf Coast Walk, which follows the coastline as far as Aireys Inlet.

Heading along the coast, **Point Addis** and the **Ironbark Basin Coastal Nature Reserve** have several marked walking trails and lookouts, while **Anglesea** is an appealing seaside resort popular with holidaying families and anglers, and has a golf course famous for its large mob of resident kangaroos. Leaving Anglesea and skirting the coast, you'll see the **Split Point Lighthouse** (1891) overlooking the small town of **Aireys Inlet**, which has fine swimming, fishing and beachcombing.

# LORNE AND APOLLO BAY

At **Lorne**, the premier holiday town on the west coast of Victoria, café society rubs shoulders with surf culture. Upstairs at 144 Mountjoy Parade, the well-stocked Lorne **tourist office** (daily 9am–5pm; ©5289 1152) can point you in the direction of the best restaurants in town, or some of the area's finest walking tracks – like those crisscrossing the Lorne section of the **Angahook-Lorne State Park**, which also has lookouts, several waterfalls, and picnic and camping areas.

> The Falls Festival is a three-day music event held each New Year in the stunning Otway Ranges outside Lorne, which has previously attracted rockers like Iggy Pop and Blondie. Tickets go on sale in October through Ticketmaster (©13/6100) and cost around $65; check out their Web site (*www.thefalls.net*) for further information.

From Lorne the road twists and turns to **Apollo Bay**, a more laid-back resort than Lorne, with a lively alternative scene. A fishing port and former whaling station, its setting is one of the prettiest along the Great Ocean Road, with a crescent-shaped bay set beneath the rounded, sometimes foggy Otway Ranges. Gentle updraughts make these hills popular with hang-gliders, who can often be seen floating lazily above the town. The pier and breakwater are usually the province of anglers, and at the base of the pier the Fisherman's Co-op sells fresh seafood. In March, the town hosts the **Apollo Bay Music Festival**, featuring jazz, rock, blues and country. For more information on this, as well as on eco-tours in the area, contact the **tourist office** at 55 Great Ocean Road (daily 9am–5pm; ✆5237 6529).

# THE SHIPWRECK COAST

Beyond Apollo Bay the Great Ocean Road heads inland, passing through the temperate rainforests and fern gullies of the **Cape Otway National Park**. In the late 1860s, loggers spread into the Otway Ranges and built a number of small townships that remain to this day, but nowadays tourism is the area's lifeblood. On the way to the hill-top town of Lavers Hill, you pass the turn-off to the **Cape Otway Lighthouse** (9am–5pm; $5). Erected in 1848 after the ship *Cataraqui* went down off the coast of King Island to the south, it is the oldest remaining lighthouse on the Australian mainland. Only nine of the 400 passengers survived – just one of many tragedies that gave the title **Shipwreck Coast** to the 130-kilometre stretch of coastline from nearby Moonlight Head to Port Fairy.

The eastern portion of the Shipwreck Coast is dominated by the narrow **Port Campbell National Park**. Windswept, heath-covered hills overlook Bass Strait and its sometimes awesome swells.·There are several places to stop along this route, the most popular being the site overlooking the **Twelve Apostles**, where the waves of the Southern Ocean have worn the cliffs into a spectacular series of offshore limestone stacks.

A few kilometres further along is **Loch Ard Gorge**. In 1878 the clipper *Loch Ard* struck a reef near here and went down, taking 52 passengers with her – most of the passengers and crew are buried in the cemetery overlooking the gorge. For more information on the coast's maritime tragedies, visit the **Loch Ard Shipwreck Museum** (daily 9am–5pm; $3) in Port Campbell, an unprepossessing town a few kilometres to the west. Beyond Port Campbell is **London Bridge**, a rock formation whose two sections were formerly connected by a central span of rock – the "bridge". In 1990, this suddenly fell down, leaving two rather startled people stranded on the outer section (they were eventually rescued by helicopter). Just beyond here, the Grotto has a path leading down to a rockpool beneath a limestone arch.

# WARRNAMBOOL TO PORT FAIRY

From nearby Peterborough, the Great Ocean Road passes through dairy country before ending just short of **Warrnambool**. Once home to sealers and whalers, it is now Victoria's pre-eminent destination for **whale-watching**: southern right whales can be sighted off Logans Beach, just east of town, between May and October, or you can take a one-hour tour with Shipwreck Coast Diving and Charters (℗5561 6108; $25). Warrnambool's excellent **Flagstaff Hill Maritime Village** on Merri Street (daily 9am–5pm; $10) is a re-created nineteenth-century fishing port, and has an excellent collection of shipwreck artefacts including the Loch Ard Peacock, an earthenware peacock washed ashore two days after the *Loch Ard* went down. On

Liebig Street, the **Warrnambool Art Gallery** (daily noon–5pm; $2.50) is another in a long line of excellent regional galleries found throughout Victoria.

West of Warrnambool is the **Tower Hill Game Reserve** (sunrise–sunset; free). After years of logging, the area was replanted in the 1950s using an 1855 landscape painting by Eugene Von Guerard as a guide. More than 300,000 trees were introduced and the reserve now has an abundance of water birds, koalas, kangaroos and wallabies, and a Natural History Centre (daily 9.30am–12.30pm & 1.30–4.30pm; free) with geological and historical displays.

A few kilometres beyond Warrnambool, **Port Fairy** is a quaint former whaling port with numerous National Trust-listed buildings and a muttonbird rookery on nearby Griffiths Island. Relaxed and low-key, it's also home to the **Port Fairy Folk Music Festival**, featuring over a hundred national and international acts, held every Labour Day long weekend in March.

THE SHIPWRECK COAST

# CONTEXTS

# A brief history of Melbourne

## Melbourne's original owners

Melbourne and Victoria's original inhabitants were the Aboriginal people, or **Kooris**, who have lived in the region for over 50,000 years. Semi-nomadic hunters and gatherers, they had a close relationship with the land, living a mostly comfortable life that was threatened only in times of scarcity. To protect themselves against the cold, Aboriginal people built fires and turf huts, and donned great possum-skin cloaks. For leisure, they played a game where two competing teams attempted to catch a round ball made of possum skins that was kicked high into the air (a forerunner to Aussie Rules football).

Victoria's Aboriginal people also had a highly ordered social life, sophisticated traditional cultures, and around ten separate languages spoken by over thirty different dialect or sub-language groups. In the Port Phillip region, five different groups shared adjoining territories, a common language, and an integrated culture and belief system, forming a nation or confederacy known as the "Kulin". Periodically, groups from the Kulin would gather in areas around present-day Melbourne. But although the Aboriginal way of life had evolved over thousands of years, they were ill-prepared for *Gubba* (white) invasion.

## Tentative beginnings

Prior to the sixteenth century, the only regular visitors to Australia were the Malays, who established seasonal camps while fishing for sea slugs along the northern coast. **European involvement** in the region began in the early seventeenth century, when Portuguese, Spanish and Dutch expeditions mapped parts of the coastline, although the land's forbidding climate and seeming barrenness discouraged the great Western powers from taking much of an interest in the country the Dutch called "New Holland".

In 1770, a British party under **Captain James Cook** sailed up the continent's eastern seaboard, which Cook christened New South Wales and claimed in the name of King George III. Even so, it wasn't until the loss of Britain's American colonies in 1783 that interest in the country gathered momentum. The government, looking for a convenient place in which to unload its criminal elements, seized upon the country's potential as the location for a penal colony. In 1788 the **First Fleet** arrived at Botany Bay, close to present-day Sydney, carrying some 800 convicts on eleven ships, and established the first European settlement on Australian soil.

The first Briton to attempt to settle the Melbourne area, **Captain David Collins** sailed from London, arriving in Port Phillip Bay in 1803 at the site of what is now the popular seaside resort of Sorrento. Less than a year later, after declaring the location unsuitable due to its lack of fresh water, Collins abandoned the settlement and travelled to Van Diemen's Land (now Tasmania). Around the same time, a party led by Charles Grimes, Surveyor-General of New South Wales, stumbled across the Yarra and had lunch on the present site of the city. James Fleming, a member of the party, was moved to write that "the most eligible place for a settlement I have seen is on the Freshwater [Yarra] River".

Across the Bass Strait, a number of Van Diemen's Land pastoralists, including John Batman and Thomas and John Henty, looking for favourable pasturage, had sought permission from authorities in London and Sydney to graze livestock on the mainland. Impetus for settlement was also spurred by the glowing reports received from whalers active in Bass Strait that suitable land could be found on the mainland. However, the pastoralists' requests were consistently refused as the authorities in both London and Sydney believed the cost of a new settlement would prove expensive. Tired of being bossed around, **Edward Henty** (Thomas's son) set out with his family and began squatting at Portland Bay on the southwest coast in 1834, thereby establishing the district's first permanent settlement.

## Into the frontier

**John Batman**, a barrel-chested former bushranger, continued to harbour plans for a pastoral settlement in Victoria. In May 1835, together with a consortium of graziers, public servants and merchants, he set out to buy land from the local Aborigines. Leading a party across the notoriously difficult Bass Strait on the sloop *Rebecca*, he reached Indented Head on the Bellarine Peninsula in Port Phillip Bay and then proceeded to walk around Corio Bay, noting that the fertile countryside was "beyond my most sanguine expectations". After reaching the mouth of a river (later to be called the Yarra), he continued along one of its tributary streams until meeting a local Dugitalla tribe with whom, on June 6, 1835, a **treaty** of his own making was signed. Batman claimed to have procured 240,000 hectares (600,000 acres), which he paid for with £200 worth of goods (knives, tools and trinkets), promising similar payments each year. Having spent a day rowing on the Yarra, Batman echoed the sentiments of James Fleming over thirty years earlier when he famously wrote: "This will be the place for a village."

Batman returned to Van Diemen's Land on June 9, leaving a small party at Indented Head to look after the land he had "bought". Days later, ensconced in the *Launceston Hotel*, Batman proclaimed he was "the greatest landowner in the world". His braggadocio was tempered, however, by the refusal of officials in Hobart and Sydney to recognize the settlement without permission from the British colonial authority. Until further instructions were received, those settling at Port Phillip (then part of New South Wales) were to be treated as trespassers.

Despite this setback, **plans for settlement** continued apace and by the end of June, Batman and his backers had formed a syndicate called the Port Phillip Association to send livestock to the mainland. However, it was another group led by the visionary **John Pascoe Fawkner** that played the major role in the establishment of Melbourne. The son of a convict, Fawkner had made his way in Van Diemen's Land as a baker, bookseller, newspaper owner (he would subsequently publish Melbourne's first newspaper, the *Melbourne Advertiser*) and publican of the *Launceston Hotel*. He had also been a member of Captain David Collins' party that landed in Sorrento. Now, 32 years later, Fawkner had bought the schooner *Enterprize* in April to ferry a new party of settlers to Port Phillip. But, having organized and financed a small group to accompany him, Fawkner was unable to leave on August 4, when he was forced to disembark for financial reasons. The *Enterprize*, under the command of Captain John Lancey, continued without him, reaching the Yarra on August 29 and berthing at a site close to fresh water near present-day William Street. Fawkner and his family arrived on October 11, with Batman – whose popularity as the city's traditional founder continues today – following on November 9.

## Growing pains

In September 1836, orders arrived allowing settlement (although Batman's purchase was declared "invalid"), sparking a monumental **land grab** as increasing numbers of settlers from Van Diemen's Land, New South Wales and immigrants from Britain flocked to the new settlement. Sir Richard Bourke, Governor General of New South Wales, visited the settlement in 1837 and chose the site where Melbourne now stands; accompanying him was the Surveyor-General Robert Hoddle, who famously mapped out the blueprint for Melbourne's spacious grid in a couple of hours. That year, the settlement was named Melbourne, after William Lamb, second Viscount Melbourne and Prime Minister of Great Britain. In 1839 **Charles La Trobe** arrived to administer the district. A precocious scholar and butterfly collector, La Trobe spent fifteen years in office, steering Victoria to self-government and establishing major public works such as the State Library of Victoria. After contributing so much to the settlement's development, John Batman died in 1839, aged just 39.

Melbourne's population grew quickly, and such was the tumult on the streets that many people were gored or crushed to death by sundry drays, bullocks and horses. By 1840, the number of citizens had reached 10,000. **Aboriginal people** also began drifting into the settlement, as their land was taken and they became increasingly attracted to tobacco and alcohol. Largely seen as a degenerate people by the European populace, Aborigines did mostly menial work, trading goods such as feathers and skins, or acting as pastoral labourers. But even though Melbourne's settlement was less violent than others in Australia (largely the result of John Batman's treaty and the Port Phillip Protectorate, which framed laws to protect Aborigines), the Aboriginal population declined from around 15,000 in 1834 to 2000 in 1850 – mostly due to massacres by white settlers, poisoned waterholes, or from European diseases such as dysentery and measles. Alcohol abuse also decelerated numbers, and by the mid-1850s there were few Aborigines left in Melbourne.

In 1842, Melbourne was declared a town and, five years later, a city. The **Port Phillip District** separated from New South Wales (of which it was still part) in 1849 and,

GROWING PAINS

two years later, officially broke from the state when it was declared an independent colony, just nine days before gold was discovered.

## The goldrush

The **discovery of gold** near Ballarat in 1851 irrevocably changed Melbourne's character. Before, Melbourne was a remote colonial town with a strongly rural character. Now, as hundreds of ships carrying fortune-seekers began flooding in from around the world, it was transformed into a convulsing, sprawling and often violent metropolis crammed with gaudy shops, brothels, flashy diggers, opportunists and no-hopers. Most migrants didn't stay long in the city but scurried off to seek fame and fortune in the goldfields: their desertion stripped Melbourne of much-needed labour, forcing even Governor La Trobe to feed and groom his own horses.

However, within a year, Melbourne's merchants were busy turning a profit from those returning out of the goldfields. The city's population exploded, and Melbourne became the fastest-growing and richest port in the British Empire. Growth came at a price, however: with no infrastructure, city streets began accumulating filth at an astonishing rate, and it was not uncommon for citizens to walk ankle deep in mud or faeces in the downtown area. In response to vigorous public pressure to clean up the city, Melbourne erected male-only cast-iron urinals in a number of locations in the 1850s, but it wasn't until 1902 – coincidentally the same year when they were granted the vote – that women's public conveniences were provided.

## Boom and bust

The 1860s to 1880s were years of great optimism and prosperity in **"Marvellous Melbourne"**. The city took over from Sydney as Australia's financial centre, rail lines and

cable trams were introduced on Melbourne's streets, telephones installed, and a night-time football match was
played under electric lighting at the Melbourne Cricket
Ground (MCG). Grandiose public developments such as
the Royal Exhibition Building (built especially to stage the
Great Exhibition in 1888) and the Melbourne Town Hall
were constructed on goldrush profits; suburbs from St Kilda
to Collingwood began to develop; and large tracts of the
city centre were set aside as public parks and gardens.
Always deferential towards the "Mother Country",
Melbourne's well-to-do modelled themselves on middle-
class English society, adopting the fashions, the furniture,
and the carefully enunciated speech, while filling their gardens with imported shrubs and trees.

During the 1890s, Melbourne's star waned as the city was
rocked by a series of strikes, sparking a devastating depression and the beginning of the **"grey nineties"**.
Melbourne's earlier lassez-faire prosperity, fuelled by dubi-
ous financial speculation, had drawn manpower from the
land, decreasing primary production. As land became
unsaleable and wool and wheat prices slumped, companies
were bankrupted and fortunes lost overnight.

## Twentieth century

By the turn of the century Melbourne had recovered, and
financial stability had returned. Following the **unifica-
tion of Australia's six colonies** in 1901, Melbourne
became the country's political capital (the first session of
the new Parliament was held in the Royal Exhibition
Building) and remained so until the specially constructed
capital city of Canberra was completed in 1927. Stability
continued through World War I and beyond, until the
city's prosperity was shattered by the **Great Depression**
of the 1930s. With unemployment rife, many people
were put to work building a series of public works,

including St Kilda Road, the Shrine of Remembrance, and the Great Ocean Road.

By the early 1930s, Melbourne had bounced back again, and began a period of intense **industrial development**. Warehousing and manufacturing moved outwards the city and into the suburbs, and families attached to these industries went to the outskirts for work and cheap housing. Following World War II, Melbourne continued its programme of development, beginning a huge **immigration programme** that attracted waves of refugees and migrants from around the world – their arrival helped transform the city from a culturally suburban, stereotypically British backwater into a sophisticated international melting pot. As the inner suburbs became crowded and accommodation scarce, Melbourne built thousands of houses in the outer suburbs for low-income earners. The drift outwards continued until the 1960s, when new city-centre developments and the revitalization of inner-city suburbs such as Carlton and Fitzroy by Melbourne's growing band of bohemians, intellectuals and immigrants helped reverse the trend. The undoubted highlight of this era was the city's hosting of the **1956 Olympic Games**. Known as the "friendly games", the event proved a watershed: not only did it lead to the Melbourne Cricket Ground (MCG) being transformed into Australia's largest and most famous stadium, but it also put the city firmly on the world map.

Progress continued until **the 1990s**, when Australia fell into recession. Melbourne, in particular, hit an all-time low as unemployment rose to record levels, factories closed, the property market collapsed and some of the city's largest financial institutions went under. The Labor Government, which had been in power for ten years, was unable to handle the state's finances, leading to a lack of trust among voters, who in 1992 elected a conservative Liberal/National party coalition under Jeff Kennett.

TWENTIETH CENTURY

## Kennett in power

Bold and occasionally boorish, Victoria's Premier **Jeff Kennett** wields almost complete control of Parliament, and has set about invigorating Melbourne by investing heavily in infrastructure. Dubbed the "Mitterrand of the South", Kennett is keen to demonstrate to the rest of the world that Melbourne is a "world-class" city with suitably aggrandizing monuments: new developments such as the Museum of Victoria and Federation Square have gone up all over the city, and in 1998 the green light was given to the 133-storey **Grollo Tower**, a soaring glass obelisk that when – or if – finished, is intended to be the tallest building in the world (construction is still dependent on the developer meeting certain financial conditions, including a $37 million upfront payment). To fund these works, Kennett's government has overseen savage budget cuts to health and education. Kennett has also come under fire for Melbourne's gambling culture, stifling democratic debate by harassing or banning the media (he once shovelled sand over a group of reporters), and making changes to the office of the auditor-general, which had previously investigated the government's dubious tender processes and credit-card abuse by its appointed officials. But despite Kennett's Thatcherite approach to the economy and propensity for antagonizing various sections of the community, his popularity as premier remains high, and he is now widely recognized as Australia's most effective politician at both a state and federal level. His activist government has continued to celebrate the state's cultural, racial and religious diversity, and his lead against the fledgling One Nation Party – a new and xenophobic force in Australian politics – has won him many admirers on both sides of the political fence. Under Kennett, Melbourne has secured major national events like the Australian Grand Prix, while his government's fiscal achievements have also been impressive, with burgeoning strengths in manufacturing, multimedia and information technology.

The years since the 1850s have also seen a remarkable rise in the **Aboriginal population** – there are now over 8000 Aborigines living in Melbourne, around the same number that existed before the European invasion. State-wide community organizations, schools such as the Galeena Beek Living Cultural Centre in Healesville (see p.236), and health and legal centres have boosted Aboriginal esteem and provided widespread employment. In addition, Victorian and federal legislation has granted control to Aborigines over some heritage and cultural sites. In 1998, the Melbourne City Council recognized the past suffering of Victorian Aborigines by issuing a formal apology during National Sorry Day.

# Books

Most of the following books are still in print, although some may be hard to find unless you visit a library, or secondhand or specialist bookshop. UK and US publishers are given where available.

## General introductions

**Jim Davidson**, *The Sydney-Melbourne Book* (Allen & Unwin). Entertaining and erudite collection of essays comparing the two cities. Topics range from politics, business, crime and education to cultural matters such as film, sport and religion.

**W.H. Newnham**, *Melbourne – Biography of a City* (Hill of Content). The best and most detailed account of Melbourne's founding and subsequent growth, with a good sprinkling of photographs and illustrations.

## History

**R. Barrett**, *The Inner Suburbs – The Evolution of an Industrial Area* (Melbourne University Press). The stuttering development of Collingwood and Richmond during the nineteenth century makes for a fascinating and grimy read, especially the warts-and-all picture of wealthy industrialists pouring noxious wastes into the Yarra.

**C.P. Billot (ed)**, *Melbourne's Missing Chronicle – John Pascoe Fawkner* (Quartet). This private journal of John Pascoe Fawkner, the industrious former publican and early Melbourne settler, traces the city's formative years in 1835–36. Somewhat scrappy but disarmingly candid, it's an invaluable work for anyone interested in Melbourne's history, and the life of one of the city's founders.

**Michael Cannon**, *Old Melbourne Town* (Loch Haven). Interesting analysis of Melbourne life up until the discovery of gold. Cannon's sequel, *Melbourne After the Gold Rush* (Loch Haven), is equally good, concentrating on Melbourne's transformation from a small shantytown into a hectic and overcrowded metropolis.

**Patricia Clancy and Jeanne Allen (ed)**, *The French Consul's Wife: Memoirs of Céleste de Chabrillan in Gold-Rush Australia* (Melbourne University Press, Aus & UK). This racy memoir of the immigrant Céleste de Chabrillan (former Parisian courtesan, circus performer and dancer) and her encounter with mid-nineteenth-century Melbourne has insightful and deliciously impertinent descriptions of society during the goldrush era.

**Graeme Davidson**, *The Rise and Fall of Marvellous Melbourne* (Melbourne University Press). Scholarly and sometimes difficult to read, but worth persisting with to gain an idea of the "Marvellous Melbourne" era, during which the city became the wealthiest and most advanced in Australia.

**Janet McCalman**, *Sex and Suffering: Women's Health and a Woman's Hospital* (Melbourne University Press, Aus & UK; John Hopkins University Press, US). A powerful and moving social history of the lives and suffering of Melbourne women since the 1850s, focusing on the nursing and medical staff at the Women's Hospital in Carlton.

**Gary Presland**, *Aboriginal Melbourne: The Lost Land of the Kulin People* (McPhee Gribble). Fascinating and readable short study of a vanished country and a remarkable way of life, with accounts of the Kulin lifestyle and the effects of white settlement on the Aboriginal population and culture.

## Art and architecture

**Maie Casey**, *Early Melbourne Architecture, 1840 to 1888* (Oxford University Press). Smallish but useful photographic representation (with brief notes) of the city's more architecturally interesting nineteenth-century buildings. Sadly, over one-third of the buildings included in the book have since been altered or demolished.

ART AND ARCHITECTURE

**Leon van Shaik (ed)**, *Architectural Monographs No 50: Tom Kovac* (Academy Editions, Aus & UK). Nicely illustrated study of the Melbourne work of the enigmatic and provocative Tom Kovac, analysing nineteen completed and unfinished projects, including the Museum of Victoria and Federation Square. The results are witty and consistently entertaining.

**Granville Wilson and Peter Sands**, *Building a City* (Oxford University Press). Meticulously researched and comprehensive general history of Melbourne's architecture.

## Fiction

**Frank Hardy**, *Power Without the Glory* (Mandarin). One of Australia's greatest and most controversial novels, *Power Without the Glory* is the semi-fictional account of the life of John Wren, a legendary criminal figure who lived in Collingwood. Hardy, who collected much of his material while working as a Melbourne journalist, had enormous difficulty in getting the work published, and was later sued (unsuccessfully) by Wren's wife for defamation.

**Adele Lang**, *What Katya Did Next: The Katya Livingston Chronicles* (Vintage, Aus; Mainstream, UK). Self-absorbed, so-in-sync-with-the-times member of the South Yarra Chardonnay set whines about her work (or lack of it), friends and sex life. The guffaw-count is reasonably high, and there is plenty of name-dropping.

**Shane Maloney**, *Stiff* (Text Publishing, Aus; Arcade, UK & US). Mixing a benighted central character (private detective and single parent Murray Whelan) with drugs, Turks and killer cars, *Stiff* is a fast and often funny thriller set in various Melbourne suburbs. First in a series that also includes *The Brush-Off* and *Nice Try*.

**Elliot Perlman**, *Three Dollars* (Picador, Aus; Faber & Faber, UK; MacMurray & Beck, US). Stirring read that goes straight for the jugular in its depiction of economic rationalism and downsizing in modern Melbourne. Collected *The Age* Book of the Year award for 1998.

**RMIT Students**, *Mean Gin: Twisted Fiction from the Gutter to the Grave* and *The Hard Word* (Vandal Press). Two well-designed collections of short stories and graphics from writing and editing graduates of RMIT. Both are hard to find, except from the RMIT bookshop.

**Christos Tsiolkas**, *Loaded* (Vintage, Aus & UK). Convincingly maps out ideas on homosexuality, ethnicity, sex, drugs and music from the perspective of Ari, the unemployed son of Greek migrants. Think Jean Genet and William Burroughs with toothache and you're already halfway there. Made into the film *Head On* (see p.278).

# Melbourne in film

Ava Gardner's wrongly attributed words famously haunted Melbourne for years. "A great place to make a film about the end of the world," she reputedly quipped in 1959, during shooting of Stanley Kramer's apocalyptic *On the Beach* (in fact, the remark was penned by a local journalist). At the time there was little film production in Melbourne, a far cry from the **turn of the century**, when the city was pioneering the latest film technology. In 1900, over two thousand people packed the Melbourne Town Hall to watch *Soldiers of the Cross*, an evangelistic film made by the Salvation Army about early Christian martyrs. Six years later, John and Nevin Tait produced *The Story of the Kelly Gang*, perhaps the first feature-length fictional film in the world. But as the Hollywood silent era churned out miles of celluloid and "more stars than heaven" (as MGM claimed), Melbourne, like the rest of Australia, succumbed to the waves of overseas imports arriving on its shores.

The city's film culture was revived in the 1950s with the founding of the **Melbourne International Film Festival** (see p.179), which helped develop an interest in alternative cinema and fostered a modest "underground" of film-makers, who took their lead from the French New Wave. During the postwar years, Melbourne also became the engine room of Australian film studies. The National Film Theatre and the Australian Film Institute were founded in Melbourne, while publications such as *Lumiere* (now defunct) and *Cinema Papers*, Australia's premier film magazine, began publication. In addition, the first film studies department was instituted at La Trobe University, and the first film school introduced at Swinburne Institute of Technology (now at the Victoria College of the Arts). Melbourne and Australia's film renaissance was given a further boost in the 1970s, when state and federal government bodies started actively supporting the domestic film industry, a process that continues in fits and starts today.

The following listing doesn't pretend to be exhaustive, but it should give you an idea of some of the films available with distinctive Melbourne qualities, or those that have their source in the city. Most can also be rented from video outlets around the city and suburbs.

**The Big Steal** (1990). Director Nadia Tass's charming romantic comedy of a high-school boy's infatuation with a girl and Jaguar cars, and getting even with a shonky used-car dealer.

**The Castle** (1997). Salt-of-the-earth saga about the battling Kerrigan family taking on big business to save their home from an airport runway extension. The nods and winks at Aussie culture might not always make sense, but the more you know about Melbourne, the funnier it gets.

**The Club** (1980). David Williamson's satirical play studies the intrigue and machismo within the ranks of Collingwood, the most famous AFL club in Australia. Perfectly adapted for film by director Bruce Beresford.

**Crackers** (1998). Low-budget film tracing the humorous goings-on within the tightly knit Dredge family, a bunch of whackos who come together for Christmas festivities.

**Death in Brunswick** (1991). Directed by John Ruane and starring Sam Neill, this black comedy revolves around Neill's no-hoper cook who works at a nightclub in the multicultural melting pot of Brunswick. New Zealand-born, Melbourne-based comedian John Clark is a scene-stealer at every turn.

**Head On** (1998). A raw and explicit story of a young "wog" (superbly played by hunky Alex Dimitriades) crashing through 24 hours of his life fuelled by vast quantities of sex, drugs and booze. Wonderfully photographed scenes of the seedier side of the city and deft insights into 1990s youth culture in multicultural

Melbourne. Based on the cult Christos Tsiolkas novel *Loaded* (see p.276).

**Malcolm** (1986). Nadia Tass again (see *The Big Steal*), who directed this delightful comedy about a social misfit inventor finding fulfilment as a criminal's offsider. Humorous, with great scenes of Melbourne and its rapidly disappearing W-class trams.

**My First Wife** (1984). Surprisingly engaging story of a tortured custody dispute amid calls for a reappraisal of the rights of the father in such cases. From Paul Cox, Melbourne's best-known author-director.

**On the Beach** (1959). Director Stanley Kramer's classic Cold War flick has Melbourne as the last place on earth that hasn't choked on the radioactive fallout of World War III. Gregory Peck, Ava Gardner, Anthony Perkins and Fred Astaire all give outstanding performances.

**Proof** (1990). Jocelyn Moorehouse's quietly paced though chilling analysis of loveless sex, betrayal and broken marriages, with a blind photographer (Hugo Weaving) caught in the middle.

**Romper Stomper** (1992). Bleak and intense tale of neo-Nazis in Footscray and their running battles with the Vietnamese community. The film divided audiences on its release, with many railing against its random acts of pitiless violence.

# Glossary of Melbourne terms

**AFL** Australian Football League, or "Aussie Rules", or simply "footy".

**Anzac** Australia and New Zealand Army Corps; every town has a memorial to Anzac casualties from both world wars.

**Arvo** Afternoon.

**Barrack** To cheer for (as in your favourite footy team).

**Bathers** Swimming costume (see "swimmers", "togs").

**Biffo** A fight.

**Bingle** Mishap or car crash.

**Bloke** Male, as in "he's a good bloke".

**Blowies** Blowflies.

**Bludger** Someone who doesn't pull their weight, or a scrounger – as in "dole bludger".

**Blue** A fight; also a red-haired person.

**Bottle shop** Off-licence or liquor store.

**Buckley's** No chance; as in "hasn't got a Buckley's".

**BYO** Bring Your Own. Café or restaurant which allows you to bring your own alcohol.

**Chunder** Vomit.

**Connies** Melbourne's late, lamented tram conductors.

**Crim** Criminal.

**Dag** Friendly term for decidedly uncool person.

**Doing a Melba** Reference to Dame Nellie Melba, famous Australian operatic soprano who retired, then made a series of comebacks.

**Dunny** Toilet; usually an outside pit toilet.

**Esky** Portable, insulated box to keep food or beer cold.

**The Espy** The perennially popular *Esplanade Hotel* in St Kilda.

**Footy** AFL.

**The G**, the Affectionate term for the Melbourne Cricket Ground (MCG).

**G'day** Hello, hi.

**Grog** Alcohol.

**Grommet** Young surfer.

**Gubba** Europeans.

**Gunzels** Tram enthusiasts.

**Gutless wonder** Coward.

**Hip and shoulder** Footy term for legal tackle.

**Hook turn** see p.31.

**Hoon** A yob, delinquent.

**Icey-pole** Ice block on a stick.

**Koorie** Collective name for Aboriginal people from southeastern Australia.

**Lavvie** Toilet, or "loo".

**Lay by** Practice of putting a deposit on goods until they can be fully paid for.

**Milk bar** Corner shop, and often a small café.

**Mystery bag** Meat pie.

**No worries** That's OK; It doesn't matter; Don't mention it.

**Onya** Good for you!

**Op shop** Short for "opportunity shop"; a charity shop (UK) or thrift store (USA).

**Pashing** Kissing or snogging.

**Pie floater** Meat pie in bowl of pea soup.

**Piss** Beer, as in "I've been on the piss".

**Pokies** Poker machines, slot or fruit machines.

**Pot** 285ml or 10oz glass of beer.

**Rattler** A train or tram.

**Rego** Vehicle registration document.

**Root** Vulgar term for sexual congress, often substituted with "pork".

**Rooted** To be very tired or to be beyond repair; as in "your car's rooted, mate".

**Scull** To down a drink (usually beer) quickly.

**Shirtfront** Another footy term for a tackle.

**Shonky** Something or someone deceptive or unreliable.

**Silverhairs** Retirees.

**Slab** 24-can carton of beer.

**Smoko** Tea break.

**Snag sausage** Usually cooked on a barbecue; not a Sensitive New Age Guy.

**Snot block** Vanilla slice.

**Southerly buster** Melbourne's much-welcomed cooling breeze.

**Speccie** Spectacular football mark, usually above a pack of players.

**Swimmers** Swimming costume.

**Thongs** Flip-flops or sandals.

**Tinnie** Can of beer.

**Togs** Swimming costume.

**VB** Victoria Bitter, the state's thirst-quenching lager.

**Vegemite** Delicious blackish-brown spread used on sandwiches.

**Waxhead** Surfer.

**Weatherboard** Wooden house.

**White mice** Football umpires, also known as "white maggots".

**Wog** Derogatory description for those of Mediterranean descent.

# INDEX

# ROUGH GUIDES: Travel

# ROUGH GUIDES: Mini Guides, Travel Specials and Phrasebooks

**MINI GUIDES**

Antigua
Bangkok
Barbados
Big Island of Hawaii
Boston
Brussels
Budapest
Dublin
Edinburgh
Florence
Honolulu
Lisbon
London Restaurants
Madrid
Maui
Melbourne
New Orleans
St Lucia

Seattle
Sydney
Tokyo
Toronto

**TRAVEL SPECIALS**

First-Time Asia
First-Time Europe
More Women Travel

**PHRASEBOOKS**

Czech
Dutch
Egyptian Arabic
European
French

German
Greek
Hindi & Urdu
Hungarian
Indonesian
Italian
Japanese
Mandarin
 Chinese
Mexican
 Spanish
Polish
Portuguese
Russian
Spanish
Swahili
Thai
Turkish
Vietnamese

AVAILABLE AT ALL GOOD BOOKSHOPS

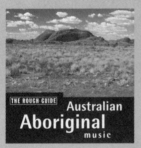

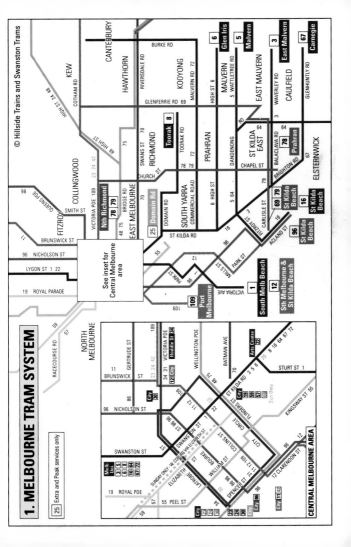

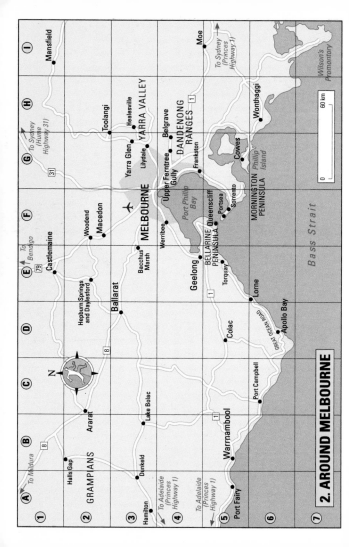

## 2. AROUND MELBOURNE